'A book that has stood the test of time. Roger Smith leads the reader through the complex history, theory and practice of youth justice with an expert's eye and a teacher's skill. First-rate and a must for all students studying this field.'

Professor Tim Newburn, *London School of Economics, UK*

'Fully updated, comprehensive in its coverage, detailed and research-focused in its content and infused with the author's insightful explanations, this is, in many ways, a new book, which is essential reading for anyone seeking to understand contemporary youth justice.'

Kevin Haines, *Professor of Criminology and Youth Justice, Swansea University, UK*

'The third edition of *Youth Justice: Ideas, policy, practice* provides an authoritative, comprehensive and completely up-to-date critical insight into the fast-moving world of youth justice. Smith's book is an invaluable resource for students and tutors alike. A "must-read".'

Professor Barry Goldson, *Charles Booth Chair of Social Science, The University of Liverpool, UK*

Youth Justice

The exciting new edition of this well-loved textbook offers a fully expanded and revised account and analysis of the youth justice system in the UK, taking into account and fully addressing the significant changes that have taken place since the second edition in 2007.

The book maintains its critical analysis of the underlying assumptions and ideas behind youth justice, as well as its policy and practice, laying bare the inadequacies, inconsistencies and injustices of practice in the UK. This edition will offer an important update in light of intervening changes, as reflected in a change of government and shifting patterns of interventions and outcomes.

This book will be a resource for youth justice practitioners and essential to students taking courses in youth crime and youth justice.

Roger Smith is Professor of Social Work at the University of Durham. As a practitioner, Roger worked as a Probation Officer, specialising in diversion with young offenders. He then spent some years as Head of Policy with The Children's Society, arguing the case for children's rights in youth justice. He has also taught at the University of Leicester, and at De Montfort University he was Professor of Social Work Research. Roger is the author of *Doing Justice to Young People: Youth Crime and Social Justice* (Willan/Routledge, 2011).

Youth Justice
Ideas, policy, practice

Third edition

Roger Smith

LONDON AND NEW YORK

First published 2014
by Routledge
2 Park Square, Milton Park, Abingdon, Oxon, OX14 4RN

and by Routledge
711 Third Avenue, New York, NY 10017

Routledge is an imprint of the Taylor & Francis Group, an informa business

© 2014 Roger Smith

British Library Cataloguing in Publication Data
A catalogue record for this book is available from the British Library

Library of Congress Cataloging in Publication Data
Youth justice : ideas, policy, practice / Roger Smith. – Third edition.
   p. cm
   Summary: "The exciting new edition of this well-loved textbook offers a fully expanded and revised account and analysis of the youth justice system in the UK, taking into account and fully addressing the significant changes that have taken place since the second edition in 2007. The book maintains its critical analysis of the underlying assumptions and ideas behind youth justice, as well as its policy and practice, laying bare the inadequacies, inconsistencies and injustices of practice in the UK. This edition will offer an important update in light of intervening changes, as reflected in a change of government and shifting patterns of interventions and outcomes. This book will be a resource for youth justice practitioners and essential to students taking courses in youth crime and youth justice"– Provided by publisher.
   1. Juvenile justice, Administration of–Great Britain. I. Title.
   HV9145.A5S65 2014
   364.360941–dc23
               2013019545

ISBN: 978-0-415-62650-7 (hbk)
ISBN: 978-0-415-62651-4 (pbk)
ISBN: 978-0-203-10263-3 (ebk)

Typeset in Times New Roman
by Taylor & Francis Books

Printed and bound in Great Britain by
CPI Group (UK) Ltd, Croydon, CR0 4YY

Contents

Illustrations

Tables

Introduction

'Dazed and confused …'

On returning to update this book for its third edition, I found that, whilst much was familiar, much, too, of the youth justice landscape had changed. Even apparently solid and recognisable features such as the Youth Justice Board no longer look or behave as they did just a few years ago and, indeed, have lost a sense of permanence. Much of the language has changed ('the Scaled Approach' and Youth Rehabilitation Orders arrived, and cautions are back), and there has been a change of government, which, of course, heralded promises of 'radical reform' and a complete rejection of its predecessor's failed policies. Practice has moved on, with perhaps a greater emphasis now on 'restorative' approaches, and less on monitoring and surveillance (box ticking); disposal patterns have revealed a significant change of direction, with the fallow years of the early 2000s succeeded by a very substantial decline in the numbers of young people formally processed, and locked up.

The challenges for the author are different, too. In the first two editions, there was (intentionally) a consistent critical thread, based on a sense of frustration and disappointment at the missed opportunities of the New Labour era, when money was available and was spent on the wrong things, with the result that the predictable (and predicted) consequences did indeed ensue. We endured a period of target-driven micro management, which imposed incomprehensible demands on practitioners, labelled and 'targeted' young people, and completely failed to address the excessive use of custody and discrimination and oppression experienced by some of those young people. It is no longer possible to sustain that straightforwardly critical narrative, because, in around 2007/08, 'something happened'. Explanations for what now seems to be a dramatic transformation are not yet certain, although it is likely that a combination of factors was responsible for a substantial refocusing of policy and practice:

> A number of factors explain the fall [in the use of custody] but it is not the case that reducing custody has been a deliberate or overt policy

objective in central government. Rather, a range of dynamics behind the scenes have worked together to reduce the number of children appearing before the courts, reducing the proportion of these children who are sentenced to custody.

(Allen, 2011: 3)

Following these changes, it is, of course, important that any contemporary narrative recognises the complexities inherent in the field of youth justice, and indeed the limits of 'prediction'. We cannot simply assume that we are experiencing a re-run of the 1980s, as a period of austerity leads to a 'rolling back' of the state, and a corresponding unwillingness to invest in the sociali- sation of a problematic group (marginalised young people) whose labour value has diminished, although this does probably offer a partial explanation for what has happened. This would, of course, be to overlook the positive achievements associated with the rediscovery of diversion, a more proactive and productive Youth Justice Board, the renewed effectiveness of 'alternatives to custody', and the possibilities offered by participatory, rights-based and restorative forms of practice.

In revisiting this terrain once again, I want to 'do justice' to the spirit of innovation and progress, which has once again emerged in the field of youth justice, whilst at the same time acknowledging the dark forces that act as impediments to genuine transformation, such as the continuing evidence of discrimination on grounds of ethnicity, the endless capacity for instant demonisation of the young (cf the 2011 'riots'), and of course the fact that, while things might have improved for young people in the specific context of criminal justice, much else has not, as the youth service is systematically dis- mantled, for instance, and as much of the infrastructure and social investment that creates a sense of opportunity and hope remains under threat or has already been lost. We should do what we can to promote and sustain a progressive youth justice system, but we should also know its limits.

The structure of the book

The organisation of this edition is broadly similar to the previous ones. The first part is effectively a detailed review of the recent history of youth justice, beginning in the 1980s, which seems increasingly pertinent, given that much that has happened recently (inside and outside youth justice) is redolent of that era. From there, I go on to discuss the 'punitive turn' of the 1990s, and the emerging consensus that supported a more intrusive and demanding model of intervention with young people who are identified as offenders. The subsequent emergence of the New Labour project is discussed in detail, and its lessons highlighted, not least because we cannot afford another period of expensive failure on such a grand scale. Then we move on to consider sub- sequent developments, and the re-emergence of 'rehabilitation', diversion, and even a renewed attempt to disturb the hegemony of the sentencing tariff.

Whilst the first part of the book focuses largely on the policy context and the influence of factors external to the youth justice system itself, the following chapters attempt to provide some insight into its organisation and operation, reflecting both on structural arrangements and the role of the Youth Justice Board, and on the practice environment, which is inevitably the point where embedded contradictions go 'live' and present very real day-to-day challenges. The tension between the actuarial, risk-based and prescriptive guidelines and tools for practice and the emerging ethos of informality, problem solving and minimum intervention becomes most acute here; it seems this is still being worked out in local practice settings ('localism' at work, perhaps?). Of course, it is in such spaces that good practice can thrive, and an emerging challenge is for us to capture and document this in the interest of future sustainability.

Taking a detour into the terrain of theory, the book will try to capture a sense of why and how young people are problematised, and what the implications are, in turn, for a constructive approach to behaviour that is identified as unacceptable, or 'criminal'. Following this, the final part will consider how the outcomes and impacts of 'youth justice' are experienced and judged from a range of perspectives, before going on to consider what these and other interests might want the system to deliver. In the final chapter, I will attempt once again to summarise the 'lessons of experience', before going on to set out some ideas about what such a system should and could look like, based on principles of equality, 'welfare rights' and social inclusion.

1   Contrasts and continuities

Youth justice in the 1980s/1990s

The meaning of history

Youth justice is, of course, a hotly contested and highly 'visible' domain, and this is by no means a recent development. It appears that the behaviour of the young has been a matter of public concern through the ages. Whether or not there has been a phase of human development designated specifically as 'childhood' (Ariès, 1962; Pollock, 1983), our predecessors nonetheless seem to have viewed the turmoil and transitions of youth with at least as much concern as is evident in the present day.

> I would there were no age between sixteen and three-and-twenty, or that youth would sleep out the rest; for there is nothing in the between but getting wenches with child, wronging the ancientry, stealing, fighting.
>
> (Shepherd, Act 3, Scene 3, *A Winter's Tale*,
> by William Shakespeare)

Others, too, have suggested that there is evidence of significant concern about youthful misbehaviour in ancient Greece (Garland, 1990), whilst Plato and Aristotle are similarly attributed with negative quotations about the juvenile delinquency (Burfeind and Bartusch, 2005).

Although the initiation and development of dedicated 'systems' for dealing with the delinquencies of children are associated more readily with the modern era, they seem only to be the culmination and rationalisation of responses to perennial fears (Muncie, 2009).

If the 'problem' of youth crime has always been with us, it does seem to become more pertinent to seek to account for changing attempts to explain and deal with its manifestations over the passage of time. Why should particular forms of response to the issue emerge and come to prevail at specific points in time? And why do they become less popular at other times? A brief historical account may help to shape our understanding of this question in two ways: first, by helping us to be clear that present-day practices are neither fixed nor necessarily the 'best' way of addressing youthful misbehaviour and, second, by providing a basis for identifying trends and trajectories, and, in turn, projecting these, cautiously, into the future.

In making a somewhat arbitrary decision to concentrate on a relatively limited 'slice of time', I am conscious of the risk of foreshortening and over-emphasising the contemporary and the new at the expense of deeper-lying and more persistent influences, particularly those to do with structure and apparently embedded certainties. However, reasons of convenience and the limitations of space do come into play, and they preclude the kind of longer-term accounts offered elsewhere by Hendrick (2006), Muncie (2009) and Hazel (forthcoming). Despite this, I do want to avoid conveying the misleading impression that only the present (or very recent past) matters; to the contrary, I believe that histories – even truncated ones – are crucial elements in the overall analysis of policy, practice and change in youth justice.

Lessons from history – what might we learn?

Before going on to consider specific aspects of the recent past in youth justice, it may be helpful just to reflect on what type of lessons could usefully be learned from history.

First, of course, things change, and these changes may be taken as evidence of more or less significant developments on a wider scale. So, for example, the transition from 'juvenile' to 'youth' justice that took place in England and Wales in the course of the late 1980s/early 1990s can be associated both with certain legislative and policy shifts – the introduction of the Youth Court, in 1991, for example; however, it can also be associated with a change in the way children and their delinquencies were conceptualised, with further implications and consequences, such as, perhaps, the later abolition of the presumption of *doli incapax*[1] in 1998.

Not only do 'things change' then, but so do ideas and it certainly seems to assist us in making sense of the present if we can locate and track the emergence and influence of specific trends in thinking about young people and their crimes. When I started to work in a 'juvenile diversion' project in the 1980s, the term 'restorative justice' was virtually unknown, and certainly did not provide us then, as it probably would now, with a conceptual framework or form of discourse to account for and justify our practice. Would it have been easier to attain a sense of legitimacy if we had had a convenient banner such as this under which to operate?

Change from 'outside' is significant, too, and is an important reminder that youth justice, like any other system, is not self-contained, and is susceptible to the impact of contingent events; perhaps especially so, given the nature of the subject matter. So, for example, the 2011 riots in England had an almost instantaneous effect on the processes and outcomes experienced by young people coming into contact with the system; similarly, earlier 'trigger' events such as the killing of James Bulger appear to have had a substantial impact.

The consequences of these events, however, lead to a further observation about the lessons of history, which is that some things don't change. Pearson's (1983) important contribution illustrates the persistence of a set of public and political attitudes that seem to exemplify hostility to young people and their behaviours as a default position. History, then, may be as much about continuity as it is about change, and this clearly acts as a helpful reminder to avoid overemphasising the meaning and significance of dramatic occurrences, especially when viewed from close at hand.

It seems, perhaps, that we should seek to understand the history of youth justice as multi-dimensional, represented both in terms of dramatic shifts, innovation and 'breaks' with the past, on the one hand, and, on the other, as the repository of much longer-standing and consistent currents of opinion and influence, which may be less immediately visible, but nonetheless of greater significance in the long term.

Back to the 1980s: another world?

The choice of the 1980s as the starting point for this contemporary historical overview is clearly somewhat arbitrary, at least in part pragmatically determined by the extent of the author's experience of working in youth justice. However, it is also a long enough period to give us a sense of continuity and change as outlined above, and it enables us to contrast periods of government, which represents a very important backdrop to our analysis.

This point in history is also a useful line of demarcation between two eras in youth justice, and therefore offers some relatively clear indicators of transition and change, which in turn help to clarify some of the persistent dynamics and tensions that will be observable over time. The preceding period, for example, had been characterised by the emergence of 'welfare' rhetoric as an influential theme, paralleled by a very substantial increase in the institutionalisation of children and young people on grounds both of care need and offending behaviour (see Thorpe *et al.*, 1980). Despite this, the incoming Thatcher government of 1979 made much of the threat to the social fabric offered by deviant young people (and other groups, such as striking miners), who collectively attracted the epithet 'the enemy within' (Milne, 2004). The polarising nature of the political rhetoric of the time, the increasing sense of 'us' and 'them', was mirrored in examples of unrest such as the 'riots' of 1981 and 1985 (Davies, 1986), and this in turn was associated with a 'racialisation' of difference, reflecting a persistent theme in 'law and order' discourses (Hall *et al.*, 1978).

Ironically, then, whilst on the one hand more and more young people were already being incarcerated, the political mood was geared towards being ever tougher on deviant behaviour in general and the crimes of the young in particular. The incoming Conservative government immediately delivered on its pre-election promise to introduce the 'short, sharp shock' regime in two detention centres for 11–14 year olds, for example (Conservative Party, 1979), an 'experiment' that was subsequently extended to other custodial settings and all detention centres (Pitts, 1988), notwithstanding evidence of its abject failure (Thornton *et al.*, 1984).

The punitive mood was also reflected in the White Paper *Young Offenders* (Home Office, 1980), which emphasised principles of individual responsibility and 'just deserts', at the expense of more welfare-oriented models of intervention. This, though, pleased some liberal critics of 'treatment'-based interventions, which had effectively drawn young people into the 'net' without the safeguards of due process (Morris *et al.*, 1980). Signposted by the White Paper and included in the subsequent Criminal Justice Act 1982 were a number of measures designed to impose tighter controls on young offenders, in the community as well as in custody. Among these were the Night Restriction Order (curfew) and Supervised Activity Order. The overall objective of the youth justice system seemed to have shifted from one of rehabilitation to one of crime control, and, indeed, risk management.

In addition to these changes in community disposals, custodial sentencing practice was also significantly modified by the 1982 Act; in particular, the indeterminate Borstal regime was replaced by a new sentence of Youth Custody, and this, alongside the 'short, sharp shock' initiative, suggested an overall shift of emphasis away from rehabilitative goals and towards 'just deserts' (McAra, 2010) and control. This change may not have led to the expected outcome in due course, but it is of symbolic significance nonetheless, to the extent that it set the tone for practice at all levels of the justice system over the ensuing period. The emergence of a relatively uncomplicated 'tariff' of disposals, allied with a commitment to crime control, suggested that the focus of interventions would be the behaviour of young people, rather than their individual needs and circumstances.

Interestingly, though, the corollary of this framework was that the measures adopted to deal with youthful misbehaviour should, indeed, be proportionate. Bottoms (1977) had already articulated the emerging logic of the justice system in general in the direction of 'bifurcation', whereby clear and wide distinctions could be made between the relatively small group of 'dangerous' offenders, whose behaviour should lead to draconian measures, and the remainder, for whom much less severe sanctions would be appropriate, given the relatively minor transgressions for which they were responsible. In practical terms, this logic was pursued by the government in the early 1980s, coincidentally a time when spending constraints were severe, and a number of measures were introduced to give effect to the aim of distinguishing between serious crimes and the rest. These included the Intensive Intermediate Treatment initiative (DHSS, 1983), which was intended to operate by 'broadening and strengthening existing non-custodial provisions', and by following the principle of greater control in the community, assisting 'the courts to avoid a custodial sentence except where one is absolutely necessary' (NACRO, 1987: 11). A sum of £15 million was made available for the development of more intensive (and credible) alternatives to custody, creating an additional 4,500 places in the community for the supervision of young people whose offences would otherwise have resulted in custodial sentences. As Hudson (1987) put it, the era of 'net-widening' was to be superseded by one of 'net-strengthening'.

Further evidence of this trend towards 'targeted' policy making emerged subsequently, with the publication of new guidance on 'cautioning' (Home Office, 1985), which actively promoted increased use of disposals short of prosecution in minor cases, also supporting the use of 'informal action' by the police. This approach followed the argument of the earlier White Paper (*Young Offenders*; Home Office, 1980), which had argued that 'juvenile offenders who can be diverted from the criminal justice system at an early stage in their offending are less likely to re-offend than those who become involved in judicial proceedings' (quoted in NACRO, 1987: 15). As well as underlining the logic of bifurcation, the 1985 cautioning guidance also introduced new elements into the mix, promoting the use of a range of interventions, including encouraging young people to make amends for their offences, by way of apologies and direct or indirect reparation to victims or the community. In this respect, it can be seen that, as McAra (2010: 292) has observed, most criminal justice jurisdictions do not reflect a 'pure' version of any one model of intervention, but usually draw from a number of alternative paradigms.

The combined effect of these policy measures enabled the then government to maintain its reputation for being tough on crime, whilst at the same time meeting other policy objectives through a 'targeted' approach, which could simultaneously keep costs down and reduce pressures on the machinery of criminal justice. By the latter stages of the decade, the government felt able to take this strategy further with the publication of the consultation document *Punishment, Custody and the Community* (Home Office, 1988), which maintained the appearance of being tough by foregrounding 'punishment', whilst at the same time maintaining the twin-track approach already in place. The document's rhetoric appealed to government supporters' sentiments with a commitment to crack down on violent crime and undue leniency in the justice process; but, at the same time, the detail was more nuanced. For:

> [o]ther, less serious offenders, a spell in custody is not the most effective punishment. Imprisonment restricts offenders' liberty, but it also reduces their responsibility; they are not required to face up to what they have done or to make any recompense to the victim or the public.
>
> (Home Office, 1988: 1)

Significantly, the notion of taking 'responsibility' for one's actions was contrasted with the experience of custody where most decisions are taken on the young person's behalf.

The ideas developed in the consultation document found their eventual realisation in the Criminal Justice Act 1991, which according to some commentators epitomised the emerging 'due process' framework for dealing with young offenders (Haines and Drakeford, 1998). The legislative provisions applicable to all ages such as unit fines, compensation orders and the de-emphasising of prior convictions in the sentencing process were all examples of an overarching strategy based on principles of equity and an offence- rather than offender-based response. This, though, by focusing on responses to the immediate problems arising from a specific offence, posed significant challenges to deeply entrenched assumptions about the sentencing tariff, and associated notions of deterrence and retribution.

Policy into practice in the 1980s: intended consequences?

The relationship between policy and practice is often complex, and the idea of 'unintended consequences' is well established in criminal justice (Cohen, 1985). On the other hand, despite the government's hard-line rhetoric, there is clearly a case for arguing that what transpired during the 1980s was consistent with national policy objectives. What is not so clear, however, is whether policy shaped practice or vice versa (see Telford and Santatzoglou, 2011, for example). What emerged, though, was a consistent and widespread 'model' of intervention that operated across the spectrum of the justice system, and appeared to incorporate a number of key principles consistently: 'minimum intervention', 'systems management', 'normalisation' and 'offence resolution' (the term 'restorative justice' was not widely in use at this time).

These principles were realised through a number of influential programmes, including diversion projects and alternatives to custody programmes. Cautioning as an option for dealing with relatively minor offences had been in use since the early 1950s, at least (Mays, 1965), and its extension had been further encouraged in the 1960s (Home Office, 1968). However, its use had remained fairly stable until the early 1980s (NACRO, 1987), despite the widespread evidence of net widening in the intervening period (Thorpe *et al.*, 1980). Perhaps significantly, the initial growth in the use of cautioning and other informal disposals was inspired by concern about the geographical disparities in the use of such measures, which prompted specific practice innovations in areas of the country such as Devon and Cornwall, Hampshire and North-amptonshire (NACRO, 1987), most of which took effect before Home Office Circular 14/85 was issued. In other words, practice appears to have pre-empted policy in this instance (Telford and Santatzoglou, 2011: 20).

The emergence of a comprehensive diversion strategy in Northamptonshire has been acknowledged as a particularly significant development in youth justice in this period, acting as a continuing influence on subsequent ideas and initiatives (Audit Commission, 1996, for example). The Northamptonshire Juvenile Liaison Bureaux (JLB) were distinctive in that they were established as arm's length, full-time teams, independent of parent agencies, and with a remit to promote alternatives to prosecution wherever possible. This involved a willingness on the part of each participating agency, particularly the police, to cede some aspects of independent authority, but, once this mode of operation had been established, the impact on the justice system was dramatic. The Wellingborough JLB, for instance, was responsible for an immediate halving of the prosecution rate for young people alleged to have offended on its inception in 1981 (from 40% to 19%), an achievement that was replicated throughout the county as the scheme was extended (Stevens and Crook, 1986). By 1992, at their peak, the JLBx received 2,399 reports from the police, relating to 1,389 young people, and only 9% of those referred were prosecuted (Bell *et al.*, 1999). Significantly, too, it was not just first offenders who were being 'diverted'; whilst the 'tariff' survived in modified form, its influence had been substantially reduced (Smith, 1989). The reduction in the number of young people being formally processed had consequential effects too, as fewer were subject to court hearings and the use of custody also declined substantially (Smith, 1989). Further evaluation also found that reoffending rates were reduced, too (Stevens and Crook, 1986; Kemp *et al.*, 2002).

Not only did the JLBx have a substantial effect in terms of numbers processed, but they also represented a significant change in the ways in which practice was conceptualised and delivered. In effect, they represented the realisation of the policy objective of shifting the focus from the offender and her/his needs and circumstances to the offence and its consequences, for all affected (Bell *et al.*, 1999). This may also have been influential in shaping subsequent thinking around the emerging principles of 'restorative justice' (Johnstone, 2002). The JLBx developed a systematic form of 'negotiated justice' (Abel, 1982), which appeared to meet the needs and interests of community, victims, statutory agencies and young offenders alike (Dignan, 1992).

The JLBx and other local diversion initiatives were substantially evaluated (Thorpe, 1984; Cheetham, 1985; Reynolds, 1985; Blagg *et al.*, 1986; Davis *et al.*, 1989; Smith, 1989; Dignan, 1992; Hughes *et al.*, 1996; Kemp *et al.*, 2002), and the studies concerned generally found that the form of youth justice being delivered was distinctive and 'successful', in that most stakeholders' interests were met most of the time. Some criticisms focused on the emergence of 'administrative justice', and the possibility that young people might be induced to admit guilt in exchange for an apparently more lenient outcome than prosecution, whilst others were concerned at the possibility of undue pressure being exerted on victims to accept less than helpful offers of reparation (Davis *et al.*, 1988, 1989). However, these fears were largely noted to be unfounded, with little evidence of 'net-widening' (Blagg *et al.*, 1986), and positive evidence that victims' interests were respected in general (Dignan, 1992).

At the other end of the scale of community interventions was the Intensive Intermediate Treatment (IIT) initiative, instigated by the Department of Health and Social Security in 1983. The earlier preventive orientation of Intermediate Treatment was by now discredited, as being neither preventive nor diversionary, and in fact contributing substantially to the recruitment of a new cohort of young people 'at risk' into the justice and institutional care systems (Taylor *et al.*, 1979). The possibility of reorienting this form of intervention to act as a genuine 'alternative' to a more punitive disposal was therefore as attractive to practitioners and managers in juvenile (youth) justice as the extension of control at low cost was to government. Building on existing practice models that once again pre-dated the implementation of formal policy change (Telford and Santatzoglou, 2011: 6), the IIT initiative was quickly 'rolled out', leading to the establishment of 110 projects throughout England and Wales, of which 95 survived beyond the initial three-year funding period (Smith, 1999). The 'flavour' of the programmes developed demonstrates a sharp contrast with the welfare-oriented projects that they superseded.

Practitioners believed that, by offering 'credible', tough and demanding interventions, they could persuade courts to opt out of custodial sentences; thus, they would need to play the 'tariff' game and offer something distinctively more intrusive and controlling than other community-based options: 'to be seen by sentencers as suitable … community corrections have to incorporate appropriate degrees of control, and offer the promise of effectiveness in stopping the delinquent behaviour' (Hudson, 1987: 153). IIT programmes thus routinely included regular attendance requirements, monitoring of young people's movements, behaviour management activities and possibly also community service of some kind to make amends for the offence. Failure to comply would incur breach procedures and return to court for re-sentencing.

Haines and Drakeford (1998: 62) have argued that what emerged from this initiative typified a 'new orthodoxy' in youth justice, based on working in a tightly focused way with young people who were 'identified offenders at a fairly high point on the criminal tariff'. Associated with this was a form of practice that concentrated on the offending behaviour exhibited by young people to the exclusion of other aspects of their lives. Accordingly, youth justice interventions were typified by:

- offence confrontation work – reinforcing the unacceptability of offending;
- developing a victim perspective – educating young people into the impact of their offending on victims;
- the offending curriculum – teaching young people how to avoid situations where offending can occur.

(Haines and Drakeford, 1998: 66)

Crucially, of course, to legitimise their rationale, these forms of intervention had to demonstrate both a reduction in the use of custody, and a reduction in offending levels amongst young people. As far as the former goes, as Haines and Drakeford (1998: 58) have demonstrated, the reduction in the use of custody during the 1980s was, indeed, paralleled by an increase in the use of community-based supervision, thus suggesting that alternatives to custody programmes were having the intended effect on sentencing practices (Bottoms, 1995).

This 'success' (Goldson, 1997) was not mirrored quite so strongly in the reported impact on offending rates, despite some evidence of positive achievements in this respect by individual programmes (The Children's Society, 1988), and very modest improvements overall amongst young people undertaking Intermediate Treatment programmes (Bottoms *et al.*, 1990; Bottoms, 1995).

Criticisms of this form of intervention have focused on the increasingly authoritarian nature of interventions (Pitts, 1988), the 'blurring of boundaries' between custody and community-based interventions (Hudson, 1987), the implicit nihilism and acceptance of the 'punishment rationale' of an approach that focuses principally on controlling immediate behaviour rather than seeking developmental change (Smith, 1999), and the loss of a focus on those other aspects of young people's lives that are almost certain to be significant influences on their prospects and outcomes (Haines and Drakeford, 1998). In other words, 'success' appeared to have been bought at a price, and one that might have longer-term consequences, as we shall see.

Measuring 'success': offending and outcomes in the 1980s

Before moving on to consider subsequent developments, it will be helpful to consider briefly the consequences of the changes in policy and practice outlined in terms of the youth justice process and its outcomes.

According to The Children's Society (1993), the 1980s saw unprecedented and parallel declines in the number of known offenders, the use of prosecutions, and the custody rate. For example, the number of young people coming to the attention of the police declined substantially overall, with the exception of 14–17-year-old girls or young women (see Table 1.1).

Whilst part of the reason for the overall fall in the number of known offenders may have been attributable to demographic changes, the rate of juvenile offenders per head of population could also be seen to be in decline, with the period 1980–90 showing a 16% reduction in this figure. In addition, the proportion of all detected offences attributed to juveniles fell from 32% in 1980 to 20% in 1991 (The Children's Society, 1993).

However, some counter-trends were also noted. Some categories of offence, such as car-related thefts – commonly associated with young people – were on the increase. Significant geographical variations could also be observed, reflecting an apparent 'north–south divide', with higher rates of offending associated with less affluent northern police areas (The Children's Society, 1993).

Table 1.1 Number of young people cautioned or found guilty of indictable offences per 100,000 population by age and sex

Gender/age	1977	1986	1991
Male 10–13	3,468	2,257	1,817
Male 14–17	7,456	7,076	6,378
Female 10–13	1,029	761	535
Female 14–17	1,553	1,706	1,973

Source: (Home Office, 1992: Criminal Statistics England and Wales 1991)

The risks involved in drawing strong conclusions from known (official) offending rates are well known, and can be illustrated by the observation that a very small proportion of crime comes to the notice of the police, and an even smaller proportion is detected and leads to the identification and processing of offenders. In evidence to the Home Affairs Committee (1993) inquiry into juvenile crime, the Association of Chief Police Officers argued that, far from being in decline, there had actually been an increase in the number of offences committed by young people over the course of the 1980s. This was partly masked, in the association's view, by the increased use of informal disposals and diversionary measures, which meant that offences were being 'cleared up', but offenders were not being formally processed as a result. In other words, the very success of the diversionary strategies of youth justice practitioners might have led to a reduction in the official figure of 'known offenders', which did not reflect the reality of criminal activity but simply a change in agency practices.

In the specific case of girls or young women aged 14–17, where the trend seems to have been in the opposite direction, explanations offered for this anomaly have been fairly tentative, but they might reflect an increasing 'awareness' of 'criminal girls' by the justice system (Worrall, 1999). Of course, these figures may also have reflected either changing patterns of behaviour amongst young women, or cultural changes in the way in which they are perceived (Walklate, 2004).

Despite the lack of certainty about the meaning of the figures relating to young people's participation in crime, the trends they suggest were paralleled by a more lenient approach to the treatment of young offenders during the 1980s. According to The Children's Society (1993), cautioning rates increased, in accordance with government policy, at precisely the same time as the overall numbers coming to the attention of the justice system were in decline.

Indeed, in the space of just over a decade, the ratio between different outcomes for young offenders had changed dramatically. Whereas, in 1977, prosecutions were brought and young people found guilty in 48% of cases dealt with formally by the police, this proportion had declined to just 21% by 1991. While prosecution was clearly the most likely option for older young offenders (those aged 14–16 inclusive prior to the changes introduced by the Criminal Justice Act 1991) at the start of this time-span, this was clearly not the case by the early 1990s. For girls and young women, despite the changes in the pattern of recorded offending, the likelihood of being prosecuted was even more remote (see Table 1.2).

Whilst it is possible at this point to distinguish clearly between male and female young offenders, it is only relatively recently that any serious attempt has been made to identify patterns of crime, victimisation and outcomes according to ethnicity. Although racism has been identified as a determining factor in a number of studies, even in the context of practices around cautioning and informal disposals (Landau and Nathan, 1983, for example), official figures shed little light on this issue until the latter part of the 1990s

Table 1.2 Changes in the numbers of young people cautioned or found guilty of indictable offences 1977–91 ('000s)

Cautioned	1977	1986	1991
Males 10–13	39.4	26.3	21.0
Males 14–16	31.3	43.6	41.0
Females 10–13	14.0	8.7	6.3
Females 14–17	10.5	14.9	14.8
Total	95.2	93.5	83.1
Found guilty			
Males 10–13	19.2	6.1	2.3
Males 14–17	59.8	37.7	17.2
Females 10–13	2.4	0.5	0.2
Females 14–17	7.6	3.7	2.2
Total	89.0	48.0	21.9

Source: (Home Office, 1992: Criminal Statistics England and Wales 1991)

when Section 95 of the Criminal Justice Act 1991 imposed a requirement on criminal justice agencies to take race and ethnicity into account when reporting on their activities (but see Chapter 8).

Despite this omission, the general picture seems to be that progressively fewer young people were being brought before the courts, both proportionally and in absolute terms over this period of time. In addition, at the point of sentencing, courts were observed to be making an increasing number of supervision orders, in line with the policy of promoting intensive community programmes (The Children's Society, 1993). According to Haines and Drakeford (1998), the use of community-based supervision increased from 15% to 20% of all court disposals between 1980 and 1990. This was not achieved uniformly, however, with the proportion of custodial sentences initially remaining fairly stable, but the net effect over the whole period appears to have been a displacement of custody by a range of community alternatives. The implication here (with resonance in the current era of Intensive Supervision and Surveillance Programmes) is that 'net widening' can be avoided where an effective systems management strategy is applied.

Changing patterns in the detection and processing of young offenders therefore had a cumulative effect in reducing the numbers being committed to custody, with quite dramatic consequences (see Table 1.3).

At the apex of the youth justice process, then, the use of custody declined by around 82% over this 10-year period. On the basis of this evidence alone, it might be concluded that the reputedly hard-line Thatcher government was, indeed, 'soft on crime' (Smith, 1995).

At each key decision point, changes in policy and practice appear to have combined to reshape the treatment of young people and their offending behaviour in a dramatic and perhaps unexpected manner: (1) fewer young

Table 1.3 Numbers and percentages of young people aged 14–16 processed by the justice system and the use of custody 1981–91 ('000s)

	Cautioned/found guilty (A)	Sentenced to custody (B)	(B) as a percentage of (A)
1981	113.7	7.7	6.8%
1986	99.8	4.4	4.4%
1991	75.2	1.4	1.8%

Source: (Home Office, 1992: Criminal Statistics England and Wales 1991)

people were the subject of formal interventions by the police; (2) a much greater proportion of those processed were being cautioned; (3) substantially fewer in number were being prosecuted; (4) relatively more community-based court disposals were being administered; (5) and so fewer young people, numerically and proportionally, were being incarcerated. The cumulative effect of these changes was thus progressively intensified. Significantly, the consequences were not just limited to minor offences or less experienced offenders:

> ... if more and more minor and younger offenders are being diverted from formal prosecution then it is increasingly the older and more serious offenders who appear in court ... If there were no changes to courts' sentencing behaviour, then an increase in diversion would be likely to lead to a proportionate increase in more severe sentences. But this did not happen in the 1980s ... juvenile justice practitioners were not just successful in reducing the custody rate, they were even more successful in reducing this rate for a relatively older and more serious cohort of offenders.
>
> (Haines and Drakeford, 1998: 60)

The evidence in support of the argument that the 1980s witnessed a clear and dramatic form of 'system change' is therefore very strong, although we are also reminded to avoid an unduly rigid adherence to the classification of youth justice 'regimes' according to specific time periods by David Smith (1999), who notes that the custody rate in 1996 was still lower than that of a decade previously, despite contrasting trends.

Overreaching ourselves: the 'punitive turn'

In presenting this schematic account of the recent history of youth justice, I am aware that this may have the effect of overstating discontinuities at the expense of those constant factors that underpin and/or overshadow the system overall. Some, indeed, have tended to emphasise such constants (Hudson, 1996; Smith, 1999; Muncie, 2000; Pickford, 2000; Burnett and Appleton, 2004), whilst others have opted for a more explicit 'change' narrative (Goldson, 1997; Haines and Drakeford, 1998; Pitts, 1999; Souhami, 2007).

Whilst accepting the argument that there are some enduring continuities, represented by structural dynamics such as 'othering' (Garland, 2001), the present account will focus initially on those changes instigated in the early 1990s that do represent, in this author's view, a substantial and disturbing reversal of the progressive developments of the previous decade. Overall, a picture will emerge of youth justice as a principled form of practice 'in retreat', where historical susceptibilities to self-righteous political populism (Hall *et al.*, 1978; Pearson, 1983) once again undermined principles of rights and social justice to the detriment of very many young people.

At the start of the 1990s, a spirit of genuine optimism prevailed in youth justice. As Telford and Santatzoglou (2011: 4) observe, 'youth justice by the end of the 1980s had travelled a considerable distance along the road towards the virtual abolition of custody (de-penalisation), and in general towards the minimisation of the formal application of criminal law in respect of youth behaviour (de-criminalisation)'. At the time, added impetus was given to these developments by events such as the death of 15-year-old Philip Knight in Swansea Prison in 1990.

Practitioners felt that they were having a real influence on the overall direction of travel in youth justice, and that the evidence supported their aspirations to the extent that it demonstrated real benefits to all those concerned with young people and their infractions of social norms. These aspirations were increasingly reflected in government policy, as noted earlier. Building on this, Home Office Circular 59/1990 (Home Office, 1990) once again endorsed the use of disposals short of prosecution for children and young people, and the Criminal Justice Act 1991 continued to develop the 'bifurcation' strategy already established implicitly. The act's sentencing framework set out clear demarcations between 'serious' and lesser offences, and endorsed the emerging offence-based perspective, which effectively downplayed offender characteristics or criminal histories:

> Arguably, the CJA [Criminal Justice Act] 1991 represented the first time that a British government clearly enshrined in a piece of criminal justice legislation a single coherent sentencing philosophy and policy.
>
> (Haines and Drakeford, 1998: 77)

The common basis of sentencing principles for both young and adult offenders also facilitated other developments, such as the alignment of the Youth Court with the provision of the UN Convention on the Rights of the Child, which defined 18 as the upper age limit of childhood.

At the same time, the behavioural emphasis of the new legislative framework was mirrored in the replacement of the more welfare-oriented Social Inquiry Reports with more offence-focused Pre-Sentence Reports to assist courts in sentencing decisions. It has also been suggested that there was an increased emphasis associated with these changes on the use of court disposals such as 'bind overs' to emphasise the importance of parental responsibility for disciplining and controlling children, again at the expense of welfare interventions (Macmillan, 1998). Indeed, it has been suggested that, ironically, it was this very erosion of concern with social and environmental influences, which had previously been welcomed by liberal interests (Stevens and Crook, 1986), that facilitated the increasingly punitive ethos of the administration of youth justice as the 1990s unfolded (Haines and Drakeford, 1998).

As previously noted, however, 'things change', and the rapid arrival of a backlash against what was perceived as an excessively liberal approach gained momentum in light of a number of coincidental events. The political sensitivity of the subject clearly played a part, and a number of changes in key personnel in government may well have contributed to the climate of uncertainty and, arguably, fear. Whatever the historical veracity of the image, the replacement of Margaret Thatcher with an apparently weaker successor, John Major, may well have been associated with a growing pressure to act 'tough'. This transition was accompanied by the appointment of a more right-wing home secretary, David Waddington, and it immediately became apparent that he was not fully supportive of the 1991 legislation, even as it passed through Parliament, emphasising its punitive aspects and contradicting his predecessors' explicit aim of reducing the prison population (Macmillan, 1998).

In addition, the early 1990s witnessed a series of 'riots' in areas that had not previously experienced the same extent of disorder, such as Cardiff, Oxford and North Shields. Of course, rioting of this kind was not a new phenomenon and, indeed, similar kinds of unrest had been in evidence periodically during the 1980s. However, these events were more likely to take place in predominantly 'white' localities, and therefore perhaps it was easier to offer 'criminalised' rather than political explanations for them; as always, it seems, young people were quickly identified as central to these outbreaks of lawlessness (Power and Tunstall, 1997).

These elements were further implicated in the process of building a 'moral panic' (Cohen, 1972) by way of a 'sophisticated campaign' led by influential figures in the police to turn attention towards 'persistent offenders' – that is, the small minority believed to be responsible for a great proportion of criminal activity and, coincidentally, the very group that was much less likely to be penalised as a result of the contemporaneous reforms in criminal justice. The campaign appears to have drawn on an array of 'evidence', including concerns arising from the outbreaks of disorder identified, the dangers posed by 'joy riding', and the exploits of particularly newsworthy individuals, such as 'Rat Boy' from Tyneside (*The Independent*, 7 October 1993).

More authoritative evidence was provided by the police to the parliamentary Home Affairs Select Committee, when arguing that, although the number of recorded young offenders was declining, crime rates had increased by 54% between 1980 and 1990 (The Children's Society, 1993). This figure was utilised to support the argument that a more liberal approach to youth offending had no effect overall in reducing crime levels, and may even have contributed to the recorded increase.

Along with the police, the courts too found the post-1991 legislative framework too restrictive, and clearly resented the limits placed on their sentencing powers (Hudson, 1996). As with the police, their primary concern was over their inability to deal with persistent offenders effectively, by increasing sentences on subsequent court appearances. The requirement to base their decisions essentially on the 'seriousness' of an offence was felt to be an example of unacceptable political interference in the sphere of judicial discretion (Goldson, 1997), and it clashed with deep-rooted assumptions about deterrence and retribution as cornerstones of sentencing practice.

Although it is often singled out as the trigger for the reversal of previous liberalising trends, the killing of James Bulger by two older boys aged 10 and 11 gave additional impetus to a movement that had already got well under way. It undoubtedly acted as an important contributory factor, and had specific consequences, such as the later abolition of the presumption of *doli incapax*, but equally, and significantly, it gained its full effect in association with a wider body of critical opinion and populist agitation.

Finally, and also of continuing relevance, was the emergence of a political consensus, at last, between the two leading political parties about being 'tough on crime'. This can perhaps be linked to the involvement of ambitious political 'heavyweights' on both sides (Kenneth Clarke as home secretary and Tony Blair as shadow home secretary), each anxious to make a reputation for himself, and to establish popular support around the issue for their own party.

In 1993, shortly after James Bulger's death, Prime Minister John Major said that 'society needs to condemn a little more and understand a little less'. This slogan has come to symbolise the conventional tone of political pronouncements in relation to youth crime, it might be thought. Writing in the *Daily Mail* at around the same time, Kenneth Clarke argued that 'the courts should have the power to send really persistent, nasty little juveniles away to somewhere where they will be looked after better and where they will be educated' (*Daily Mail*, 22 February 1993). Later in the year, in the bid to gain the political high ground, his opposite number Tony Blair observed: 'no one but a fool would excuse the commission of a crime on the basis of the offender's upbringing; and no one but a bigot would ignore the impact of that upbringing on the individual's behaviour' (*Daily Express*, 31 August 1993). Despite the acknowledgement of the influence of external factors and the aspirations for better outcomes for young offenders, these statements were clearly designed, first and foremost, to attract public support for a tough and essentially punitive stance on youth crime. Little attempt was made to add any real depth to the discussion about social causes and effective interventions. Such posturing has, indeed, tended to become the norm in party political debates about the problem of youth crime.

The government subsequently announced plans to tighten up on persistent young offenders on a wider scale. Within months of abolishing custody for 14 year olds under the 1991 Act, incoming Home Secretary Kenneth Clarke was announcing plans to create 200 new places in Secure Training Centres, which could be utilised for children as young as 12:

> The Government are determined to continue to strengthen the powers of the courts to deal with persistent offenders. We must also take measures to tackle the problem on a broader front ... The secure training orders will be different from anything that has ever been provided before.
>
> (House of Commons Debates, col. 139–40, 2 March 1993)

In line with this commitment, the government's first step was to reintroduce by way of the Criminal Justice Act 1993 the capacity for courts to take fuller account of offenders' previous criminal histories by simply inserting two words into section 1(2) of the Criminal Justice Act 1991, so that now 'one *or more*' (my emphasis) 'offences associated' with the one under consideration could now be taken into account in the sentencing process.

With the subsequent appointment of an avowed right-winger to the post of home secretary, Michael Howard, there was no doubt as to which way government policy was heading. Speaking at the Conservative Party conference in 1993, he proclaimed famously that 'prison works' (Rutherford, 1996). Significantly, he advanced only two justifications for this claim: that incarceration protects the public from 'murderers, muggers and rapists'; and that it acts as a deterrent (a claim that is unsupported by evidence). Absent was any attempt to justify its use in a reformative, rehabilitative or correctional manner. Evidence as to the effectiveness or otherwise of custody did not seem to be of particular concern in this context (Rutherford, 1996).

In keeping with these sentiments, further legislation was introduced in the form of the Criminal Justice and Public Order Act 1994, which, among other things, added to the range of custodial options available to sentencers, introducing Secure Training Orders of up to two years for 12–14 year olds, of which half would be served in the newly commissioned Secure Training Centres. Neither their cost (£75 million to build, £20 million a year to run: The Children's Society, 1993), nor the implicit disregard for the relevant international convention on the administration of juvenile justice (the 'Beijing Rules'; United Nations, 1985), acted as any kind of deterrent.

The same legislation also extended the capacity of courts to sentence young people to longer terms in custody, whilst it was also made easier for courts to override the presumption in favour of bail originating with the Bail Act 1976. Further announcements, of the establishment of 'boot camps' and of more stringent forms of 'punishment in the community', followed (Home Office, 1995).

At the other end of the spectrum, the increasingly punitive ethos was reflected in the revised guidance on cautioning, issued as Home Office Circular 18/94, which effectively put a stop to repeat cautioning, except in very tightly defined circumstances. This measure also sought to ensure that the nature of the offence would also be taken into account, and that 'serious' offences would automatically result in prosecution. Effective multi-agency strategies, such as that developed in Northamptonshire, were perceived to be under threat: 'although previous Home Office circulars on cautioning ... had positively encouraged the police to consult with multi-agency partners ... this circular went a long way in retracting this policy commitment' (Bell *et al.*, 1999: 99).

The net (widening!) effect of this policy shift was always likely to be an increase in the numbers of young people being formally processed and taken to court. As always, it seems that, whereas liberalising initiatives need copious evidence to demonstrate that they 'work' (Burnett and Roberts, 2004), moves in a punitive direction can be determined on the basis of hearsay or whim, as seems to have been the case here. Macmillan (1998) has suggested that this particular step was prompted by a BBC television programme, in which a young offender spoke of a caution being meaningless, and in which police and magistrates speculated about a link between increased use of cautioning and higher crime rates, despite the continuing absence of any evidence to support these assertions (Smith, 1989; Kemp *et al.*, 2002).

For youth justice practitioners, these represented challenging times. Having already committed themselves, sometimes explicitly, to a strategy of systems management, and having accepted the 'just deserts' approach embraced by government in more favourable circumstances, they now found it increasingly difficult to articulate an effective argument against government policies that claimed to be applying very similar tariff-based considerations of proportionality, but calibrated against very different calculations of what fair and appropriate disposals might constitute. Having accepted arguments for 'punishment in the community', and more restrictive alternatives to custody in order to establish 'credibility', there was little room for manoeuvre when the home secretary still insisted on dismissing community-based sentences as a 'soft option' (Muncie, 1999a).

Even in its last days, this Conservative government sought to toughen its approach yet further, by way of the Crime (Sentences) Act 1997, including provisions to extend the use of curfews, and to 'name and shame' convicted juvenile offenders.

Practice in a hostile climate

The abrupt shift in government policy and rhetoric in the early 1990s clearly signalled a change of mood. However, it is not always the case that public pronouncements, or even legislative changes, lead directly and logically to the desired outcomes. Similar rhetoric had been evident during the 1980s, of course, with the 'short, sharp shock' detention centres appearing very similar in intent to the 'boot camps' announced by Michael Howard in 1995; yet, practitioners and managers had found ways of working and developing services that confounded populist sentiments. So, what else changed to force practitioners onto the defensive and undermine their earlier achievements?

Bateman (2011a), too, has been concerned to address this question. He argues that there are four elements that combined to shape the working environment, and which therefore set the terms according to which practitioners operated: namely, 'increased public concern about the nature and scale of youth crime'; the convergence of political responses between the two main political parties; the reaction of the courts and other criminal justice decision-makers; and legislative change 'encouraging more intrusive responses to young people in trouble' (Bateman, 2011a: 118). Even in combination, though, these do not fully account for changes in practitioner behaviour, which are also associated with the changing dynamics of youth justice in the 1990s. Using the example of 'breach', Bateman illustrates the extent to which the notion of 'routinely' returning young people to court for non-compliance with community orders 'was not regarded as part of the job' by most youth justice professionals (ibid.: 120), but that this position was progressively eroded, such that between 1992 and 1998, for example, 'the number of custodial sentences imposed for breach – aggregated for adults and children – rose by 199 per cent' (ibid.: 127). However, he argues that this was not a simple product of automatic and unthinking compliance with new rules and expectations. There was evidence of resistance and a sense that practitioners were clinging on to cherished principles such as 'minimum intervention', but at the same time these principles were adapted to fit the new realities of this period:

> If the establishment of a 'custody free zone' was no longer a viable objective, it made less sense for practitioner philosophy to be focused in the same way around an anti-custody orthodoxy.
>
> (Bateman, 2011a: 124)

He concludes that what was in evidence was a 'progressive watering down' of practitioners' commitment to keeping children out of custody (Bateman, 2011a: 128), rather than a simple abandonment of this kind of fundamental principle.

Ironically, too, it may well have been the enduring commitment to such principles that led to an extension of punitive sanctions into the community, in a vain attempt to maintain community disposals as alternatives to custody. Not only were more and more requirements and surveillance measures imposed on young people, but, at the same time, this, too, increased the risk of failure through non-compliance. The Audit Commission (1996) provided an example of one such programme, with young people required to attend for 30 or 60 days. Attendance was reported as being strictly monitored, with two failures resulting in an automatic return to court for breach proceedings. The programme's content comprised five 'compulsory modules', covering offending behaviour, social skills, numeracy and literacy, job search/education, and substance abuse and HIV. Other optional components were also offered, including the ubiquitous 'constructive use of leisure time', and information technology.

In providing a strict and explicit correctional framework, this project could be said to be meeting the concern of the government of the time to ensure that the controlling aspects of community supervision programmes were enhanced. Thus, by the middle of the decade, there were 'over 150 diversionary community programmes operating in England and Wales designed to address offending behaviour through victim awareness, anger management, drug awareness and positive leisure schemes' (Muncie, 1999b: 283).

Perversely, however, the example cited by the Audit Commission did not appear to be fulfilling the aim of providing a direct alternative to custody. Only 38 (25%) of 153 young people considered suitable for this particular scheme were accepted onto it. Of the remainder, only 34 (22%) received a custodial sentence, whilst the rest were made subject to a range of less punitive disposals, including supervision or probation orders without conditions attached (29%), and in some cases fines or even Conditional Discharges. Not only was this project relatively unsuccessful at persuading the courts to make use of it, but it also seemed to be some way from offering a pure alternative to custody, given the diversity of outcomes recorded for potential participants. Indeed, for those not at risk of custody, but who subsequently breached the conditions of the programme itself, the result would have been an increased risk of being locked up. We cannot rely too heavily on one example (even one cited, rather surprisingly, as an illustration of 'good practice'), but it does at least illustrate quite sharply the point that a strategy of intensifying 'punishment in the community' (Hudson, 1996) can hardly be justified if it cannot demonstrate that it is genuinely acting as an alternative to custody.

Not only was the political climate increasingly hostile to inclusive and welfare-oriented practice, but there was also a sense in which organisational and structural changes were impacting on services at the same time. This can partly be attributed to contextual factors that ensured that attention and, indeed, resources were directed elsewhere. It may be that the achievements of the 1980s contributed to an assumption that the battle for progressive youth justice was won, and for hard-pressed local agencies money and personnel could be redeployed, for instance into child protection, or towards the implementation of community care (in 1993). In addition, the substantial investment of money and energy represented by the 1983 IIT initiative had gradually tapered off, and the 100 projects established under that programme were either wound up or incorporated into mainstream services (Smith, 1999). There is perhaps something also in the argument that the nature of the task had changed, from one of developing and proving the value of new forms of intervention, to one of 'managing' these interventions as part of established practice. Some (for example, Muncie, 1999a) have argued that this shift is also consistent with wider trends towards 'managerialism' in the delivery of public services, which can be seen as part of the Conservative legacy, stemming back as far as 1979. Indeed, Pratt (1989) has argued that even the debates between 'welfare' and 'justice' positions were themselves merely a smokescreen for the emergence of a 'corporatist' agenda, which was primarily concerned with efficient, effective (and cheap) service arrangements.

This emerging influence was associated with new forms of public management, which emphasised common strategic and organisational characteristics, rather than substantive differences of purpose or service context, so offering one rationale for the parallel development of multi-agency partnerships in youth justice as in other areas:

> By the 1990s such corporate, multi-agency strategies were to become subsumed within a much broader process of public sector managerialization. This ... has generally involved the redefinition of political, economic and social issues as problems to be managed rather than necessarily resolved.
>
> (Muncie, 1999b: 288)

A further development, which resulted in more explicit expectations of those responsible for direct practice, was the initial publication of National Standards for the Supervision of offenders by the Home Office (Home Office, 1992). This set in motion a conveyor-belt, which periodically delivers a new or revised set of standards almost as a matter of course (Youth Justice Board, 2000, 2004a, 2010a). The consequences have been highly significant in terms of the imposition of centralised constraints and procedures on practitioners, albeit in the name of consistency, fairness and good practice.

A major issue to emerge from these developments is the sense in which youth justice appears to have been 'depoliticised' (Muncie, 2009). The challenge becomes one of finding the best and most effective way of delivering an agreed package of assessments, service management, record-keeping and intervention, which is based on universal principles of best practice. The scope for alternative perspectives and professional discretion becomes extremely limited in this context:

> Social issues were depoliticised. Policy choices were transformed into a series of management decisions. Evaluations of public sector performance came to be dominated by notions of productivity, task remits and quantifiable outcomes.
>
> (Muncie, 1999b: 288)

Accounts of practice began to portray this kind of preoccupation, being more likely to highlight improvements in efficiency and 'system management' than the development of new models of intervention, or the promotion of social justice through service developments. Thus, The Children's Society (1993) reported an inter-agency initiative in South Wales that had claimed, as success indicators, a 'speeding up' of the judicial process, and a reduction of offending whilst on bail. Another initiative mentioned in the same report listed as its principal achievement the adoption of a comprehensive approach to managing the youth justice system, with no mention of substantive outcomes beyond this. Although these achievements may have some merit, they can only be seen as meaningful targets within a broader strategy to promote crime reduction or social inclusion.

Nevertheless, during this period there were initiatives put in place that sought to modify the worst consequences of the punitive agenda. These interventions were largely confined to the voluntary sector, with organisations such as the Howard League, through its Troubleshooter Project, and The Children's Society taking the lead (see, for example, Ashton and Grindrod, 1999; Moore and Smith, 2001; Moore and Peters, 2003). Both organisations remained explicitly committed to ending the use of custody for children, and sought to promote and preserve their rights in the youth justice context. In this sense, they represented a spirit of continuity with the 'anti-custody', justice-oriented movement of the 1980s identified by Haines and Drakeford (1998). Unlike providers located within statutory agencies, they did not experience the same constraints of rationalisation and prescription, and they began to develop a role as defenders of the key elements of a 'liberal' approach to youth justice. Thus, they sought to find ways of protecting and promoting the interests of children and young people at the most acute pressure points, specifically targeting the arbitrary and discriminatory use of custody.

Processes and outcomes: upward trends

General trends in the incidence of crime may help to provide a context for our analysis of changing practices in youth justice, although this relationship is, indeed, problematic for a number of reasons. Estimates of the level of offending from both official records and surveys of the general population suggest that this reached a high point in the early 1990s (Home Office, 2001b). Recorded crimes, for example, rose from 4.5 million in 1990 to 5.6 million in 1992, although by 1998/99 they had declined again to 4.5 million annually, at which point new counting rules took effect. The revised figures after this date suggested that the crime rate had levelled out over the next two years. It is extremely difficult to extrapolate from these headline figures any meaningful estimates of the proportion of offences carried out by children or young people, although the Audit Commission (1996) estimated that, based on the relative proportion of known offenders under the age of 18, this figure can be put at around a quarter. Subsequent estimates have suggested a rather higher figure than this, at just over a third (Budd and Sharp, 2005). Of course, we know, too, that the profile of offences committed by young people is also likely to be different from that of adult offenders, given differences in culture, lifestyle and opportunity (Budd *et al.*, 2005; see also Chapter 7).

At the same time that the rate of offending appeared to stabilise, detection rates were falling, whilst police also continued to make use of informal warnings in some cases (Home Office, 1996). The net effect was a reduction in the proportion of young offenders who were the subject of formal action (cautions or prosecutions) over the course of a 10-year period (Home Office, 2001b). This is not the same, of course, as suggesting that the number of offenders decreased in reality, or that we can infer anything about wider patterns of behaviour (Muncie, 2004). It does mean, however, that a pattern emerged of progressively fewer young people coming to be processed formally by the machinery of the justice system.

For those who were cautioned (replaced in June 2000 by Reprimands/ Final Warnings) or prosecuted, there were significant changes in the pattern of disposals. In common with other trends, cautioning as a proportion of outcomes increased to its highest level in the early 1990s for all age groups and for both sexes (Home Office, 2001b: 105), but then declined steadily to the year 2000. Cautioning rates, too, fell for all categories of indictable offences between 1990 and 2000, except criminal damage and robbery (see Table 1.4).

With the rate at which children and young people were proceeded against falling, and the cautioning rate moving in the same direction, the net effect was that the number of cautions administered was dropping quite sharply over this period.

On the other hand, the *number* of those aged 10–17 being taken to court for indictable offences was on the increase. After an initial decline in this figure from 66,000 in 1990 to 60,000 in 1993, there was a steady rise to 81,000 by 2000. While the overall number of those being dealt with by way of formal proceedings did not change substantially, the balance had clearly shifted very significantly towards a much greater relative emphasis on prosecutions rather than pre-court disposals.

This change was paralleled by a much greater use of the most punitive options by the courts, with an increase in the rate of custodial sentencing over

Table 1.4 Cautioning rates (offenders cautioned as a percentage of all those cautioned or found guilty), 1990–2000

Year	Males			Females		
	10–11	*12–13*	*15–17*	*10–11*	*12–13*	*15–17*
1990	95	84	53	99	93	73
1992	96	86	59	99	96	81
1994	95	81	56	100	94	77
1996	94	77	51	99	91	72
1998	91	72	48	97	88	67
2000	86	68	43	95	86	63

Source: (Home Office, 2001b: Criminal Statistics England and Wales 2000)

the period 1990–2000, from 10% to 15% of all disposals in respect of 15–17-year-old males, and (a threefold increase) from 2% to 7% for 15–17-year-old females. In numerical terms, these trends are even more striking, with an increase from 3,600 to 5,200 for young men, and 100 to 400 for young women in this age group.

For 12–14 year olds, custodial options had only been available at the start of the decade under Section 53 of the Children and Young Persons Act 1933, in respect of the most serious of offences. With the introduction of Secure Training Orders from 1997, this became a much more widely used form of disposal. Importantly, this also illustrates the lesson that, whatever safeguards are in place, if a punitive disposal is available, it is likely to be used, sometimes with enthusiasm. By 1994, for instance, the percentage of sentenced 12–14-year-old boys sent to custody had decreased to an insignificant figure; however, by 2000, this had increased again to 6%, of which 4% was represented by Secure Training Orders (repackaged as Detention and Training Orders under the Crime and Disorder Act 1998). Females in this age group were also now receiving custodial sentences where they had not previously (2% in 2000) (see Table 1.5).

In short, the 1990s, and particularly the latter part of the decade, saw a rapid reversal of the 'double gain' identified in the previous decade (Haines and Drakeford, 1998). Previously, diversionary strategies had reduced the number of young people coming to court, and at the same time greater availability and use of alternative to custody schemes had reduced the proportionate use of custody, achieving a kind of multiplier effect across the system as a whole. However, these achievements were thrown precisely into reverse by the end of the 1990s: fewer young people were being diverted from court, and as a greater proportion were being dealt with by the courts, so the higher rate of custodial sentencing again had a compound effect, accelerating the trends towards increased levels of incarceration.

At the same time, there were also big increases in the use of community sentences (Supervision Orders, for example), but these were at the expense of other lower-tariff disposals, such as fines and discharges (Home Office,

Table 1.5 Custody rates (percentage of children and young people receiving custodial sentences as proportion of all those sentenced), 1990–2000

Year	Males			Females		
	10–11	*12–14*	*15–17*	*10–11*	*12–14*	*15–17*
1990	0	2	10	0	0	2
1992	0	3	11	0	0	2
1994	0	0	14	0	0	4
1996	0	1	16	0	1	4
1998	0	2	15	0	0	6
2000	1	6	15	0	2	7

Source: (Home Office, 2001b: Criminal Statistics England and Wales 2000)

2001b). Such trends looked certain to be further exacerbated with the effective removal of the Conditional Discharge as an option for anyone who had previously received a Final Warning under the Crime and Disorder Act 1998.

The cumulative evidence from this brief review of trends in the exercise of police discretion and courts' sentencing behaviour suggests that the youth justice system did take an increasingly punitive turn from the early 1990s onwards and, indeed, that this shift was not modified in the short term by the change of government in 1997.

Alongside this, another key message becomes apparent for those engaged in management and practice within the youth justice system. It is of considerable importance to retain an awareness of how the 'system' as a whole operates, and how its various elements interact. Good practice in one context can easily be negated elsewhere, either as a result of 'unintended consequences' (Thorpe *et al.*, 1980), or because of deeper changes, which effectively transform the whole working environment – so that, for example, diversionary practice is progressively undertaken with increasingly inexperienced offenders, responsible for more and more minor offences.

The 1980s and 1990s: a simple tale of advance and retreat?

The empirical evidence appears to support the argument that this period of roughly 20 years can be divided fairly straightforwardly into periods of progressive advance, on the one hand, and a dramatic reversal of this movement, on the other. Pitts (2001b: 17), for example, describes the extension of custodial regimes for 12–14 year olds as 'a death blow to the non-interventionist delinquency management strategies of the 1980s'. Similarly, Goldson (1997: 79) has suggested that in the 1990s 'a reactionary U-turn was launched which rapidly dismantled the successful practice orientation of the previous decade'.

Others, though, are careful to stress the continuities that are apparent, despite the obvious shifts in patterns of intervention and disposal. Pratt (1989) argued at the time that the key development was the emergence of 'corporatist' principles, as evident in the establishment of multi-agency collaborations, measures to standardise practice and the increasing dominance of managerial rather than professional orientations towards practice. 'Welfare' remained discredited as a rationale for intervention, whilst practitioners continued to express a commitment to an 'anti-custody' philosophy (Haines and Drakeford, 1998). For Bateman (2011a: 125), too, the 1990s are better seen as a period of retrenchment, at least on the part of practitioners, rather than abandonment of principles of minimum intervention, advocacy and arguing 'against custody as far as possible for as long as possible'. Matthews (2005: 193) also argues against the dangers of over-simplification, suggesting that there 'is a preoccupation with limited oppositions and polarities that fail to do justice to the diversity, contradictions, reversions and tensions in current crime control policy'. By the same token, Muncie (2002: 156) argues that youth justice as it is constituted and practised, effectively incorporates a series of competing and potentially contradictory rationales, and it is the interplay between these that is significant in determining the precise configuration of interventions, decisions and outcomes at any particular point in time.

Undoubtedly, though, the experiences of this 20-year period (1980–2000) offer a number of important lessons for those concerned with the contemporary shape and future possibilities of youth justice. First, under the right circumstances and acting effectively in collaboration, practitioners can make a difference at a strategic level (Telford and Santatzoglou, 2011); second, young people and their misdemeanours are, and will remain, a focal point for public concern and political agitation; third, ideas, discourses and practices do not always interface coherently or consistently (an 'anti-custody' philosophy may thus inadvertently underpin greater levels of 'punitiveness', for example); and, finally, over-simplification is unhelpful (as in the wholesale rejection of 'welfare' as a relevant consideration for young offenders).

Note

1 According to the presumption of doli incapax, young offenders aged 10–14 were deemed not to be fully responsible for their crimes unless this was shown to be the case.

2 The New Labour experiment

'Tough on crime, tough on the causes of crime …'

As we have already observed, the 1990s was a period in which a consensus emerged between the two leading political parties in the UK over youth crime. This was an issue on which Labour had historically been seen as unconvincing in the eyes of the general public, and where the party came to the view that it must shift its position as part of a wider strategy of becoming 'electable' (Pitts, 2003; Solomon and Garside, 2008). In order to try to establish a distinctive position, Tony Blair, as shadow home secretary, sought to establish a coherent link between the expectation that young people would take personal responsibility for their behaviour and that, in return, they could expect help from government and the community to integrate them effectively into society. Thus, by linking the criminal act with its causes, and promising to be 'tough' on both, the party hoped to achieve the dual task of assuaging fear of youthful delinquencies, whilst reassuring supporters that it also recognised the need for social investment to counter the criminalising effects of inequality and discrimination.

This, in turn, enabled Labour to develop a twin-track approach, developing a range of policies to control and minimise 'crime', whilst locating these within a broader strategy aimed at promoting social inclusion and tackling those social problems associated with disadvantage and inequality, as part of a 'joined up' policy agenda (Clark, 2002).

In seeking to achieve this aim, the tactic adopted was to re-affirm commitment to 'popular Conservative law-and-order themes', whilst promising to do a much better job of meeting these aspirations, by offering 'vastly improved economy, efficiency and effectiveness' (Pitts, 2003: 88). Thus, the elision of populist objectives and managerial methods of delivery lay at the heart of New Labour's 'new youth justice' (Goldson, 2000), and this, perhaps, helps to explain why one of the party's 'five pledges' in the 1997 election campaign was simply to 'speed up' youth justice processes.

Indeed, true to its word, on coming to power, New Labour acted very swiftly to introduce its proposals for youth justice (Home Office, 1997a, 1997b) and then legislate accordingly. However, we should also acknowledge that this was not just an isolated initiative, but was linked in various ways to the government's goal of tackling social exclusion (Social Exclusion Unit, 1998, 2002) and, in particular, reducing crime through broader intervention programmes. It will be helpful here to consider the relationship between these wide-ranging social programmes and specific youth justice measures in order to gain a sense of the inter-relationship between the two, their combined impact and the 'legacy' (Goldson, 2010) left by New Labour on its departure from office.

Getting 'tough on the causes of crime'?

In many respects, the approach adopted by the incoming Labour government in 1997 deviated very little from a long-established consensus, linking the incidence and distribution of youth crime with a range of associated factors, including various features of social exclusion, including 'inadequate parenting', 'lack of training and employment', 'unstable living conditions' and 'drug and alcohol abuse' (Audit Commission, 1996; Farrington, 1996), a consensus that has evidently persisted to the present too (Centre for Social Justice, 2012). The then government established its Social Exclusion Unit (SEU) immediately on coming to power, with a view to developing an integrated ('joined-up') strategy to understand and then address these and other related issues, both in their own right and in relation to their compound effects, especially in certain geographically defined communities:

> The poorest neighbourhoods have tended to become rundown, more prone to crime, and more cut off from the labour market. The national picture conceals pockets of intense deprivation where the problems of unemployment are acute and hopelessly tangled up with poor health, housing and education.
>
> (Social Exclusion Unit, 1998: para. 1)

The apparent interconnectedness of these problems, and their concentration amongst particular groups, led to the assumption, in turn, that the benefits of developing integrated intervention strategies were self-evident. This, it was suggested, would be an innovative approach:

> Above all, a joined-up problem has never been addressed in a joined-up way. Problems have fallen through the cracks in Whitehall Departments or central and local government. And at neighbourhood level, there has been no one in charge of pulling together all the things that need to go right at the same time.
>
> (Social Exclusion Unit, 1998: para. 7)

Outside the UK, though, it appeared that there was evidence to support the kind of preventive initiative envisaged, with the prospect that appropriately targeted interventions would have a generic impact in reducing social problems, both for individuals and for their communities. There could be a 'virtuous circle' of beneficial outcomes. This was exemplified for New Labour, in particular by the Headstart (High/Scope) programme from the USA, first introduced in the late 1960s, and subject to detailed subsequent evaluation. This demonstrated that a comprehensive early years service could generate long-term improvements against a number of key objectives, including improved educational attainment and higher employment rates, as well as reduced levels of offending (Schweinhart, 2003). Thus, the major investment in Sure Start undertaken by the government at this time was itself partly justified by the belief that it would contribute to a future reduction in the levels of youth crime (Sure Start, 2000).

More detailed analysis of the relationship between social exclusion and youth offending seemed to offer support for the principle of 'joined-up' policy and practice development. Youth offending has been found to be strongly associated with 'non-attachment to school' and lack of 'parental supervision', for instance (Graham and Bowling, 1995). High-crime areas themselves have been observed to demonstrate characteristics of *'compound social disloca-tions* – that is, an accumulation of social problems alongside crime, including drug-misuse, family violence, teenage pregnancy, children taken into care, and school failure' (Hope, 1998: 53).

These areas are also characterised by *'concentrated poverty'*, where 'low-skilled' young people are systematically excluded from the labour market. In these circumstances, Hope (1998: 52) argues, the conditions are established for 'vulnerable victims and potential offenders' to be brought together. Of course, subsequent work has also established that there is a strong likelihood of young people's experience of victimisation itself being associated with their involvement in offending at the individual level (Smith, 2004). As we shall see, Merton's (1957) work provides a plausible sociological explanation of the dynamics that may underpin these outcomes.

The policy implications identified by the Social Exclusion Unit, and accepted wholeheartedly by government, were that only a systematic and comprehensive response to the problems facing many disadvantaged groups and neighbourhoods would be effective, echoing another prime ministerial soundbite: 'Joined up problems demand joined up solutions' (Blair, 1997). The view that interventions needed to be both comprehensive and systematic naturally also lent itself to the assumption that such measures would need to be tightly specified and closely managed, pre-figuring an intensification of 'managerialism' at the point of delivery (Clarke *et al.*, 2000).

So, these broader strategies and programmes can be seen as acting in a complementary manner with the more focused measures directed specifically at 'youth crime', which we will consider shortly (Home Office, 1997a, 1997b; Solomon and Garside, 2008).

During its time in power, the New Labour government sustained its com-mitment to tackling social exclusion, periodically 'renewing' its approach (HM Government, 2006), but largely retaining its overarching analytical and strategic framework. Thus, in restating the five 'guiding principles' of its approach, it notably enumerated 'better' problem identification, promoting multi-agency ('joined-up') working and improving 'performance' (HM Government, 2006: 8, 9), thus reinforcing the perception that the primary concern was with more and better management rather than changes in social relationships or, say, the promotion of a rights-based approach to inclusion.

This broad strategy was echoed from within youth justice, with an acknowledgement that the 'objectives of reducing social exclusion are complementary to those of preventing offending, and vice versa, and an extremely important policy area for youth justice' (Ashford, 2007: 25). Although it is clear from such policy pronouncements that the overall interconnectedness of social problems, including youth crime, lay at the heart of the government's approach, as the focus shifts to consider initiatives in more detail, it is also apparent that policy can be differentiated, according to the way in which problems were classified. The Social Exclusion Unit itself set out to focus on discrete areas of concern within its overarching framework (for example, Social Exclusion Unit, 1999b, 2002). As a result, it seems that government was pursuing its objectives of prevention and inclusion on a number of distinct levels (see HM Government, 2006: 58, for example): generalised prevention programmes, targeted schemes for 'at risk' groups, and individualised interventions directed specifically at those known to be involved in problematic behaviour. In terms of youth crime prevention, this, in turn, led to a differentiated model of resource allocation and intervention (see Table 2.1).

Generalised crime prevention

The New Labour government promised a 'revolutionary approach' to the problems of disadvantage and deprivation in specific neighbourhoods. This would be triggered by the creation of a £900 million Neighbourhood Renewal Fund, and programme targets included improved educational attainment and reductions in crime, notably domestic burglary (to be cut by 25% over the period 2001–05). The National Strategy for Neighbourhood Renewal (Social Exclusion Unit, 2001b) set out to provide substantial funding for the benefit of entire communities on the assumption that focused universal provision of this kind would provide mutually reinforcing gains, improving the quality of life generally, at the same time as producing measurable achievements such as a reduction in crime and anti-social behaviour.

New Labour also undertook a wide range of initiatives directed at various aspects of social exclusion with a more or less explicit link to the perceived risk of youth crime, including: truancy and school exclusion; neighbourhood renewal; teenage pregnancy; youth unemployment and children in care (Social Exclusion Unit, 2001a, 2003). For instance, a series of initiatives was introduced to tackle school exclusion and truancy at a cost of £300 million

Table 2.1 Government youth crime prevention initiatives

Level	Generalised	Targeted	Individualised
Object of intervention	Disadvantaged neighbourhoods, problem populations, 'crime' in general	'At risk' groups, marginalised young people, families 'causing anti-social behaviour'	Known offenders, anti-social individuals, 'at risk' individuals
Methods of intervention	Family support, community development, education and training	Leisure schemes, project work, employment schemes, learning opportunities, Family Intervention Projects	Offending behaviour management programmes, surveillance, restrictions of freedom
Intervention programmes/ mechanisms (e.g.s)	Sure Start, Connexions, Neighbourhood Renewal Programme, inclusive education	'On Track', Youth Inclusion Programme, Community Safety Partnerships	Final Warning programmes, Youth Inclusion and Support Panels (YISPs), Intensive Supervision and Surveillance Programmes (ISSPs), Acceptable Behaviour Contracts, Intensive Fostering
Outcome targets	Long-term overall reduction in crime figures	Medium-term, area-based reduced fear of crime, reduced rates of reported crime	Short-term, stop/ reduce/prevent individual offending

over the period 1997–2001, keying in with the government's wider emphasis on educational achievement. This programme included the establishment of Learning Support Units, additional places in Pupil Referral Units and the addition of incentives to encourage schools to 'hold on' to students at risk of exclusion. In addition to these broadly supportive measures, however, the government also brought in a number of specific (targeted) schemes to emphasise the *responsibilities* of children and parents in this context, including 'truancy sweeps', to be negotiated between Local Education Authorities and the police, which involved an extension of police powers in December 1998.

It was subsequently reported that 'in York, when truancy sweeps were launched in 1999, youth crime fell by 67 per cent, and in parts of Newham, car crime fell by 70 per cent' (Social Exclusion Unit, 2001a: annex B, para. 16). Here, the link between promoting positive educational outcomes and preventing youth offending is made quite explicit, and the reduction in youth crime is advanced as one of the major justifications for getting young people back into school. Interestingly, however, subsequent research questioned the ease with which a causal connection between school exclusion and youth crime has been assumed (Berridge *et al.*, 2001; Hodgson and Webb, 2005). Even though this is clearly identified as a 'joined up problem' (Berridge *et al.*, 2001: 48), patterns of cause and effect are complex, and thus simplistic responses are unlikely to provide a complete answer.

Concerns about the implications of unemployment for young people were also addressed quite early in the SEU's lifespan (Social Exclusion Unit, 1999a), and this led to the establishment of the Connexions Service.[1] This was set up as a universal programme, unlike other initiatives, such that every young person would have access to information and assistance in making key decisions about the transition into further education or training and the world of adult responsibilities. Connexions was launched in 2000 with a spending commitment of £420 million, to:

> provide information, advice, support and guidance to all teenagers through a network of Personal Advisers based in schools, further education colleges and elsewhere. The service has a range of ambitious targets to improve participation and achievement in education and training, and to reduce drug abuse, offending and teenage pregnancy rates.
>
> (Social Exclusion Unit, 2001a: para. 5.22)

Once again, the link is made between the overall programme objective and a series of apparently connected social problems, including, of course, youth crime. Even a universal programme such as Connexions was partly to be judged according to its achievement in reducing offending. Indeed, evidence from early pilots suggested that this was a realistic aspiration:

> Thirteen Connexions pilots have already demonstrated how a Personal adviser can make a real difference. There are examples within the pilots of young people at risk being pulled back from the brink of chaos and set up to achieve greater success in later life.
>
> (Social Exclusion Unit, 2001a: annex E, para. 3)

By 2006, the government was in a position to review progress and launch a further 'Action Plan' on social exclusion, which spoke of building on progress up to that point (HM Government, 2006), although it was much less specific than previous policy documents about how it would go about doing so. In relation to youth crime prevention, the plan referred to the aim of further increasing investment in parenting support (ibid.: 62), thematically linked to a range of other initiatives intended to 'improve' parenting across the childhood years (ibid.: 60). This, in turn, may have been informed by the emerging evidence that, despite all the opportunities to improve their lives provided by New Labour up to that point, 'a minority of families – around 2% of the population – have simply not been able to take advantage of these opportunities' (Armstrong, 2007: 1).

Targeted youth crime prevention

The New Labour government also sought to develop a range of targeted programmes, seeking to address those young people 'at risk' in various ways. Some of these were pragmatic developments, based on schemes already in place, such as drug education and crime prevention in schools, Safer Cities projects, and other existing initiatives, focusing on bullying, graffiti and vandalism (Home Office, 1997b). Some were quite specific, and appeared designed to attract popular support, such as the 'local child curfew', proposed by the new government, with the dual aim of protecting children in particular areas from the risk of harm and preventing 'crime and disorder' (Home Office, 1997b: 16).

These ideas were supplemented by other strategies promoting a 'joined-up' approach at local level, including a new requirement for local authorities and the police to work together to reduce crime and improve community safety (through the establishment of Crime and Disorder Reduction Partnerships). Specifically, it was stated that 'the Government expects that measures to tackle youth crime will figure wherever that is a problem locally' (Home Office, 1997b: 10).

Additional funding was provided by government to address the issue of young people 'at risk' of offending through other policy streams, aimed at specific target populations. On Track was one such development, launched in December 1999, and aiming to put in place a range of preventive options for children aged 4–12. The suggested menu of interventions included 'home-school partnerships, home visiting, parent training, structured pre-school education and family therapy' (Children and Young People's Unit, 2002).

Similar aspirations were evident in the Youth Inclusion Programme (YIP), intended to target 'the most disaffected young people in the 13 to 16 age range' (Morgan Harris Burrows, 2001: 1). The objective of this initiative, launched in 2000, was to identify the 50 young people at greatest risk of offending in the highest crime areas in England and Wales, and to include them in a variety of activities alongside other young people, including holiday schemes, sport, after-school projects, informal education and social skills training. The initial results from the YIPs were said to be highly encouraging (Morgan Harris Burrows, 2001), with a 32% fall in crime reported in Doncaster and 14% falls in Gateshead and Wrexham, where schemes were in place. However, subsequent follow-up suggested that these initial achievements had not been sustained (Morgan Harris Burrows, 2003: 14).

Further developments included 'Splash', initiated by the Youth Justice Board in 2000 to provide summer activities for young people at risk – borrowing, it seems, from the much-praised French model of the *étés jeunes* (Pitts, 2001b).

In a quite different context, the teenage pregnancy initiative prompted by an earlier SEU report (Social Exclusion Unit, 1999b) also made links to youth crime:

> A module on sex and relationships for young offenders has been developed as part of the Life Skills package with the Prison Service. The Sex Education Forum has produced supporting materials. The sexual health education course for young offenders will be rolled out from April 2001 ...
>
> (Social Exclusion Unit, 2001a: annex D, para. 8)

The assumption here appears to be that promoting a sense of personal responsibility in one aspect of one's life may contribute to a broader embrace of pro-social behaviour. It also points to an underlying concern about the apparent 'joined-upness' of social problems, in that it becomes possible to apply quite damning generalisations to those whose behaviour may be a cause of concern in just one respect. In this sense, it might even become easier to find validation for the notion of a composite 'underclass', sharing a catalogue of inadequate characteristics and undesirable behaviours (Murray, 1996).

Within the broader framework of the government's generalised strategy, these targeted schemes appear to have demonstrated a degree of internal coherence, being based on the principle of systematically identifying those most likely to offend according to common characteristics (see McCarthy *et al.*, 2004); and then providing intervention programmes aiming to re-engage them in mainstream activities, which also offered opportunities for personal growth and development, social integration and achievement. Whilst there have been criticisms of the negative connotations of 'targeting' (Percy-Smith, 2000), the pragmatic and empiricist assumptions underlying 'administrative' approaches to tackling deep-rooted structural problems (Clarke *et al.*, 2000), and the potential 'net-widening' effects of notionally preventive strategies (Solomon, 2009), these programmes appear to have offered both a substantial investment and a clear commitment to an inclusive approach to crime prevention among young people.

By the time New Labour came to revisit its overall youth crime strategy, its detailed prevention objectives were clearly aligned with the shifting focus of the social exclusion agenda; and the 'targeted' aspect of the revised Youth Crime Action Plan 2008 (HM Government, 2008) clearly prioritised the '110,000 families with children identifiably at risk of becoming prolific offenders', each of whom would be the subject of 'a targeted intervention as a result' of the new measures to be put in place (HM Government, 2008: 7). The new catchphrase to encapsulate the government's intentions was 'non-negotiable support and challenge' (ibid.: 1). Families 'with the most complex and entrenched problems' who 'tend not to look for support themselves, and can sometimes be resistant to offers of support' would be required to engage in programmes of parenting support 'with non-negotiable elements' if they should 'refuse to engage' (ibid.: 31).

By 2010, when a Youth Crime Plan Update (DCSF, 2010) was published, immediately before the government was voted out, great claims were being made for the 'Family Intervention Projects' (FIPs) established in every local authority area. A '64% reduction in anti-social behaviour, a 58% reduction in problematic school behaviour, a 70% reduction in drug abuse and a 53% reduction in alcoholism' were stated to have been achieved for the first 1,030 families to 'complete a FIP' (DCSF, 2010: 8; Dixon *et al.*, 2010: 5).

The increasing emphasis on preventive work with parents and families is perhaps of significance here, and clearly finds echoes in subsequent developments associated with the coalition government that followed (Centre for Social Justice, 2012, for example, and the 'troubled families' initiative); essentially, though, the notion of 'targeted' prevention and the continuing development of programmes consistent with this approach represents a continuity of the kind of thinking articulated from the early days of the New Labour project (Straw and Michael, 1996).

Individualised crime prevention

A recurrent problem for crime control strategies that prioritise 'prevention' is that they are inevitably unable to prevent all criminal activity. In light of this, and in line with the managerial logic of New Labour, it became necessary to develop forms of intervention designed to address the specific risks posed by individuals identified as potential or actual offenders. Whilst prevention remained the overarching objective, and set the terms for such interventions, the emphasis shifted much more explicitly towards measures to identify the level of threat posed by specific young people, and take action to contain or manage their behaviour in order to reduce crime.

From the start, New Labour's White Paper *No More Excuses* (Home Office, 1997b) proposed a range of options under the heading 'Effective Intervention in the Community', which aimed to identify and address children and young people identified as being 'at risk' of offending, and their parents. Thus, 'the child safety order is designed to protect children under ten who are at risk of becoming involved in crime or who have already started to behave in an anti-social or criminal manner' (Home Office, 1997b: 15). Presumably here the word 'protect' is intended to imply the words 'from themselves'! The proposed order (aimed at children below the age of criminal responsibility, it should be stressed) would allow courts to require children to comply with specific instructions, such as 'to be home at certain times' or to attend 'a local youth programme', with the option of instituting care proceedings for failure to comply.[2]

This measure would be complemented by the parenting order under the government's proposals, which could require parents to attend specific training programmes as well as require them to secure the good behaviour of their children. The justification put forward for this provision was that: 'inadequate parenting is strongly associated with offending – in a Home Office study,[3]

42% of juveniles who had low or medium levels of parental supervision offended, but only 20% of juveniles with a high level of supervision' (Home Office, 1997b: 12). Measures were subsequently put in place by the Crime and Disorder Act 1998, and succeeding legislation, to compel parents to engage in the process of controlling their children's behaviour, once evidence of some form of transgression emerged.

Subsequently, this strategy was further intensified, most notably through various mechanisms of surveillance, prohibition and enforced compliance embedded within the justice system. Thus, for example, known and persistent young offenders were subjected to greater scrutiny through the introduction and later extension of the Intensive Supervision and Surveillance Programme (Beaumont, 2005; and see below), put in place with an explicit commitment to reduce reoffending (Youth Justice Board press release, 18 March 2004).

At the other end of the spectrum the invention, extension and enthusiastic promotion of the Anti-Social Behaviour Order, and associated paraphernalia such as the Acceptable Behaviour Contract, focused on those whose behaviour may have been demonstrably problematic, but who need not have been the subject of formal criminal proceedings (Burney, 2005).

Further measures such as Intensive Fostering, introduced by the Criminal Justice and Immigration Act 2008, shared the same agenda, being:

> based on the Multi-dimensional Treatment Foster Care (MTFC) model which has been used successfully with offenders in Oregon since the 1980s. This model is based on a system of points and levels which reward appropriate behaviour.
>
> (Ministry of Justice, 2012e)

In sum, New Labour's evolving youth crime prevention strategy incorporated three distinct levels, operating within and in concert with an overall 'tackling social exclusion' agenda, informed by a rationale that sought to identify and intervene with certain populations or communities known to be 'at risk' of incubating crime or anti-social behaviour, at one level, and at another, to address potential and then known perpetrators directly by imposing a range of measures of containment and control on them and their parents. These latter options would, of course, be supplemented further by the extensive range of criminal sanctions also put forward under the government's developing reform programme for youth justice, to which we shall now turn.

The end of tolerance – the roots of reform

The central project of tackling youth crime, which formed such a significant element of the incoming government's overall project in 1997, and continued to do so thereafter, can be traced back to a number of emerging strands, linking political expediency, research evidence and direct experience. These elements coalesced to form a purportedly coherent and politically attractive change strategy, which was set out in detail in the White Paper *No More Excuses* (Home Office, 1997b).

It had become increasingly apparent over a number of years that the impact of young people's behaviour was a major issue of social concern, which necessarily forced it up the political agenda. 'Left realists' had argued that the attribution of 'criminality' should not be seen simply as the consequence of the imposition of state control on young people in particular, but also as a feature of the everyday experience of most communities, and especially those experiencing other social disadvantages (Lea and Young, 1984; Kinsey *et al.*, 1986). Not only do the official figures fail to recognise a huge number of unreported offences, but these are also likely to affect certain sectors of the population disproportionately, with poorer people demonstrably more likely to be burgled and young black men more likely to experience violent assaults, for example (Lea and Young, 1984: 22). The fact that these constituencies were seen as being 'Labour' led to a significant reappraisal of the party's response to the issue of crime. The victimisation of specific groups, such as women and ethnic minorities, and the concentration of specific types of crime in poorer areas, were seen as requiring a range of proactive responses, in order to demonstrate a commitment to social justice:

> Law and order ... is a radical issue. It is an issue for the poor and the old, least able to resist the impact of crimes that ... may appear trivial. It is an issue for ethnic minorities suffering racial harassment and racial attacks. It is an issue for women suffering ... male harassment and violence ... All these social groups, despite their many differing interests, have a common interest in combatting crime.
>
> (Kinsey *et al.*, 1986: 73)

This realisation, driven initially by academic research, found echoes in the direct experience of Labour politicians, national and local, notably those 'from working class backgrounds' (Taylor, 1981). They tended to represent those very areas that were experiencing the multiple impacts of a series of social disadvantages, including the kind of 'intra-group' (Lea and Young, 1984) crimes that compounded the sense of injustice and abandonment that they felt. This recognition, combined with Labour's traditional vulnerability to the accusation of being 'soft on crime', led to a significant reappraisal during the party's long period in opposition from 1979 to 1997.

The first clear signs of a shift in emphasis emerged with Tony Blair's contributions to the debate in the prevailing climate of moral panic in the early 1990s (Blair, 1993). Moves to develop a new and credible centre-left position on crime, and particularly youth crime, were further intensified with the promotion of Jack Straw to the position of shadow home secretary in 1994. It seems that his willingness to take action in this area derived at least

partly from his own history and experience. He had been brought up in relative poverty, and he had been made particularly aware by his own constituents
of their concerns about crime. As a result, he found less room for excusing the
acts of offenders than might have been expected, perhaps. A visit to New York
in 1995 enthused him with the idea of 'zero tolerance' policing (Newburn and
Jones, 2001). According to the principles of this approach, any and all signs
of anti-social behaviour and community disintegration must be tackled swiftly
and resolutely (Kelling, 1998). This message was relayed bluntly, and with a
distinct shift of emphasis, away from the causes of crime and towards its
manifestations:

> In conjunction with tackling the underlying causes of crime, the commu-
> nity has a right to expect more responsible and less anti-social behaviour
> from its citizens. That means less intimidation, bullying and loutish
> behaviour on the streets and in our towns and city centres.
>
> (Straw, 1995, quoted in Charman and Savage, 1999: 198)

These clear statements of intent were quickly translated into policy commitments prior to the forthcoming general election, at least partly to neutralise
the Conservatives' perceived electoral advantage in this area of the political
landscape (Pitts, 2001b). Thus, by 1996, the language of 'blame', 'responsibility' and 'punishment' had been purposefully introduced into the rhetoric of
Labour politicians. In seeking to take the initiative, the party's document on
youth offending stated that:

> Recognising that there are underlying causes of crime is in no way to
> excuse or condone offending. Individuals must be held responsible for
> their own behaviour, and must be brought to justice and punished when
> they commit an offence.
>
> (Straw and Michael, 1996: 6)

Equally importantly, the historical concerns of Labour to prioritise children's
welfare (in the Children and Young Persons Act 1969, for example) were now
being de-emphasised: 'the welfare needs of the young offender cannot outweigh the needs of the community to be protected from the adverse consequences of his or her offending behaviour' (Straw and Michael, 1996,
quoted in Goldson, 1999: 9). The contrast with Labour's commitment to
address offending behaviour *by* meeting welfare needs under the 1969 Act
could not be starker.

The consequences for government policy when New Labour took power
were evident. Youth offending would be dealt with directly in its own right,
and at face value. It was subsequently noted that: 'the (re)politicization of
youth crime has ushered in a new agenda moulded and fixed around
the imperatives of punishment, retribution and re-moralisation' (Goldson,
1999: 9).

The Crime and Disorder Act 1998 and the micro-politics of control

Hot on the heels of *No More Excuses*, the New Labour government introduced its 'flagship' legislation, the Crime and Disorder Act 1998, despite the intense concern generated already by the policy changes signposted in the White Paper (Crowley, 1998; Newburn, 1998).

The Act itself built on *No More Excuses* directly, particularly in areas such as the creation of inter-agency arrangements to plan, implement and oversee local youth offending services. The establishment of Youth Offending Teams (YOTs), local inter-agency partnerships and statutory plans to tackle youth crime were all put on a statutory footing. The Act thereby created the structures to support a 'corporatist' approach to the delivery of youth justice (Pratt, 1989).

The structural framework was further supported by an extensive range of mechanisms and procedures setting out precisely detailed and highly prescriptive rules for implementation, as could be expected from an administration with a commitment to a strategy of 'micro-management' (so extensively demonstrated during its time in office; Muncie, 2006).

The precise nature of the Act's provision for linking specific interventions to the circumstances and offending patterns of individual young people is also of note. The room for professional discretion or creativity was highly diminished under this policy regime, for both youth justice practitioners and, indeed, the judiciary. Thus, for example, the progression through pre-court disposals, by way of Reprimands then Final Warnings, for early career offenders left virtually no room for manoeuvre, as some YOTs found to their cost (Pragnell, 2001), and despite evidence that demonstrates the potential value of discretionary use of alternatives to prosecution (Stevens and Crook, 1986; Kemp *et al.*, 2002; Smith, 2011a).

By the same tariff-bound logic, the 1998 Act also sought to rule out the use of Conditional Discharges in respect of young people who had already received a Final Warning, presumably on the basis that they had already exhausted their entitlement to a 'second (or third) chance'. The subsequent introduction of the Referral Order by the Youth Justice and Criminal Evidence Act 1999, to be located only at the point of a first court appearance, seemed merely to compound the arbitrary fettering of judicial discretion. These measures collectively bore uncanny similarities to the framework for the realisation of social control anticipated by Michel Foucault (Smith, 2001). In this way, the machinery is put in place to treat every infringement of the penal code as part of an unbroken continuum, leading from minor acts of disobedience (pre-delinquency) to the far end of the spectrum in the form of the carceral institution, operating to the same forensic logic of corrective behavioural control:

> Continuous gradation of the established specialized and competent
> authorities ... which, without resort to arbitration, but strictly according

to the regulations, by means of observation and assessment, hierarchized, differentiated, judged, punished and moved gradually from the correction of irregularities to the punishment of crime.

(Foucault, 1979: 299)

Tightening control

If anything, the changes introduced by the Crime and Disorder Act represented an intensification of the processes of criminalisation and punitive actions against young people, at all levels of the justice system. This process was accompanied by a steady flow of florid rhetoric from successive home secretaries (Jack Straw, David Blunkett and Charles Clarke), as well as the prime minister. In one such example, the support of the electorate was courted graphically:

> One of the biggest challenges we face is how to deal with young offenders who believe that their age makes them untouchable, who flout the law, laugh at the police and leave court on bail free to offend again. The public are sick and tired of their behaviour and expect the criminal justice system to be able to keep them off the streets.
>
> (David Blunkett, Labour Party Election Broadcast, 24 April 2002)

Whilst the sceptical observer might note that this says little for the preventive reform programme already undertaken by the self-same administration, of greater significance is that the persistence and consistency of this kind of reputedly authoritative pronouncement can only serve to reinforce a hegemonic (Gramsci, 1971) view of what the problem is and what the solutions are. A series of policy documents and legislative measures followed, informed by, and to some extent also validating, these politically driven arguments (Home Office, 2001a, 2003a, 2003b). For example, the government's review of the entire criminal justice system, *Criminal Justice: The Way Ahead*, issued in 2001, proposed a series of changes focusing on the restriction, containment and surveillance of young offenders, including the introduction of more intensive community supervision programmes, tighter surveillance and monitoring of bailees (Home Office, 2002a), and increased availability of places in custody. In announcing the new Intensive Supervision and Surveillance Programme (ISSP) with funding of £45 million from April 2001, the emphasis on control and rigour was made clear:

> The Youth Justice Board is making grants to around fifty YOTs [Youth Offending Teams] (or groups of YOTs) for each to work with 50–60 hard core repeat young offenders a year.
>
> An ISSP will last at least six months for each offender. It will combine close surveillance by the police and other agencies with a highly structured intensive daily programme tackling the causes of offending. During

the first three months the supervision programme will be for at least five hours a day on weekdays with access to support during the evenings and weekends.

The whereabouts of each young offender on the programme will be checked at least twice daily with 24 hours a day, seven days a week surveillance where this is necessary. Techniques may include electronic tagging, voice verification ..., tracking ..., and intelligence led policing.

(Home Office, 2001a: 32)

Clearly, here, the focus is entirely on surveillance, containment and crime control and there is no consideration of any underlying factors linked to the young person's offending, or the issues of need and personal and social development.

The ISSP was launched initially in 41 areas of England and Wales, and subsequently its coverage was extended to young people on remand, thus ensuring that a highly intrusive programme would be imposed on young people prior to conviction or sentence. By 2003, plans were afoot to expand the number of ISSP places to 4,200, three-quarters of which would be available post-conviction (Home Office, 2003b). Although ISSP was promoted by the Youth Justice Board and others as an 'alternative to custody' (NACRO, 2005), this number was actually in excess of the total number of young offenders in custody at the time, strangely.

In addition to ISSP, proposals were included in *Criminal Justice: The Way Ahead* for a further extension of courts' powers 'to refuse bail to youngsters with a history of committing or being charged with imprisonable offences' (Home Office, 2001a: 32). This appeared to represent a further toughening of the government's position, and represented a clear dilution of the commitment to the underlying presumption in favour of bail, established in principle by the Bail Act 1976. This proposal was implemented by Section 130 of the Criminal Justice and Police Act 2001, which enabled courts to impose a 'security requirement' where a young person had a 'recent history' of repeat offending, and where in the court's opinion they must be kept in a secure setting to prevent the commission of further offences. Earlier restrictions based on the seriousness of the alleged offences, or the level of risk posed to the public, were effectively removed by these new powers. As the supporting guidance stressed, 'the courts have not previously had the power to remand into secure detention those young people who have committed, or who are alleged to have committed, repeated offences of a less serious nature' (Home Office, 2002b: 2).

In addition, the same piece of legislation provided courts with the additional power to require 'electronic monitoring' (tagging) of young people on bail or remanded to local authority accommodation (Sections 131 and 132).

Finally, in this bundle of measures to 'strengthen' the youth justice system, the government made a commitment 'over the next five years to build 400 additional secure training centre places, providing intensive supervision and high quality programmes for young people in custody' (anticipated Home Office, 2001a: 32). Presumably, these were partly intended to offset the need for 600 places in local authority secure units necessary to accommodate the increased numbers of young people detained on remand (*The Guardian*, 16 April 2002).

If these measures are to be seen as part of a coherent programme, then there can be no doubt that government initiatives targeted at *individuals* involved in crime or anti-social behaviour represent a strategy of intensifying levels of control and restriction of liberty, whether in community-based forms of intervention, or in secure settings. This, as we have seen (Chapter 1), stands in marked contrast to earlier commitments to minimise the use of custody and other punitive measures, thus continuing the trends originating in the 1990s of eroding the safeguards for young offenders, especially at the younger end of the age scale.

The catalogue of prescriptive and restrictive initiatives continued unabated, indeed, with the introduction of further legislation, including the Criminal Justice Act 2003 and the Anti-Social Behaviour Act of the same year. In both cases, the trends were similar. Yet more powers were provided to the police, courts, youth justice services and others to impose requirements on children and their parents across a range of activities and settings. Thus, under the former (Sections 322 and 323), it became possible to attach Individual Support Orders to Anti-Social Behaviour Orders, in effect to impose compulsory intervention programmes on young people whose behaviour might not necessarily have constituted an offence. In addition, powers to make Parenting Orders were also to be extended to be available in cases where Referral Orders were made on young people (Section 324), thus further compromising the 'restorative' principles underpinning this particular disposal.

Burney (2005: 37) comments that the Anti-Social Behaviour Act incorporated a 'raft of new controls' on parents, and incorporated a 'rag-bag' of proposals based on the preceding White Paper *Respect and Responsibility* (Home Office, 2003a), including the ability to impose curfews on children under the age of 16.

The green shoots of ambiguity

In some respects, though, New Labour's policy initiatives demonstrated at least a hint of an alternative discourse. Whilst the punitive logic of micro-control was extended into the area of children's 'anti-social' behaviour, at the same time modifications of the rigorous logic of progressive punishment were apparent in the relaxation of the rules on the use of Referral Orders (Home Office, 2003b) and the introduction of pick 'n' mix-type community orders (first the revised and broadened Action Plan Order, and later in 2009 the Youth Rehabilitation Order, or YRO), which offered an alternative to the notion of a progressive tariff. On the other hand, the principles of micro management seem to have been retained to the extent that an ever-increasing number of elements could be prescribed under the aegis of such catch-all orders (extending to 18 distinct options under the YRO; www.justice.gov.uk/youth-justice/courts-and-orders/disposals/youth-rehabilitation-order, accessed 18 June 2012).

These slight nods towards alternative purposes for the youth justice system were developed further by New Labour, in subdued counterpoint to the heavily dominant preoccupation with close control. These developments were partly inspired by a relentless refusal on the part of the government to allow its own initiatives time to settle and to become effectively embedded in practice. The sense in which 'reflexive modernity' (Giddens, 1991; Beck, 1992) had taken hold was striking, but, for those affected, the everyday challenge remained to make sense of and try to respond to the maelstrom of constant innovation:

> The issue always is, in that process of change, how do you keep all of your day-to-day functional services operating and not take your eye off the ball, because it's like you're having to do two things at once, isn't it? Because you're keeping the operational service going but you're reconfiguring some of its relationships or its structural set up, and for me the issue then always is the capacity and it's almost a more risky time going through the change.
>
> (Children's services representative, quoted in Fielder *et al.*, 2008: 16)

Nonetheless, there did appear to be a sense in which, perhaps, alternative but coherent rationales for practice were emerging (Muncie, 2002, for example). In particular, there was a palpable air of enthusiasm about restorative justice and the potential for extending its limited role in the wider justice system (Home Office, 2003c).

The first significant reorientation of the government's strategy, following 1998, came with the introduction of the Referral Order the following year. The order had been signposted by the White Paper, *No More Excuses*, and it put in place a means for young offenders to be dealt with outside the conventional sentencing framework on their first court appearance. If pleading guilty, they should be referred to a 'youth panel' for their offence(s) to be addressed through the application of the principles of 'restorative justice' (Johnstone, 2002; Crawford and Newburn, 2003). Although the subject of some debate (Dignan, 2005, for example), according to the White Paper these were:

- *restoration*: young offenders apologising to their victims and making amends for the harm they have done;
- *reintegration*: young offenders paying their debts to society, putting their crime behind them and re-joining the law abiding community; and

• *responsibility*: young offenders – and their parents – facing the consequences of their offending behaviour and taking responsibility for preventing further offending.

(Home Office, 1997b: 32)

This attempt to provide a rationale for the government's preferred model for the Referral Order seemed somewhat eclectic, and at the same time glossed over a lively and continuing discussion about the nature of restorative practice (Haines, 2000). For the moment, however, it was this interpretation that informed the subsequent legislation and its implementation.

Thus, on an admission of guilt, a young person would be referred to the youth panel,[4] and s/he and her/his parents would be required to attend a 'panel session', with others in attendance, including the victim and any other relevant participants. The panel itself would be representative of the community, and would therefore reflect 'lay' rather than judicial interests. Legal representation would not be allowed, in order to ensure that the panel itself was able to engage 'directly' with the young offender.

The proposal for the new order suggested that a 'contract' should be drawn up between the panel and the young person, setting out the requirements to be placed on her/him and her/his parents. These would 'always include an obligation to make *reparation*. This might be achieved through a letter of apology or a direct meeting with the victim; by putting right any damage caused by the offence; or through financial compensation' (Home Office, 1997b: 32). Reparation could also be made to 'the community' where direct methods were deemed inappropriate, for instance if a victim declined to become involved. In addition, the contract might be expected to include requirements to participate in specific activities, such as counselling or drug rehabilitation, unpaid community work or educational provision. The agreement might also specify that the young person should not participate in certain activities, or visit particular places. According to the White Paper, although the court would have no control over the content of the programme, it could determine the length of time for which it should apply (between three and twelve months), subject to three-monthly progress reviews by the panel.

These proposals were enacted by Part I of the Youth Justice and Criminal Evidence Act 1999 (itself subsequently consolidated in the Powers of Criminal Courts (Sentencing) Act 2000), so that referral to a 'youth offender panel' became mandatory on a young person's first court appearance (and admission of guilt), except where the court might intend to impose a custodial sentence (or hospital order), or deal with the matter by way of an absolute discharge. Thus, on the one hand, the youth offender panel and the Referral Order were established as central features of the youth justice system, to which virtually every young person appearing in court for an offence would become subject, but, on the other hand, clear limits were imposed on its intrusion into the established judicial structures and procedures, in that the order would only be available at this point in the young person's offending career (with limited exceptions in the case of further offences whilst subject to the order).

In addition to these constraints, the issue of compulsion and failure to comply also poses some challenging questions in relation to Referral Orders. Although highly punitive sentences are not imposed as a matter of course when offenders do not attend, fail to agree a contract, do not comply with the contract or reoffend (Crawford and Newburn, 2003: 140), additional sanctions are available to the courts in these circumstances. This, along with the fairly standard menu of interventions on offer, may indicate that the young offender's experience of the Referral Order was likely to be little different from that of other forms of disposal. So, whilst the Referral Order apparently moved restorative ideals centre stage, it:

> represents both a particular and a rather peculiar hybrid attempt to integrate restorative justice ideas and values into youth justice practice. It does so in a clearly coercive, penal context that offends cherished restorative ideals of voluntariness.
>
> (Crawford and Newburn, 2003: 239)

The state of policy under New Labour: all things to all people?

At this point, it might be helpful to take a step back and reflect on the meaning and impact of changes in youth justice policy as developed by the New Labour government over its first decade in office.

The first question to consider here is that of the *intent* of the government's activities in the field of youth justice. As we have already observed, this is a highly politicised and contentious subject, and it is one on which the Labour Party historically felt itself to be vulnerable, and therefore a certain amount of political manoeuvring might be expected. It is on this basis that we might then ask the question as to whether the government was really committed to some of the draconian measures introduced, or merely wished to appear 'tough on crime'.

For example, the New Labour government sought to distinguish between measures intended to reduce crime by improving the quality of life and promoting social inclusion, on the one hand, and those 'targeted' at the problematic behaviour of specific individuals and groups, on the other. These various initiatives were at times presented as coherent and compatible parts of an integrated overall strategy (Home Office *et al.*, 2002: 30). According to Prime Minister Blair:

> Re-balancing the system means tackling the causes of crime – striving to give everyone in our society the rights and the opportunities they need to avoid a life of crime.
>
> It means tough legislation – backed up with police on the streets – to reduce crime and anti-social behaviour and reinforce people's responsibility to society.

It means bringing our courts into the twenty-first century and making sure that they serve victims and witnesses as well as they serve defendants.

And it means sentencing that keeps the public safe from the most dangerous prisoners, and which rehabilitates those who can be diverted from re-offending.

(Blair, 2002)

Vision statements of this kind were elaborated in a series of policy documents, stemming from the mid-1990s through the period of New Labour's term in office, including *No More Excuses, Justice for All* and *Respect and Responsibility*. At the same time, the panoply of authoritarian reforms of justice systems and processes is matched by an equally extensive range of policy and spending initiatives intended to promote community well-being and prevent crime. The recurrent theme was that 'rights' to welfare support and other forms of socially beneficial intervention should be matched by the exercise of individual 'responsibilities', but with severe sanctions in place for those who did not accept this implicit 'deal'.

Of course, there is a difference between simply presenting a series of disparate measures as a coherent and unified programme and being able to demonstrate that this is the case. This is clearly a pertinent question in this context.

First, it has been suggested that the overall 'managerial' tone of the government's approach to policy making reflects a misunderstanding of the structural nature of the problems being addressed. For example, Pitts has argued that dealing with superficial 'manifestations' of poverty is unlikely to provide real or lasting solutions to the 'structural economic and political problems at the heart of social exclusion' (Pitts, 2001b: 147). In other words, the New Labour government's approach focused primarily on symptoms, rather than causes of social disadvantage and crime. As a result, intervention strategies concentrated on easily identifiable and measurable 'risk factors', which have, at best, only a partial relationship to the causes of offending

Table 2.2 'Tough on crime, tough on the causes of crime' – the government's 'integrated' strategy

Tough on crime	Tough on the causes of crime
Catching and convicting criminals	Sure Start
Prosecuting and rules of evidence	Neighbourhood Renewal
Review of the criminal courts	The Children's Fund
What works (prison service reform)	Raising standards (education)
A better deal for witnesses	New Deal(s)
Anti-social behaviour measures	Anti-Drugs Coordination Unit
Stronger sentencing powers	Youth activity programmes

Source: (Adapted from Home Office, 2001a: 22)

behaviour (Pitts, 2001a). Thus, concerns with 'social exclusion' were trans-lated into programmes automatically designed to manage and eradicate only its visible representations, in the form of '"[poor] parenting", "truancy", "drug abuse", "homelessness", "low income" and the like' (Pitts, 2001a: 9). As a con-sequence, initiatives to tackle these issues, like 'truancy sweeps', are based on, and indeed reinforce, causal assumptions that are not evidence-based. In fact, these approaches actually divert attention away from more plausible explanations of disadvantage and anti-social behaviour. Managerial indicators of 'risk', pro-gramme performance and outcomes serve only to gloss over key questions about both the underlying purpose and efficacy of the strategies adopted. Thus:

> we are little nearer understanding the causes of youth crime and our choice of methods of intervention must remain haphazard. In the event, this, by no means insignificant, problem has been resolved by a process of political and scientific attrition.
>
> (Pitts, 2001a: 9)

Associated with these concerns about the limitations of a programme based on managerial assumptions is the prospect that dealing with social problems by way of a 'targeted' approach will itself result in a number of unintended consequences. These interventions may, indeed, run counter to the intentions of more generic, universal services. There are likely to be problems with both the techniques of 'targeting' and the consequential impact on those individ-uals and communities who are highlighted in this way. It is, as Percy-Smith puts it, very difficult to find sufficiently accurate and sensitive tools to 'iden-tify individuals, groups or areas who should be the focus of targeted actions' (Percy-Smith, 2000: 18). In addition, because these mechanisms are crude, people are inevitably going to be wrongly classified, with some alleged troublemakers being targeted incorrectly, and others, whose behaviour may be more problem-atic, being missed (McAra and McVie, 2005). Indeed, it may be that more subjective concerns about what is problematic come to determine apparently *objective* decisions about what is acceptable and unacceptable, especially in an era of increasing concern with the anti-social as well as the criminal (Squires and Stephen, 2005: 202).

As the Audit Commission (1996: 58) has acknowledged, there is 'no way of predicting accurately which individuals are going to offend'. As Pitts (2001b) reminds us, 'risk factors' linked to youth crime operate in quite different ways depending on the context. Furthermore, apart from the practical difficulties associated with identifying just which individuals and groups should be the subject of particular interventions, there may be other, counterproductive consequences. The result can be the exacerbation of 'negative perceptions of particular areas or groups' (Percy-Smith, 2000: 18). This, in turn, can generate additional problematic consequences, such as racial stereotyping and general stigmatisation of entire communities and neighbourhoods (Pitts, 2008: 63). The risks of such 'unintended' outcomes of youth justice policy are of real significance, given the recognition that young black men continue to be over-represented at all stages within the justice system (see Chapter 8).

Notes

1 One example of an increasing divergence between England and Wales in terms of social policy developments has been the growing use of different terminology to describe apparently similar programmes. The Welsh equivalent of the Connexions Service was launched under the heading 'Extending Entitlement' (National Assembly for Wales, 2000).
2 Although this provision was implemented under the Crime and Disorder Act 1998, the Children Act 2004 modified the Child Safety Order, so that care proceedings could no longer be instituted for failure to comply – on the basis that it contravened the principles and procedures of the earlier Children Act (1989).
3 A study carried out by Graham and Bowling (1995).
4 These became Youth Offender Panels under the subsequent legislation.

3 Coming full circle?

The legacy of New Labour

The period between 1997 and 2007 was a time of unprecedented activity in the world of policy relating to young people and their (mis)behaviour, with powerful consequences at all levels of the justice system, as Souhami (2007) has demonstrated. As the mood of the times changed, with the oncoming economic downturn, and a new prime minister (Gordon Brown), so there also seemed to be another significant change of direction in youth justice, from 2008 onwards. Whilst it will be important to consider the drivers and consequences of change at this point of time, it will also be helpful first to set this apparent refocusing of youth justice against the backdrop of 10 years' concerted attempt to promote 'radical' reform.

It is helpful, too, to recall just what was heralded in 1997 when Labour came into government, and promised to overhaul the system of justice that it had inherited. In a 'remarkable' transformation of both its own reputation as historically 'soft on crime' and the machinery for 'managing' the problem of youth crime, New Labour set out its ambitions to prevent crime through a programme of early intervention, to improve and speed up the functioning of the machinery of justice, to deliver swift and effective interventions where needed, and to ensure greater coordination and efficiency of the youth justice system overall (McLaughlin *et al.*, 2001: 307). In short, better management would lead to more certain and thus more impactful outcomes, with offenders being left in no doubt as to the consequences of their behaviour, and left with no hope that endemic inefficiencies would 'let them off the hook'. Just by making things work better, a step change would be achieved in the quality of intervention, and its effectiveness in controlling delinquent behaviour and preventing reoffending. The logic and rhetoric of justice need not be questioned, according to this argument, as these improvements alone would guarantee an enhanced quality of life for communities, victims of youth crime and even those engaged in offending and their families. By simply making the system work better, rising crime rates could be halted, and 'the restoration of law and order could be achieved by rebuilding the foundations of a strong civic society' (McLaughlin *et al.*, 2001: 304).

As we have seen, though, this was not exactly how things played out in practice. In a sense, it was the very logic of tighter management and closer control of unruly behaviour (Foucault, 1979) that created the conditions for the emergence of problems further down the line. This can perhaps be illustrated in two ways: through the emergence of the 'ASBO nation' (Squires, 2008), and the 'scorecard' of New Labour's achievements over the period of a decade (Solomon and Garside, 2008).

A growth industry: dealing with 'anti-social behaviour'

The government responded to calls from communities and local authorities to provide greater powers to tackle anti-social behaviour through Section 1 of the Crime and Disorder Act 1998, supported by some hard-hitting ministerial rhetoric. This was: 'a triumph of community politics over detached metropolitan elites' (Home Secretary Jack Straw, 8 April 1998, quoted in Burney, 2002: 471). The aim was to provide measures that would give a range of local agencies powers to control and prevent behaviour short of a crime that was causing significant neighbourhood disruption. Although these were not targeted solely on young people, provision was made for action to be taken against them within the legislation and supporting guidance (Burney, 2002: 474).

The Anti-Social Behaviour Order (ASBO) was implemented in April 1999, although initial take-up was fairly low, with only 466 orders being made in the first two-and-a-half years (Burney, 2002: 475). Significantly, however, 58% of these were made on under-18s. In addition, even at this stage, there was clearly a wide variation in their use geographically.

Any thought that government might merely have introduced these measures as a form of posturing was dispelled by the enthusiasm shown for ASBOs by a succession of ministers, including further legislation to extend their use, for example through the Police Reform Act 2002 and the Anti-Social Behaviour Act 2003. As early as October 1999, the home secretary wrote to local authorities reminding them that the order had been introduced at their instigation and urging them to make greater use of it (Burney, 2005: 32). Both Jack Straw and his successor David Blunkett continued to promote ASBOs, culminating in the announcement that: '"ASBO Ambassadors" would be despatched to those areas deemed not to be making sufficient use of the orders' (Squires and Stephen, 2005: 74).

Although the ASBO was introduced as a civil power, a number of aspects of its operation appear to have blurred the distinction between civil and criminal disposals, and it seems clear that this distinction had little value in the minds of ministers. So, an easy elision began to be made between anti-social and criminal behaviour, thereby justifying tighter measures of control:

> The anti-social behaviour of a few damages the lives of many. We should never underestimate its impact. We have seen the way communities spiral downwards once windows get broken and are not fixed, graffiti spreads

and stays there, cars are left abandoned, streets get grimier and dirtier, youths hang around street corners intimidating the elderly. The result: crime increases, fear goes up and people feel trapped.

(Blunkett, 2003: 2)

The rise of the ASBO

As Squires and Stephen (2005) have pointed out, the basis for the use of measures such as ASBOs was somewhat uncertain, allowing for a 'range of activities' to be included within the definition of anti-social behaviour (ibid.: 38). On one day, 10 September 2003, no fewer than 66,107 incidents were recorded by more than 1,500 organisations. However, of these, more than half were already defined as criminal acts. Thus:

> ASB comprises not a new range of problems to which modernity has lately become subject but rather a range of very familiar crimes and disorders defined largely by reference to a new range of enforcement processes.
>
> (Squires and Stephen, 2005: 38)

The substantial overlap between criminal behaviours and the vague and extensive list of other issues of concern, such as 'loud music' or 'climbing on buildings' (Home Office, 2004a: 4), suggests very wide scope for interpretation in the application of legislative powers in this area. As a result, there was a 'large area of enforcement leeway' (Squires and Stephen, 2005: 38), with the process of enforcement itself acting to apply the label 'anti-social' to a particular form of behaviour (which thereby also justifies its use).

Understandably, perhaps, in the light of this, there was considerable variation both over time and by geographical area in the processes of obtaining and implementing ASBOs. Initial findings (Campbell, 2002) suggested that ASBOs were not being granted in very large numbers (see above), but that they were very rarely refused on application to magistrates (only 18 (4%) turned down between April 1999 and March 2001). In addition, in the early days of implementation, the great majority of orders made were on young people (74% aged 21 or under), prompting the comment that 'This bears out the common perception of ASBOs as largely combating anti-social youth' (Campbell, 2002: 8).

Significantly, too, ASBOs were far more likely to be administered to young males than their female counterparts (a ratio of 14:1 was reported; Campbell, 2002: 9). Applications were received almost equally from police and other agencies, and the most common concern was about behaviour committed as part of a 'gang'. At least 18 different types of behaviour were targeted, including some that were clearly 'criminal' (such as assault and racial harassment), and others that may simply be annoying ('noise' or 'public disturbance').

Other observations were also made in this study about the characteristics and antecedents of those made subject to ASBOs. Over 60% of those for whom information was available had 'mitigating factors' that might have contributed to their behaviour (Campbell, 2002: 18), and a large number also had previous convictions. This appears to support the view held elsewhere (Burney, 2005; Squires and Stephen, 2005) that the distinction between anti-social and criminal behaviour has become blurred.

Equally, this initial study found that ASBOs were relatively ineffective in terms of achieving the objective of preventing the repetition of problematic behaviour. Of a small follow-up sample, 36% were found to have breached their ASBOs within a year of the order being made (Campbell, 2002: 75). For those who were breached for failure to comply with the terms of the ASBO, custodial sentences were administered in 46% of cases, including a number of young offenders. Whilst the numbers were not large, this appeared to indicate the possibility of custodial sentences being made for behaviour falling short of a crime, thus incorporating a 'tariff-jumping' effect, which creates an 'artificially steep and slippery slope into custody' (Squires and Stephen, 2005: 109).

Such evidence-based concerns did not appear to inhibit the government, however, given that it proceeded to widen the scope for obtaining ASBOs, and continued to exhort agencies and police to extend their use. Introducing the Anti-Social Behaviour Bill to the House of Commons in 2003, the home secretary proclaimed this as 'very important legislation, which will empower people across the country once and for all to get a grip on the scourge that bedevils their communities: the anti-social behaviour that makes other people's lives a misery' (David Blunkett, quoted in Burney, 2005: 34).

Dismissing the legislation as based on a 'rag-bag collection' of community concerns, and lacking any real definition of 'anti-social behaviour' at its core, Burney anticipated the 'targeting of certain types of problem people, some of whom – beggars, youths – become anti-social simply by being in the street. Linked to this is the theme of sanitised public space' (Burney, 2005: 36). In light of this, it was striking that one of the 'case studies' given great prominence on the relevant government website reflected exactly this kind of scenario (see the archived website, attributed to the Home Office, at webarchive.nation alarchives.gov.uk/20100413151441/http://asb.homeoffice.gov.uk/members/article. aspx?id=7668, accessed 16 July 2013).

Following an initially slow take-up, the use of ASBOs accelerated rapidly, with a total of 14,972 reportedly issued by December 2007 (Berman, 2009). These were concentrated both geographically (Manchester and Greater London alone accounted for 3,450 orders between them; ibid.: 18), and demographically with 41% of those issued being taken out against juveniles where age was known (ibid.: 8). The breach rate overall was calculated as 54%, and for 'juveniles it was 64%' (ibid.: 14).

Investigations by the Youth Justice Board (2004b, 2005a) suggested that a considerable proportion (36%) of young people had breached ASBOs in the period June 2000 to December 2002, and, of this number, 41% (71) were sentenced to custody. Nevertheless, the Youth Justice Board concluded that this did not mean that failure to comply was recruiting a 'whole new group' of young people into the prison population, since many of these cases concerned young people who were already likely to be 'considered prolific offenders', with an average of 42 previous offences (Youth Justice Board, 2004b). Even so, the board expressed its concern about both the length and the nature of the restrictions imposed by ASBOs, which were 'quite challenging'.

Given the level of interest and its own commitment, it is perhaps surprising that the government appears to have gone cold at this point on evaluation and dissemination of the impact of ASBOs, with substantial criticism being made of its reluctance to issue up-to-date figures on breaches, for example (asboconcern, 2006). This may partly be connected with the parallel concerns emerging about the effectiveness of this 'targeted' measure, with its additional 'tailored' options of Individual Support Orders (introduced under the Criminal Justice Act 2003) and Acceptable Behaviour Contracts. In practice, evidence was beginning to build up of ASBOs being used in a simplistic attempt to control behaviour with complex and deep-seated antecedents (BIBIC, 2005; Fletcher, 2005). Children with identifiable learning difficulties, for example, appeared to be made subject to orders, regardless of the origins or prognosis of their 'problem behaviour'. Thus, the British Institute for Brain Injured Children (BIBIC) found that Youth Offending Teams (YOTs) had identified 35% of those under 17 subject to ASBOs as having a 'diagnosed mental health disorder or accepted learning difficulty'. In one case, a 14-year-old boy with a language impairment and suspected ADHD (Attention Deficit Hyperactivity Disorder) had been subject to an ASBO for two years, during which time he had broken its terms on 13 occasions. Despite having committed no additional offences during this time, he had spent a considerable period in custody as a result.

As we shall see subsequently, the change of government in 2010 led to a recognition that the ASBO was not fit for purpose, and a rethink of policy in this area, but its emergence and use as a specific tool of intervention under New Labour does exemplify in stark terms the meaning and consequences of an obsession with the micro management of problem behaviour.

'How did we do?' New Labour's scorecard

Helpfully, the Centre for Crime and Justice Studies did carry out an audit of the government's achievements in youth justice over the period 1997–2007 (Solomon and Garside, 2008), judging its performance on its own terms, rather than from an explicitly critical perspective, and the conclusions drawn were not positive:

> Overall, most of the targets have been missed and success in achieving the desired outcomes has been far more elusive than the government claims.

In reality, the record on youth justice reform is at best mixed. Despite the huge investment, self-reported youth offending has not declined ...

(Solomon and Garside, 2008: 11)

The authors of the study reviewed four key areas: youth justice spending, the incidence of youth crime, the youth justice process and meeting the needs of young people in the justice system.

On spending, they noted that, between 2000/01 and 2006/07, 'spending on youth justice has increased in real terms by 45 per cent' (Solomon and Garside, 2008: 9), although the pattern of spending was skewed heavily in favour of meeting the costs of custody, representing over 12 times the proportion of the budget dedicated to prevention. It was noted, too, that this funding increase represented a shift in the balance of welfare spending into youth justice, given that much of the bill for local youth justice services was met from local authority social services budgets.

In relation to youth crime, the study noted that there had been falls in the number of young people being convicted for offences such as vehicle crime and burglary, but that these simply replicated wider falls in the number of offences recorded by police. These developments in turn reflect long-term crime rate trends, and this 'places in some doubt confident claims that the falls in youth convictions for these offences are related to recent government reforms' (Solomon and Garside, 2008: 37), in youth justice or other areas of policy. On the other hand, self-reported crimes by young people had remained stable, and the government's target in this respect had not been met, an outcome which was 'far from impressive' (ibid.: 37).

Turning to the youth justice process itself, the findings of the audit were that, whilst there had been some progress towards the recently intro-duced target of reducing the number of 'first-time entrants', the overall number of young people being drawn into the system had increased, over the three-year period from 2003 to 2006, by 19% for serious offences, and by 39% for lesser offences (Solomon and Garside, 2008: 41). This was partly attribu-table, in Solomon and Garside's view, to the targets set by government for 'Offences Brought to Justice' by the police, with one policy objective being in direct contradiction to another. At the same time, at the other end of the scale, the use of custody for children and young people had not declined in line with the government's target; indeed, between May 2000 and May 2008, the average under-18 custody population rose from 2,804 to 2,898 (Ministry of Justice, 2012a). In addition, claims of success in relation to reoffending were considered to be methodologically suspect (Solomon and Garside, 2008: 50).

Finally, the audit report noted that targets relating to the welfare needs of children in the justice system were not being met either, particularly in areas such as mental health, accommodation and educational provision, which was believed to be particularly surprising, given that 'it was widely expected that' the multi-agency composition of Youth Offending Teams would constitute 'a considerable advance over the previous arrangements for the delivery of health, education, substance misuse and mental health services to young people who are convicted' (Solomon and Garside, 2008: 64).

This pessimistic view of the impact of the government's programme was replicated elsewhere. Significantly, the respected then chair of the Youth Justice Board, Rod Morgan, resigned early in 2007, citing concerns that the government was not supportive of an enlightened approach to youth offending, and expressing fears over the trend towards drawing greater numbers of children into the system and its implications for the 'gratuitous criminalisation' of young people (Morgan, 2007a: 5). He pointed out that many practitioners and magistrates were of the opinion that many of the young people brought to court should not be there, but that the 'automaticity' embedded in the system inhibited the exercise of professional and judicial discretion to seek alternatives. This excessive rigidity was further compounded in his view by the 'Offences Brought to Justice' target, which created a powerful incentive for the police to 'criminalise' relatively minor but easily detectable misdemeanours, thereby propelling young people into the early stages of the justice system unnecessarily: 'A lot of this is minor stuff and we're dragging more and more behaviour into the criminal justice system to meet the target' (ibid.: 6). However, it was not just a misconceived target to which he attributed the increasingly punitive nature of the youth justice system. Noting that there were 'twice as many' young people locked up as 12 years previously, he argued for 'a degree of responsible leadership. Doing things which will not work, which won't increase public safety, just to pander to some populist short-termist agenda is irresponsible' (ibid.: 8).

Similar criticisms of a failure of leadership were to be found elsewhere (Chambers *et al.*, 2009, for example). Government's excessive interference in the minutiae of delivery had been counterproductive whilst also leaving a strategic vacuum at the helm, it seemed, and the removal of local discretion in favour of a 'graduated approach' could be seen to have heightened the likelihood of children and young people being drawn into the system whilst also sensitising the general population more fully to the issue of youth crime. As acknowledged elsewhere: 'This rigid approach risks undermining efforts to divert large numbers of young people from the youth justice system' (Whitehead and Arthur, 2011: 476).

The government's 'respect agenda' (Respect Task Force, 2006), with its promise of 'swift, summary and straightforward justice' (Allen, 2007: 25), was similarly criticised for its inherent tendency to problematise young people (Chambers *et al.*, 2009: 18). Despite taking a positive view of some aspects of the government's 'inclusion' strategy (see previous chapter), Allen concluded that there were:

> some developments of which we really should be ashamed – in particular aspects of the way we lock up children, the gross over-representation of racial minorities in custody, the demonization of young people involved

in anti-social behaviour, and the coarsening of the public and political debate about how to deal with young people in trouble.

(Allen, 2007: 25)

In his almost weary analysis, Goldson observes that the culmination of New Labour policy over this 10-year period is remarkable for its ready defiance of the available evidence (despite claims to be guided by 'what works'), and its over-readiness to respond to 'the political imperative to appear "tough"' (Goldson, 2010: 171), notwithstanding the wealth of 'criminological expertise', research evidence and expert experience that points in quite a different direction. Nonetheless, like Fergusson (2007), and earlier Muncie (2002), he recognises that policy and its interface with operational reality do not exist in a straightforward or linear relationship; indeed, one of the key features of New Labour policy when examined in detail is its 'uneasy hybridity' (Goldson, 2010: 168); hence, for example, the tension between the target to increase throughput of 'solved' crimes on the part of the police and the parallel objective of reducing the number of young people formally processed; similarly, the ambiguity of 'early prevention' coexisting with the anti-social behaviour agenda is readily apparent.

Another 'U' turn?

Despite the apparent equilibrium established over the 10-year period up to 2007, it may well be that the inherent tensions and ambiguities identified represented deeper-lying instabilities. At the start of the 1980s, it seems that one of the triggers for the startling developments of that decade was an emerging consensus that too many young people were indeed being criminalised for relatively minor misdemeanours, based on detailed evidence (Thorpe *et al.*, 1980). It is certainly possible that similar unease began to coalesce by around 2007. This was the message expressed very publicly by Rod Morgan, the departing chair of the Youth Justice Board, for example, and it seems to have been picked up elsewhere, too.

Indeed, it was from perhaps an unexpected source that the impetus came for a significant change in the processing of alleged offenders. A major review of policing conducted during 2007–08 observed that the perverse incentives of the government's 'Offences Brought to Justice' target had resulted in an overuse of formal means of processing relatively insignificant misdemeanours:

An emphasis on sanction detection levels has undoubtedly to a degree produced the unintended effect of [police] officers spending time investigating crimes with a view to obtaining a detection even when that is clearly not in the public interest. An example of such would be a low-level playground assault.

(Flanagan, 2007: 10)

It was further argued that the government's drive to increase the number of 'Offences Brought to Justice' had disproportionately impacted on young people, because their behaviour often resembled 'low-hanging fruit', being more often visible, and therefore more easily 'detected'. As a consequence, much of this easy-to-spot but not hugely problematic behaviour meant young people 'ending up in the youth court where magistrates complain that many cases do not warrant their attention' (Morgan, 2007b; see also Bateman, 2008).

In response to the interim report on policing in 2007, the government revised its approach to the processing of alleged offences, introducing Public Service Agreement 24 (HM Government, 2007a), with effect from April 2008, which shifted the emphasis towards more serious offences, and the change of direction was underlined in the final report issued by the Chief Inspector of Constabulary: 'The centre must ensure that these [Offences Brought to Justice] targets are not reinstated and ACPO [the Association of Chief Police Officers] must ensure that this behaviour no longer manifests at force level' (Flanagan, 2008: 56).

The impact of this change in policing policy was subsequently manifested in equally striking terms in the official figures. Thus, for example, *Youth Justice Statistics 2010/11* (Youth Justice Board and Ministry of Justice, 2012: 4) states that, since 2007/08, 'there are 55 per cent fewer young people coming into the system', noting, too, that the custodial population had fallen by 30% over the same timescale, and the 'frequency' (but not the rate) of reoffending had also declined by 29%.

For Reprimands and Final Warnings, the decrease in the number administered from the peak figure in 2006/07 of 131,660 to the 2010/11 figure of 49,407 represented a fall of 62% (Youth Justice Board and Ministry of Justice, 2012: 4). It was noted, too, that the reduction in the use of formal proceedings mirrored a longer-term trend, if rather less dramatic, and that this was to be observed across the spectrum. Thus, 'first time entrants' to the youth justice system had fallen by 50 per cent from 2000/01 to 2010/11 (ibid.: 6), but, similarly, the number of custodial disposals had fallen by almost the same proportion over that period of time (49%).

This pattern of significantly reduced use of the formal machinery of youth justice suggests however that the causes may be quite complex and that it therefore 'cannot be explained by one factor alone' (ibid.: 6). Although the redefinition of the Offences Brought to Justice target in April 2008 appears to have had some effect, the start of the decline from the 2006/07 peak slightly pre-dates this, and the decline accelerated subsequently to such an extent that the number of children and young people being formally processed by 2010/11 was dramatically lower than in 2001/02, at the point when the government first established targets for 'bringing offenders to justice' (Crown Prosecution Service, 2006).

Understanding the trends

Bateman's (2012a) forensic analysis of trends in youth justice closely evaluates the relationship between behaviour, processes and policy, noting that the backdrop for the 'oscillations' in patterns of formal intervention is a continuing decline in the rates of recorded crime by children and young people, and that this trend is mirrored by the decreasing levels of victimisation reported by the British Crime Survey from 1995 onwards, and the more recently identifiable drop in the 'proportion of children in mainstream schooling who self-report offending within the previous year from 26% in 2004 to 23% in 2008' (ibid.: 5). Yet, whilst the use of formal mechanisms for processing youth crime showed an 'oscillating' pattern, during the early part of the decade, the use of custody remained relatively constant, until 2008/09, when this figure, too, went into sharp decline, falling from a peak of 3,072 in June 2008 to a figure of 1,744 in May 2012. As Bateman notes:

> Between 2000/01 and 2008/09, the annual average number of children behind bars had fluctuated between 2745 and 3029. In December 2008, the population was lower – at 2715 – than at any point since April 2000 ... the subsequent trend was uniformly downwards.
>
> (Bateman, 2012b: 37)

As Bateman also observes, the sudden reversal of established patterns of disposal had not been anticipated: 'most commentators remained pessimistic' about the prospects for securing a reduction in the number of children and young people in custody, as indeed many had been in the early 1980s (Morris and Giller, 1987). The effect of replacing the Offenders Brought to Justice target might have explained part of what happened, and particularly the decline in the use of formal sanctions for what might be seen as relatively minor infringements; however, the momentum built up and, as time went on, the process of de-penalisation at all levels of the youth justice system proceeded apace, in contrast to its adult equivalent (see Berman, 2012, for example).

Bateman (2012b) suggests that the effect may have been twofold, in the sense that changing policy had both a direct effect on systems and processes, but it may also have had a subtler impact in terms of affecting the climate of opinion, at least within the justice system, about what constituted fair and proportionate treatment of young people in trouble with the law. Thus, in particular, the introduction of the new target by government in October 2007, to reduce the number of 'first time entrants' to the youth justice system (HM Government, 2007a), not only changed the way in which agencies and the police were incentivised to respond to reported offences, but also had an effect on the prevailing 'mood':

> in addition to channelling literally tens of thousands of children away from formal criminal justice responses, the new indicator could also be read as intimating that harsh responses for children who broke the law were no longer *de rigueur* – alternatives were available and should be used.
>
> (Bateman, 2012b: 45)

Certainly, as he notes, there must be some way to account for the discrepancy between developments post-2008, when targets suddenly appeared to be influential and achievable, and the apparent lack of any discernible impact of the Youth Justice Board's earlier targets to reduce youth custody (Bateman, 2012b: 39).

Government policy remained highly contradictory (Bateman, 2012b: 45). Indeed, for a brief time (October 2007–April 2008), two diametrically opposed objectives (to increase the number of offences processed – Public Sector Agreement 24; and the reduction in the number of first-time entrants – PSA 14) ran in parallel; this continuing state of confusion was also reflected in the mixed bag of the *Youth Crime Action Plan* (HM Government, 2008), especially when read in conjunction with the overarching *Children's Plan* (HM Government, 2007c).

The *Youth Crime Action Plan* certainly had a veneer of toughness, by now seemingly mandatory in Labour government policy pronouncements. The document incorporated a 'triple-track' strategy, intended to combine 'enforcement and punishment where behaviour is unacceptable, non-negotiable support and challenge where it is most needed, and better and earlier prevention' (Smith *et al.*, 2008: 1). On the face of it, this did not appear massively different from the kind of robust rhetoric, or indeed the three-pronged approach to crime reduction (see Chapter 2), adopted in the early days of New Labour. However, perhaps deliberately buried in the detail of the plan, interestingly included under the rubric of 'prevention', and couched in some rather tortuous logic, the government stated that:

> Our desire to see an improvement in the support services to children in, or at risk of entering, the youth justice system is underpinned by Public Service Agreement (PSA) objectives to reduce new entrants to the youth justice system and to reduce overall offending.
>
> (HM Government, 2008: 11)

This, then, was the legitimation for the establishment of the new target to reduce the number of first-time entrants to the system; however, it does not, in itself, account for subsequent developments, and the fact that this target in particular appeared to 'stick'.

Allen (2011) argues that it is important to consider the combination of factors in play at any one time to obtain a satisfactory explanation of this kind of sharp change of direction in youth justice practice and outcomes. He suggests, indeed, that the falls in the use of custody observed between 2008 and 2011 were not associated with a 'deliberate or overt policy objective' (ibid.: 3) on the part of central government, notwithstanding the Youth Justice Board's previous aspirations in this regard. Ironically, in fact, the board is reported to have dropped its target to reduce the use of custody in 2008, at just the point where the decline in usage began (*Children & Young People Now*, 16–22 October 2008). Allen's analysis is based on the observation that 'a range of dynamics' had coincided to create cumulative momentum for a change of direction. We have noted already the frustration of enforcement agencies and the courts with having to deal formally with very minor offences, but also apparent were changing relationships and structures within government, with responsibility for youth justice transferring from the Home Office to the Ministry of Justice and the Department for Children, Schools and Families jointly; both structural and personnel changes led to a more liberal perspective on youth justice within government, and this is partially, if ambiguously, reflected in the planning documents mentioned previously.

Other factors that Allen (2011: 3) believes may be relevant are changes in the law and sentencing guidelines, although he notes that the decline in the use of custody for children pre-dated these particular developments. More significant might have been 'a greater engagement between the Youth Justice Board and Youth Offending Teams on the one hand and courts on the other, which may have developed a shared view that custody should be a last resort' (ibid.: 4). This could certainly help to account for the evidence that the percentage of recorded young offenders sentenced to custody did not increase over the period in question, despite the reduction in the number of children coming to court for minor offences, in his view.

Allen (2011: 9) suggests that it is difficult to attribute changes in practice to a change in public mood or 'overt political enthusiasm', and, although the Criminal Justice and Immigration Act 2008 included new requirements placed on courts to justify the use of custody rather than an Intensive Supervision or Intensive Fostering requirement when making such a disposal, this can only be credited with reinforcing changes already under way. Further reinforcement, too, could perhaps be found in the new sentencing guidelines published for consultation in late 2008 and finalised in 2009, which re-emphasised the internationally agreed principle that custody should only be employed as a 'last resort', and that 'welfare' needs of children should be taken into account in sentencing decisions (Sentencing Guidelines Council, 2009).

Other policy instruments, such as the establishment of a local authority performance indicator promoting a reduction in rates of young people sentenced to custody, may have had an impact to the extent that it 'endowed [this objective] with a good deal more significance for local authorities than hitherto' (Allen, 2011: 11). Although local authorities were not directly responsible for sentencing, clearly, Allen believes that this may have encouraged them to be more proactive in providing community alternatives to custody and pursuing other preventive measures.

Allen believes that the reduction in custody numbers can also be attributed to the 'improved performance and focus' of Youth Offending Teams, which were credited with taking a more systematic and targeted approach to the provision of alternatives to custody, whilst also working to improve their credibility with the courts (Allen, 2011: 20). This argument parallels similar suggestions regarding the achievements of the 1980s, when youth justice practitioners were widely credited with playing a key part in the sustained decarcerative trends of that period (Haines and Drakeford, 1998). Interestingly, too, Allen believes that these achievements were directly linked with a 'targeted' approach by the Youth Justice Board, which jointly with the chair of the Magistrates Association's Youth Court Committee wrote to YOTs and the courts in high custody areas, asking them to 'meet and discuss their use of custody compared with other areas' (Allen, 2011: 21). This approach appeared to be consistent with continuing findings of wide geographical variations in both court sentencing practice and the orientation of youth offending practitioners, in terms of their willingness or otherwise to recommend custody, for instance (Bateman, 2011b).

There is a fairly wide consensus that the revised targets already mentioned were significant in changing the direction of practice and outcomes in youth justice (Evidence to House of Commons Justice Committee, 21 June 2012), although Bateman (2012b) also notes that the seemingly arbitrary nature of these changes raises wider questions about the underlying dynamics of the system. As he observes, if the 'punitive turn' of the 1990s represented a deeper ideological shift, or retrenchment, then moves in a different direction are hard to explain in the apparent absence of any parallel transformation in the 'organising ideas' (Gramsci, 1971), which appear to dominate public discourse on the subject:

> Critics of the 'culture of control' have objected, perhaps with reason, that in some formulations it can appear over deterministic; unable, for instance, to allow for falling crime rates …
>
> (Bateman, 2012a: 46)

If we were simply in the grip of a uni-directional drive towards ever greater intensification of the mechanisms of control and punishment in youth justice, there would be no end to the continuing 'increase in the deployment of punitive or emotive' sanctions (Matthews, 2005: 182). Does this mean that we should reject the notion of a 'punitive turn', then? Or is it possible, as Bateman (2012a: 46) suggests, to retain a more nuanced view of recent developments, including wider 'global and social' changes, which have indeed contributed to a lessening commitment to the role of welfare in youth justice, whilst not necessarily implying a continuing and inexorable ratcheting up of the severity of treatment of those who fall foul of the law. According to this line of argument, punitiveness may represent the dominant ethos, whilst still being 'mediated' by the varying contextual and operational factors that shape youth justice outcomes, including 'institutional frameworks, cultural constructions, professional dynamics, and local political or economic considerations' (Bateman, 2012a: 46). Short-term deviations from the longer-term 'direction of travel' may be explained by contingent factors, such as revised targets, restricted budgets, changes in government structures and policy, or practitioner innovation and campaigning. Although 'welcome', a decline in the formal processing and custodial sentencing of young people can only be taken as a sign of fundamental change when a 'more general climate of penal tolerance' can be seen as having established itself, in Bateman's view.

This, though, suggests that the recent trends towards less punitive treatment of young people by the justice system are better viewed as contingent consequences of a number of pragmatic decisions, and enabling factors, in association with which more liberal elements in the administration of youth justice could utilise the perennially available rhetoric of proportionality, child well-being and fairness. In this sense, and to the extent to which any gains are provisional and capable of being reversed, the trends emerging from 2008 onwards may be viewed as simply a re-run of the liberalisation of the 1980s. However, it is important to acknowledge that contemporary developments are not simply a reversion to this earlier shift of emphasis towards diversion and minimum intervention. First, the changes of 2008 were not associated directly with an incoming neo-liberal government, and the principles of non-interference in civil society that might be associated with this. It is plausible, though, that the impending financial crisis had been recognised, and at least some influence can be accorded to a perceived need to prioritise spending, whether by police or other agencies.

In this sense, there are parallels, perhaps, but, unlike the 1980s, there seems to have been little evidence of a practitioner- or agency-driven movement towards a different approach to practice, or a conscious articulation of a set of operating principles such as those informing the 'alternatives to custody' movement (Rutherford, 1996). The Youth Justice Board may be thought to play something of a similar role, having promoted practice innovations, such as ISSP, and, as observed previously, having been willing to articulate a desire to see fewer young people locked up, and to target high-custody areas accordingly. As in the 1980s, campaigning groups and academics have also continued to express their opposition to the 'punitive turn' and its consequences (Muncie, 2008, for example), although, once again, it would be plausible to ask why their influence should have an impact in the late 2000s in view of their relative ineffectiveness over the previous 15 years or so. It is interesting, though, to reflect on the possibility that change is driven here, as elsewhere, partly by the shared agendas of unlikely collaborators: whereas those of a radical persuasion might call for a less oppressive approach to young people in trouble, others interested in 'rolling back the state' (or, more prosaically, saving money) might, at least in the short term, also be persuaded of the value of intervening less in order to reduce the drain on public finances. The 'payment by results' initiative launched by the incoming coalition government in 2010 was predicated on this kind of trade-off, for example (Ministry of Justice, 2010).

The drivers of change and the limits of possibility?

As Bateman (2012b: 48) notes, the 'current situation is ... one fraught with contradiction'. The combination of influences, which appears to point towards a less intrusive response to the perceived misdemeanours of young people, is always at risk of being fractured in the face of a rapid change of mood. The 'riots' in the summer of 2011 inspired a series of knee-jerk political reactions, and prompted a brief upsurge in the use of custody for young people (Ministry of Justice, 2012a), who were punished particularly severely for their part in these occurrences (*The Guardian*, 2 December 2011). However, within a few months, the previous downward trend had reasserted itself and the number of children and young people in custody had reached 1,744 by May 2012.

Thus, it seems, a new wave of punitiveness was unable to assert itself at this point, despite the angry voices of the prime minister and others (Pitts, 2011). Perhaps the wider context is the more likely to exert a determinant influence, and the economic crisis and the dramatic scaling back of state spending continued apace through this period. Was it, then, a phase to be equated to the 1980s in the sense that the state (consistent with the electoral interests of the ruling party/ies) had no interest in those areas more likely to be affected by the crimes of the young (Pitts, 2011: 89)? Did this suggest perhaps that keeping a tight rein on spending was more in keeping with dominant interests than addressing the concerns of people experiencing disorder in poorer neighbourhoods (Lea and Young, 1984)? On the other hand, if times of relative affluence give rise to ham-fisted attempts to 'crack down' on disorder by means of the Anti-Social Behaviour Order, the alternative appears equally discouraging.

This analysis suggests a fairly bleak reading of trends and developments in youth justice over time. If progressive practice is only able to gain any purchase at times of economic decline, what are its achievements? If the achievement of 'minimum intervention' represents an effective withdrawal of resources from communities that are in difficulty, this suggests that we must temper our enthusiasm and our inclination simply to judge 'success' in terms of doing less, albeit doing less that is harmful to young people's interests.

To answer the question posed in the chapter's title, yes, it does appear that we have been here before to a substantial degree; however, there are differences, too, in that a new dimension has emerged with the continuing privatisation of intervention and the new feature of 'payment by results'. Private Sector interests are unlikely to welcome a system that prides itself on doing less and not spending money, so perhaps interventionism is set to make a reappearance, under the guise of 'prevention' and the savings notionally associated with that.

4   Where are we now?

Bringing policy into line with practice?

As we have seen, despite widespread agreement that New Labour's approach to youth justice had for some time been wasteful and ineffective, the latter years of the 1997–2010 administration saw a substantial shift in the way in which young people in trouble were treated, in the direction of less intensive and more proportionate disposals. It appears that this was inspired initially by a pragmatic decision to move increasingly scarce resources away from processing offences that were viewed as relatively minor. The post-2008 achievement of increased levels of 'diversion' was probably not a victory of principle, but a by-product of tightening financial controls.

It is clear though that this position has been maintained and even improved on through a change of government, even though the rhetoric of the incoming administration made much of its predecessor's failings, and its commitment to introduce radical change, much as New Labour had done some 13 years previously. Describing the Labour government's record as being one of 'moral failure', David Cameron pronounced that 'Something is broken. Society is broken. The broken society is not one thing alone. It is not just the crime. It is a whole stew of violence, anti-social behaviour, debt, addiction, family breakdown, educational failure, poverty and despair' (Speech, 27 April 2010); although in making this claim he was only doing what New Labour had done prior to coming to power in 1997 (Muncie, 2006: 270).

Cameron's April 2010 speech, which also launched the idea of the 'Big Society', was nonetheless noteworthy for appearing to mark out and define a new 'caring' conservatism, which would 'help' criminals to stop reoffending. The social contract would be redefined, and he claimed: 'We are going to do all that we can to support every family – and every kind of family. After all, show me the boy smashing up a bus stop, and I'll show you a boy who feels worthless. And show me an inmate doing time for a violent crime, and I'll show you the man who never knew the love of his father.' Families must meet their responsibilities, but in return they could expect to be helped by the 'most family-friendly government you have ever seen in this country'. This aspirational message certainly seemed like a change of heart on the part of the

Conservative Party, and may have led to expectations of a more liberal approach to youth crime, despite the party's prevailing image of intolerance.

In due course, we found ourselves entering new terrain when the 2010 election resulted in a hung parliament and a Tory-Liberal Democrat coalition. It might have been anticipated that the newly liberal approach signposted by Cameron and his colleagues would generally find favour with the junior partners in the coalition. In 2008, the Liberal Democrat home affairs spokesperson promised 'a system of social support-led prevention that tackles the underlying social and personal problems that send young people off the rails. This would be supported by a system of community and restorative justice, tailored to local needs and designed to keep young people out of the youth justice system' (Miller, 2008: 2). We could therefore reasonably safely anticipate a less intrusive and perhaps less punitive approach from the new government.

So, is youth justice likely to have seen a significant change of direction as a result of the election of the coalition government in 2010, or does policy remain substantially detached from the world of practice, and largely represent a series of repeated attempts not to lead, but to catch up and take credit for events principally driven by other factors?

Taking the reins: the rhetoric of radical change

Although the establishment of a coalition government in 2010 marked the beginning of a distinctive phase as far as the UK is concerned, there was no less evidence than usual of the frenetic desire to 'hit the ground running' when power changes hands. As always, the subject of crime and justice came near to the top of the agenda, given its consistently high profile. The appointment of Kenneth Clarke, widely recognised in his own party as something of a liberal, perhaps gave some indication of the intended policy direction. From the start, Clarke set out the basis for his rejection of the previous consensus on the merits of incarceration. He spoke of the then current population of 85,000 in prison as being 'astonishing' and a figure that it would have been 'ridiculous' to predict at the time of his previous term as home secretary in 1992–93 (*The Guardian*, 30 June 2010), when the average prison population was just over 44,000.

In this way, he seemed to be marking out a decisive break from the position adopted by his predecessors in both main political parties, using language that might suggest that he and the new government were committed to 'radical' changes that would lead to a 'rehabilitation revolution'. He expressed his desire also to break away from the political stalemate whereby policy making in criminal justice had been reduced to a competition over which government could spend more and lock up more people for longer. Whilst he offered pragmatic justifications for the change of direction signposted, such as the cost of custody, and the damaging consequences of excessive use of imprisonment, he also began to speak of the purposes and objectives of the justice system in terms that had not been used quite so openly for some time: 'rehabilitation' was rehabilitated, and concerns for offenders' 'jobs', 'homes' and 'families' also came to the fore.

Of course, one powerful speech alone could not be expected to shift the balance of opinion, either within or beyond the confines of the minister's own party – especially because Clarke's analysis was immediately attacked by his opposite number, Jack Straw, who was only too ready to re-enter the competition about who could lock up more offenders for longer: 'Does anyone seriously believe that crime would have come down and stayed down without those extra prison places [created by Labour]?' he asked (*Daily Mail*, 30 June 2010), conjuring up echoes of the familiar phrase 'prison works', associated with the former Conservative home secretary of the mid-1990s, Michael Howard. Howard himself was quick to join the fray, being quoted on the same day reasserting his belief in the importance of custody: 'I am not convinced by his [Clarke's] speech. Serious and persistent criminals need to be put in prison. When I was home secretary crime went down as the prison population started to go up' (quoted in *The Guardian*, 30 June 2010).

The task facing Clarke, then, was to try to create some sort of political consensus in the face of this prevailing orthodoxy, and in particular to address the concerns of sceptics who undoubtedly formed the majority within his own party, whose views were more akin to Howard's than his own.

So, his next step, in a speech to the judiciary, was to begin to dismantle this wall of opposition, by referring first to the absence of any clear correlation between prison numbers and crime rates. He observed that crime had fallen 'throughout most of the western world in the 1990s', irrespective of the prevailing sentencing practices in the countries concerned (*The Guardian*, 14 July 2010), suggesting instead that economic prosperity might be a more likely contributor to such trends (and, by the by, claiming credit for this as the former Chancellor of the Exchequer at the time!).

Joining him on the offensive was the Home Secretary Theresa May, who was also keen to associate excessive use of criminal sanctions with the over-intrusive, micro-managerial ethos of the previous New Labour administration. May chose the Anti-Social Behaviour Order (ASBO) and associated measures as the focal point for her attack, suggesting that Labour had introduced a 'ludicrous list' of sanctions targeted at anti-social behaviour, which were poorly understood, even by professionals, variably applied depending on the area of the country concerned, 'too complex and bureaucratic', and that 'they too often criminalised young people unnecessarily, acting as a conveyor belt to serious crime and prison' (*The Guardian*, 28 July 2010). Excessive use of such intrusive interventions was thus carefully associated with the failings of the previous government, in respect of its supposedly excessive interventionism, its wasteful use of resources and its ineffectiveness (in the sense of criminalising young people rather than preventing crime). Like Clarke, the home secretary was beginning to speak of measures that would be rehabilitative and 'restorative' rather than 'criminalising and coercive'.

What was emerging here appeared to be a carefully orchestrated portrayal, conflating the reputed failures and excesses of the previous government with an expensive and unsustainable overuse of counterproductive and coercive sanctions that could not hope to achieve their stated aims. Thus, in addressing the party faithful at the Tory conference in 2010, Clarke began by highlighting again the 'disgraceful waste' that his government had inherited from its predecessor, framing his new justice policy principally in the context of a need to reduce costs. However, for him, it would not simply be a matter of 'doing less of' what the previous Labour administration had done, but doing 'better' with less.

Nodding in the direction of his party's hardliners, he reiterated the view that 'career criminals and violent, dangerous criminals should be in prison – not roaming our streets' (Speech to Conservative Party Conference, 5 October 2010), bringing to mind a similar pronouncement (see Chapter 1) from his earlier spell as home secretary when he announced an expansion of the secure estate for 'really persistent, nasty little juvenile offenders' (*The Independent*, 28 February 1993). In fact, the rhetorical devices being employed here suggested that a well-established 'hegemonic' (Gramsci, 1971) strategy was being brought into play yet again, namely the distinction being made between the 'criminals who should be locked up' because their offences are serious, or because they are 'dangerous', and those who 'don't need to be locked up', for whom 'tougher and more effective' community disposals are the appropriate option (Speech to Conservative Party Conference, 5 October 2010). 'Bifurcation' and dichotomous arguments based on this principle have been a recurrent feature of policy making in criminal justice (Bottoms, 1977).

In constructing an alternative model of intervention, the two ministers were clearly also guided by what they deemed to be 'acceptable' ways of representing intervention strategies, in employing the language of reform and prevention. Later in his conference speech, Clarke again drew on the imagery of 'need' and disadvantage to justify his favoured (welfare-oriented) approach, referring to the very many prisoners with mental health problems or educational difficulties.

Clarke subsequently committed himself to reducing the prison population by at least 3,000, with Treasury support, significantly (*The Guardian*, 20 October 2010). Money would be saved, at the same time as the 'rehabilitation revolution' would be initiated. The aim of the new welfare measures outlined (see Ministry of Justice, 2010: 68) would be to provide the most effective means of working with 'difficult, inadequate, not very nice' people to make sure they do not reoffend (*The Guardian*, 30 June 2010), rather than simply the most punitive. The reference to cost savings is clearly significant to the extent that it might appeal to otherwise strongly punitive and, in this sense, interventionist Conservatives, whose visceral instincts might be outweighed by the apparent urgency of the need simply to save money.

The strategy adopted here to 'organise consent' appears to have incorporated three strands. First, the position inherited by the incoming government was associated with the failures and inefficiencies of the previous New Labour administration, and so the 'overuse' of custody can be attributed to its excessive desire to interfere in the workings of civil society, as opposed to the much less persuasive argument that it had been too 'tough on crime'. Second, there was a renewed emphasis on the need to distinguish ('bifurcate') between serious and dangerous criminals and those who were simply clogging up the system, to their own but also to the wider community's detriment, in the sense that incarceration seems to have either no, or a negative, impact on the likelihood of reoffending (Centre for Social Justice, 2012). Finally, this latter group becomes ripe once again for 'welfarist' arguments, which emphasise the importance of rehabilitation and reform, and their preventive qualities. Notably, these are strategies that have been deployed in various forms over an extended historical period, and this may thus indicate the limits of the repertoire of available justifications for policy change.

At this point, restorative interventions, by contrast, had been given a brief mention by ministers in the new government, but did not seem to have displaced traditional polarities. The principal focus of the policy proposals set out specifically for young people by the justice secretary was articulated in terms of 'a joined up approach to address the multiple disadvantages that many young offenders have and the chaotic lifestyles that many lead' (Ministry of Justice, 2010: 68).

Support for the approach being developed by the justice secretary was already available elsewhere, and helps to create a sense of direction for this policy agenda. For instance, the 2010 Conservative election manifesto made commitments to 'reduce the causes of crime', to 'deal with anti-social behaviour without criminalising young people unnecessarily' and to '*help* young offenders go straight' (Conservative Party, 2010, my emphasis). Authoritative support was also offered by the right-leaning think tank the Centre for Social Justice (CSJ), which had by then already expressed concern about the social factors linked with youth offending, and acknowledged that custodial settings act as 'colleges of crime' (CSJ press release, 4 February 2010).

The liberal flavour to many of these pronouncements from the incoming government may be surprising to some, but it clearly represented a concerted attempt to create the impression that government was taking the initiative to change direction, and that it could do so in a way that met the expectations of quite a wide constituency, from the Liberal Democrat wing of the coalition all the way across the political spectrum to those libertarian free-marketeers whose primary interest was in rolling back the state, rather than investing ever more heavily in state spending of any kind, even in the shape of carceral institutions.

A more cynical view might be that the government's strategy was more reactive than proactive, and that many of the new directions signalled were in reality aligned with trends that had already been established, and in fact pre-dated the change of government.

Room for innovation? The Big Society and restorative justice

One area in which the new government nonetheless did aspire to build on, rather than reject, the achievements of its predecessor was the development of restorative justice. The idea of 'making amends' perhaps fits well with market principles, and the idea of (literally) paying for one's crimes, and this aspect of the restorative justice philosophy appeared to suit the ideological bent of many in government. The Green Paper *Breaking the Cycle* (Ministry of Justice, 2010) certainly confirmed a continuing commitment to restorative practice. The emphasis on early, informal interventions with young people advocated by the Green Paper was framed in terms of young offenders facing up to 'the consequences of their crime', providing 'reparation for victims' and preventing reoffending (Ministry of Justice, 2010: 68). Rejecting the wasteful approach of the previous government, and the 'automatic' escalation of repeat offenders up the intervention tariff, the coalition approach proposed devolving greater discretion to police and prosecutors, and putting 'our trust in the professionals who are working with young people on the ground' (ibid.: 69). Partnership working between the police and other agencies could lead to referrals to appropriate services, or reparation, 'depending on the severity of the offence and the circumstances'. The Green Paper also promised that restorative justice would be used more widely in Referral Orders, stating that 'Restorative justice is already a key part of youth justice and we want to encourage this across the youth justice sentencing framework as a whole, drawing on the experience of youth conferencing in Northern Ireland' (Ministry of Justice, 2010: 69).

The government's view of restorative justice, and its place in relation to wider policy agendas, was subsequently elaborated further by other ministers. In early 2011, for instance, the minister for policing and criminal justice explicitly linked the concept to one of the government's 'big ideas':

> I would like to take the opportunity ... to talk about the Big Society. In particular, why I think restorative justice is a reflection of what we are talking about when describing the Big Society. Above all, I would like to talk about ... how we embed it at the heart of the criminal justice system.
>
> (Herbert, 2011)

Linking these themes to the aim of reinstating 'professional discretion' and eradicating the prevailing 'top-down culture', the minister stressed the importance of 'partnerships with the public' and re-emphasising the 'responsibility of the offender'; the route to achieving these aims, in turn, would be to take justice out of the 'narrow confines' of the formal justice system and 'putting it into the community'. By recognising the interests of victims, by returning power to the community and facilitating restorative practices, he argued that this was to represent 'what the Big Society should be about'. Restorative justice should become 'mainstreamed' as a central component of the societal response to crime and anti-social behaviour. Criticisms that this reflected a 'soft' approach were anticipated and headed off with the claim that this would, instead, be 'real justice'. Quite radically, the minister then went on to argue that we should 'stop talking about "diverting" reported offenders from the justice system, because the principles of restorative practice should become "embedded" as a central operating principle of intervention, throughout the system, and not as an optional "alternative"'.

Speaking some time later, another minister reiterated this broad aim, arguing that 'the increased use of restorative justice needs to be rooted in local needs ... It needs to be driven by how practitioners, victims and communities want to respond to crime in their area' (Lord McNally, Speech to All-Party Penal Affairs Parliamentary Group, 3 July 2012). Once again, the aspiration appeared to be towards embedding restorative practices more fully throughout the justice process, including '[p]re-sentence restorative justice' and 'more regularly' in community sentences. In summary, then, restorative justice was argued to represent the 'triple benefit of victims avoiding the trauma of future crimes, the tax payer not having to foot the bill for more crime, and a rehabilitated offender making a positive contribution to society'. Notable here is the explicit linkage between restorative practices and monetary savings, which is perhaps suggestive of a degree of 'financial expediency' (Rodger, 2012: 18), to which loftier principles appear to be conveniently aligned. Other commentators have been similarly forthright:

> There is no doubt that increasing pressure is put on government to cut down the costs of imprisonment and recidivism. Suspicion is therefore created as to the reasons behind institutional and policy reform.
>
> (IARS and Gavrielides, 2011: 9)

Financial imperatives: payment by results

Alongside the strong endorsement of community-based restorative justice, and to some extent aligned with its potential to generate savings, the incoming government also sought to introduce a new element to the terrain of criminal justice, namely, 'payment by results'. Connected to restorative practices by the thread of 'greater professional discretion', the payment by results approach was straightforwardly designed to create performance-based rewards for those forms of intervention that were most successful in reducing reoffending. As with restorative interventions, this was also claimed to be a 'localising' initiative when the idea was first announced in 'Breaking the Cycle':

> This is a radical and decentralising reform which will deliver a fundamental shift in the way rehabilitation is delivered. It will make the concept of justice reinvestment real by allowing providers to invest money in the activity that will prevent offending ...

To do this we will give providers the freedom to innovate to deliver results, paying them according to the outcomes they achieve and opening up the market to diverse new players ...

(Ministry of Justice, 2010: 38)

It was noteworthy here that the proposed reform focused on means to rehabilitate offenders, suggesting an implicit assumption that welfare interventions represent the most appropriate means to reduce reoffending. Much was made of the principle of 'tailoring' payment by results models to 'different groups of offenders', and several pilot schemes were established, with a specific focus on reducing the use of custody (*Children & Young People Now*, 7 September 2011). Ironically, rehabilitation was not the central objective of these pilots; perhaps the high cost of custody was a more immediate influence on this aspect of the policy implementation process.

Indeed, one of the striking features of the 'payment by results' initiative is its relatively low-key beginnings, and the absence of any substantial evidence of 'new players'; in the first phase of the pathfinder, all those taking part were local authorities, individually or in groups, and it is likely that their motivation was as much to do with limiting their losses from funding cuts as with initiating major practice innovations (see *Children & Young People Now*, 7 September 2011). Marketisation of youth justice therefore got off to a slow start, but this did not mean that the pace of change could not rapidly accelerate in more auspicious circumstances, with 'troubled families' perhaps becoming the targets of profit-making interests.

'LASPO': one step forward ...?

The passing of the Legal Aid, Sentencing and Punishment of Offenders (LASPO) Act 2012 was not greeted with the same kind of fanfare as its New Labour equivalent, the Crime and Disorder Act 1998. This is partly because it did not, in the end, demonstrate the same kind of ambition, despite the initial zeal of 'Breaking the Cycle'. Nonetheless, the Act did incorporate a number of significant reforms, some of which, at least, were consistent with the 'rehabilitative' aspirations initially espoused by government ministers. As always, we must be cautious about simply 'reading off' the direction of change from law and formal policy pronouncements, especially where there are both 'positive and retrogressive' elements in the mix (National Association for Youth Justice, 2011). Some aspects of the new legislation appear to have been designed to play to populist sentiments, including criminalisation of squatting, and mandatory custodial sentences for 16–17 year olds threatening someone with a knife. Equally, provision was made for longer curfews (up to 16 hours a day) where imposed as a component of a Youth Rehabilitation Order, potentially amounting to virtual house arrest for up to a year.

Whilst these measures offered no indication of a 'rehabilitation revolution', others were clearly geared towards this kind of goal, with greater scope for offences to become 'spent', over a shorter timescale in the main. Breaches of Detention and Training Orders could now be dealt with by way of a period of supervision instead of custody, and Youth Rehabilitation Orders could be ended once their requirements had been met (and extended where this was not the case).

Perhaps of most significance in this respect, though, were the new arrangements for children and young people on remand 'otherwise than on bail', who would all now be subject to a 'single remand framework', becoming 'looked after children' in the process (now also including 17 year olds), and with the associated costs transferring to the relevant local authority. Although clearly associated with the government's general strategy of getting expenditure off its own books, this move was also argued to represent an 'incentive' to local authorities to use secure remands more sparingly, and by extension to seek alternatives more suited to the needs of a 'looked after child'.

Concerns had repeatedly been expressed about the 'overuse' of custodial remands for children and young people (Gibbs and Hickson, 2009; NACRO, 2011), and it was noted in particular that as many as 75% of those remanded in custody by magistrates' courts were either subsequently acquitted or received non-custodial sentences (Gibbs and Hickson, 2009: 13). As the youth custodial population fell, the proportion represented by those on remand remained stubbornly high, and the Youth Justice Board (YJB) made it clear that it saw that the application of cost pressures on local authorities could, in turn, promote a greater emphasis 'on finding alternatives to custody and supporting children much better in the community' (YJB Chair Francis Done, *Local Government Chronicle*, 19 September 2012). At the same time, however, concerns persisted about the perverse incentives still embedded in a system where the costs of local authority secure remands remained much higher than their custodial equivalents, which are demonstrably less able to address the welfare ('rehabilitative') needs of children and young people.

Equally, if not more evident in the LASPO Act were measures designed to promote informal responses to young people's offending, whether through a new range of cautioning (and repeat cautioning) options, or through extending the scope of the Referral Order. These measures all seemed to point in the direction of greater use of community-based offence resolution measures of one kind or another. Although some aspects of these changes appeared to offer a more central place for restorative measures, it seemed more likely that they could lead to an effective extension of the disposal tariff, with Reprimands and Fnal Warnings replaced with the option of repeat cautions, as well as conditional cautions, and at sentencing stage by creating greater flexibility over the use of Conditional Discharges and Referral Orders. The hegemony of the tariff itself is also called into question, with the introduction of a power to apply a lesser sanction (caution or conditional caution) even following a prior conviction. Whilst such measures do not by any means guarantee a de-escalation of the justice process, at a time of financial stringency they appear at least to be permissive in this respect.

With most of the provisions of LASPO due for implementation in late 2012 or early 2013, its precise impact is uncertain, although there is a clear sense of continuity between the legislation and the wider aspirations of the coalition government: less micro management, greater local discretion, cost savings and the 'Big Society'. Equally, it seems to fall into line with a number of trends that clearly pre-date its implementation, such as the reduction in the number of 'first time entrants' to the justice system, and the corresponding reduction in custody levels (Bateman, 2012a). On the other hand, there is less on offer for those on the right, and this might in turn lead to renewed calls for a more 'punitive' approach. The replacement of Kenneth Clarke with a less liberal alternative in September 2012 may be seen as offering a 'sop' to this strand of opinion in the Conservative Party, certainly.

The road ahead ...

Drawing on what we know of recent developments in order to predict what might happen next is inevitably a risky task, and in many ways there is less certainty about the direction of travel in the 2010s than there was at the turn of the century (see Smith, 2001, for example). Nonetheless, there does appear to have been some measure of consistency in some aspects of the emerging trends.

First, and perhaps most influentially, at least in the very short term, are the financial circumstances of the UK. Reducing costs has been the mantra for all aspects of public spending and state activities for a number of years, and, given that the perceived crisis has eased the ideological constraints on cuts in areas such as defence and education, then similarly it becomes easier to justify liberalisation of youth justice in the face of punitive rhetoric. The argument that scarce time and effort should be redirected away from less serious matters is persuasive, and clearly finds its echo in the 2012 legislation, which effectively validated a series of pragmatic measures already adopted, and taking effect from 2008 onwards.

Second, and perhaps similarly associated with the effects of cuts in public spending and economic decline, acknowledgement of the intense pressures on families and their consequences has become more explicit, and the paternalist, 'welfarist' strand of Conservatism has found renewed articulation; hence, perhaps the re-emergence of 'rehabilitation' as a central rationale for youth justice interventions. Increasingly tight budgets will 'encourage' much greater integration of services, with the potential for closer alignment of welfare and youth justice services at the local level, too. Here again, the coincidence of these developments with the government rhetoric of 'localism', and provision for greater exercise of 'discretion', may lead to a more inclusive and sensitive approach to service delivery, but only where it can be afforded, of course.

Associated with these trends, the diminution of centralised control and prescription associated with both legislative and contextual developments may help to create the space for a reassertion of principled and creative practice, as Allen (2011) has previously indicated.

Whether these potentially positive developments can be sustained against the potentially damaging impacts of marketisation, by way of payment by results, remains to be seen, but cautionary notes have already been aired by the National Association for Youth Justice, which believes that a market model could:

- encourage a risk averse practice at the expense of interventions intended to enhance the wellbeing of children;
- focus on short term reoffending at the expense of other longer term, developmental, measures;
- require that issues of proportionality and children's rights are sidelined as material rewards come to take priority ...; and
- generate a range of unintended consequences without delivering the promised reductions in offending behaviour.

(NAYJ, 2011: 2)

On the other hand, the introduction of market mechanisms is essentially dependent on whether or not there is a 'market' and the potential for profit, which seems increasingly unlikely in the context of pervasive cost cutting. It may well be that the core principles of effective practice in youth justice are more likely to come under threat in times of greater affluence, when the market for expensive and unworkable solutions is itself likely to be much more buoyant. Meanwhile, good and principled practice is alive and ..., well, alive at least, as we shall see.

5 Inside the machine

Between policy and practice

The previous chapters have considered the recent history of youth justice, and effectively set it in contrast to the changing shape of youth crime policy. One message emerging clearly from these observations is that the relationship between formal policy and lived practice is not straightforward, or easily predictable. Indeed, it is important to try to make sense of the ways in which pure policy goals are mediated and transformed by way of the strategic and operational arrangements and the procedures that establish the terrain in which practice is carried out. We cannot simply assume that policy as set out by government or quangos such as the Youth Justice Board (YJB) translates directly and straightforwardly into standardised programmes and interventions; this is so even in a context where it frequently feels as if practitioners are being addressed directly by government, over the heads of responsible agencies and managers. For example, Harris and Webb (1987), in their study of secure accommodation for young people, advanced the proposition that there is a dynamic relationship between each of three levels, the 'macro', 'mezzo' and 'micro'; thus, policy originating at the 'macro' level is interpreted, developed, revised and in some cases bypassed, ignored or subverted as it is translated into operational guidance and practice itself.

Inevitably, there is a degree of tension between the generalised aims of policy and the practical challenges of making these aspirations 'work' on the ground. Indeed, this may seem obvious; broad prescriptive statements cannot offer enough detail or precision to inform interventions across a wide range of very different settings. In addition, it is quite likely that some aspects of policy may come into conflict with each other at the point of implementation. Hard choices have to be made, and organisations have to find ways of mediating between competing expectations, such as the imperative to reduce delays in bringing cases to court, as against the statutory requirement (and professional responsibility) to carry out detailed assessments of young people and their circumstances.

We should also expect room to be allowed for variations in the application of policy depending on local circumstances, or the specific characteristics of the population. Attempts to apply blanket policies in 'colour-blind' fashion will only compound inequalities and discrimination experienced by certain groups (see, for example, Bowling and Phillips, 2002; Feilzer and Hood, 2004). It is also the case that policy is sometimes self-defeating, with a tendency to generate its own contradictions and unintended consequences (Muncie, 1999a). For example, the increasing use of formal procedures at the early stages of the justice process (Reprimands and Final Warnings) was in itself a potential source of administrative complexity and procedural delays, working against the intended aim of providing an immediate and proportional response 'close' to the point at which the offence was committed (Keightley-Smith, 2009). This sort of procedural frustration may well have added to the pressure to find ways of reintroducing more informal disposals.

There are, therefore, a number of essentially pragmatic reasons for expecting policy in the form of law and guidance to be developed and modified first by agencies and managers and then by practitioners as they are translated into concrete interventions. This, in one sense, is a relatively benign interpretation of the way in which 'bureaucracy' (Weber, 1957) adapts the intentions of the state in order to ensure that they are fair, realistic, practical and deliverable. This in turn suggests one criterion by which the machinery of youth justice can be evaluated; that is, it can be judged according to the extent that it is efficient and effective in delivering the practices and outcomes prescribed by government, such as the 'principal aim of preventing offending by children and young people' (Home Office, 1998), introduced under the Crime and Disorder Act 1998.

At the same time, there are other, rather less benign interpretations of the mechanisms and procedures put in place for the delivery of youth justice, which must also be considered. Muncie (1999b) and Pratt (1989, 2000), for example, have suggested that an increasing emphasis on the apparatus of management and procedural compliance should be seen as part of an emerging pattern of closer and more pervasive forms of control, which themselves bind agencies and practitioners together in a strategy of containment and coercion. This is seen as the:

> 'dark side' of modernity. That is to say, the seeming humanity and rationalist side of punishment in the modern world camouflaged a more intrusive and extensive modality of social control, based around tactics of discipline and surveillance: and at the forefront of such deceptions were the penal experts and the penal bureaucracies.
>
> (Pratt, 2000: 143)

Thus, in a sense, the machinery of justice develops an internal logic of its own, which is concerned with 'performance' rather than substance, and demonstrates a tendency towards indifference as to the effects or consequences of its operation. 'Managerialism' (Clarke *et al.*, 2000; Fergusson, 2007) was, of course, particularly associated with New Labour, but its influence and ethos are not restricted to that era alone; in certain respects, such as the introduction and continuing influence of 'National Standards' in criminal justice, managerial approaches can be seen more as a feature of the modern era, rather than of a particular political administration.

It could still be argued, however, that the intervening structures and agencies between the state and practice are essentially and necessarily mediating bodies, the task of which is to elaborate and interpret broad aspirations and directives so that they are deliverable 'on the ground'. It could be argued, for instance, that New Labour's reforms essentially established a framework of common goals and processes (targets and procedures), within which it was possible to accommodate both situational diversity and the capacity to develop creative and innovative services to address the problems associated with youth crime. As part of this delivery structure, the establishment of a body such as the Youth Justice Board might be seen as having contributed significantly to this function, by virtue of its role as both the agent of government, as an expert interpreter of policy goals and as a source of experience, expertise and new ideas to inform effective practice.

The delivery of youth justice has also been mediated by the establishment of local Youth Offending Services and Teams, under the provisions of the Crime and Disorder Act 1998. Multi-agency by design, and yet governed by shared objectives and operating conditions, these, too, act as a site for negotiation, contestation and creativity in the delivery of 'youth justice'. Whilst the cynical view might be that this sort of arrangement shifts much of the complexity involved in delivering service goals (and, of course, the blame should things go wrong) outside of government, by the same token the space is therefore opened up for independent initiatives, innovation and risk taking. This is a fine line, because engaging in these structures and processes might lead to the incorporation of professional and policy interests that would otherwise be directly critical of some aspects of the youth justice reform programme. This reflects the way in which the structures for the delivery of youth justice constitute contested territory. It remains possible to argue that there is 'all to play for' in terms of constructing and delivering progressive forms of practice, on the one hand; whilst, on the other, these innovative arrangements might also be taken to indicate that practitioners have been co-opted by ruling interest, as an effective means of extending hegemonic control into the detailed workings of the system (Foucault, 1979). In order to unravel these problematic questions, it is important to consider the evidence, such as it is, arising from the actual development and implementation of the procedures, structures and mechanisms for the delivery of youth justice in the early part of the twenty-first century.

The changing face of 'National Standards'

Aside from the structural and organisational arrangements established for the delivery of youth justice, there has been evidence of a move towards prescription of standardised expectations of practice, in youth justice as else-where in criminal justice and other areas of public service. The specific vehicle for this has been the successive iterations of National Standards, issued first by government, but subsequently by the Youth Justice Board. Despite their centralising tendencies and associations with micro management, national standards in criminal justice significantly pre-date New Labour, and their origins can be traced back further, at least to the early 1990s. It was at this point that the criminal justice system began to witness the publication of a range of standards for interventions with offenders (Smith, 1999). In par-ticular, the progressive development of National Standards for work with young offenders from 1992 onwards represented an attempt to set clear and consistent expectations as to the levels of control to be applied across the range of interventions. This appears to have been a progressive process, with successive versions of the standards representing an increasing emphasis on behaviour management, and a reduced level of concern with meeting welfare needs. The standards thus prioritise compliance and responsible behaviour on the part of offenders. As Smith points out, by 1995, the needs of young people had been subsumed within the aim of reforming them, effectively prefiguring the sentiments expressed by New Labour in *No More Excuses* (Home Office, 1997b). Supervision Orders, for example, were now expected '[t]o encourage and assist the child or young person in his or her development towards a responsible and law-abiding life, thereby promoting the welfare of the offender' (Home Office, 1995, quoted in Smith, 1999: 148).

These developments, he suggests, emphasise young offenders' criminality, according them no substantive recognition as children or young people. In arguing for a creative response to the uniform requirements of practice stand-ards, he argued for 'the recovery of forgotten possibilities, memories of social work's past which have been all but eradicated from practice today by man-agerial diktat and the rule-bound proceduralism of National Standards' (Smith, 1999: 163).

Smith's concerns were further substantiated by the progressive hardening of Home Office policy towards enforcement and compliance, which promoted greater use of punitive sanctions in cases where orders were breached (Home Office, 1997b). Thus, the implementation of tighter and more prescriptive prac-tice standards could be seen as part of an escalating trend towards control and coercion at the expense of a concern with young offenders' personal welfare, delivered within a corporatist managerial framework (Muncie and Hughes, 2002).

Over the ensuing period of time, National Standards have remained a subject of keen interest, with no fewer than four versions being published between 2000 and 2012 (Youth Justice Board, 2000, 2004a, 2010a; Walker, 2012). The changes in their organisation and content offer some interesting insights into the precise consequences of shifting 'positions' taken by government and its agents, in which role the YJB was clearly cast in this context.

In their initial form, these standards undoubtedly set out to create the impression that practice would be driven by a spirit of rigour and certainty

(Youth Justice Board, 2000). Reiterating the principal aim of the youth justice system (the prevention of offending by young people), six objectives were specified:

- the swift administration of justice so that every young person accused of breaking the law has the matter resolved without delay;
- confronting young offenders with the consequences of their offending, for themselves and their families, their victims and the community and helping them to develop a sense of responsibility;
- intervention that tackles the particular factors that put the young person at risk of offending;
- punishment proportionate to the seriousness and persistence of the offending and which strengthens protective factors;
- encouraging reparation to victims by young offenders; and,
- reinforcing the responsibilities of parents.

(Youth Justice Board, 2000: 1)

The general tone of this corporate document, setting the 'required standards of practice which youth offending teams and others are expected to achieve' (Youth Justice Board, 2000: 2), was highly prescriptive, and clearly underlined the priorities of punishment, responsibility and behavioural change. Whilst the preamble also made some gestures in the direction of children's rights and avoiding discriminatory practices, these were no more than rhetoric in light of the prevailing ethos of the document.

With a change in the chair of the Youth Justice Board, there was also something of a change in tone of the second edition of the National Standards for Youth Justice Services (Youth Justice Board, 2004a). From this point, practice would be expected to support the 'principal aim' by:

- preventing crime and the fear of crime by ensuring that services are targeted at children and young people at high risk of offending, and meet the needs of victims and communities;
- ensuring that young people who do offend are identified and dealt with without delay, with punishment proportionate to the seriousness and frequency of offending; and
- promoting interventions with young offenders that reduce the risk factors associated with offending, increase the protective factors and reinforce the responsibilities of parents.

(Youth Justice Board, 2004a: 3)

Perhaps this represents a slight shift of emphasis with the insertion of a responsibility to address 'protective factors', although the language of 'targeting', 'risk' and 'punishment' retains a strong flavour of offence-oriented behaviour management.

By 2010, a substantially more detailed edition of the publication was launched. In the same way as the ever-expanding child protection guidance appeared to demonstrate, this epitomised the New Labour preoccupation with prescribing intervention to ever-finer levels of detail, following the trajectory anticipated by Beck (1992). By this point, it was claimed:

> The National Standards aim to prevent offending by children and young people by ensuring that:
> - there is effective governance, planning and performance management within YOTs [Youth Offending Teams] to support the delivery of youth justice services;
> - all children and young people entering the youth justice system benefit from a structured needs assessment to identify risk and protective factors associated with offending behaviour to inform effective intervention;
> - court orders are managed in such a way that they support the primary aim of the youth justice system, which is to prevent offending, and that they have regard to the welfare of the child or young person;
> - reports prepared by the YOT for courts and youth offender panels are effective and of a high quality;
> - the needs and risks of young people sentenced to custodial orders (including long-term custodial orders) are addressed effectively to enable effective resettlement and management of risk;
> - services provided to courts are of a high quality and that magistrates and the judiciary have confidence in the supervision by YOTs of children or young people who offend;
> - those receiving youth justice services are treated fairly regardless of race, language, gender, religion, sexual orientation, disability or any other factor, and actions are put in place to address unfairness where it is identified;
> - strategies and services are in place locally to prevent children and young people from becoming involved in crime or anti-social behaviour;
> - out-of-court disposals deliver targeted interventions for those at risk of further offending;
> - comprehensive bail and remand management services are in place locally;
> - restorative justice approaches are used, where appropriate, with victims of crime and that restorative justice is central to work undertaken with young people who offend; [and]
> - all relevant information is captured and recorded accurately on the YOT case management information system.
>
> (Youth Justice Board, 2010a: 5)

The list grew ever longer as yet more essentially incompatible expectations were piled on agencies and practitioners by way of the array of detailed instructions accompanying these grand aims. There was a greater acknowledgement of the rights and needs of young people, certainly, and restorative justice had come to be more strongly emphasised, but these aspirations sat amongst a whole series of procedural requirements aimed at securing greater efficiency rather than principled objectives.

In keeping with its broader critique of the micro-management ethos of its predecessor, the incoming 2010 government immediately found fault with what it saw as a barrage of rules and procedures, noting that:

> The most recent (2009) edition of youth justice national standards contains over 500 standards. Many of these focus on processes rather than outcomes. In line with green paper proposals, it was clear that we needed to review the extent of prescription within national standards and consider opportunities for greater freedoms and flexibilities for YOT practitioners.
>
> (Ministry of Justice, National Standards trial 2012, www.justice. gov.uk/youth-justice/monitoring-performance/national-standards/ national-standards, accessed 22 October 2012)

As a result, a revised, cut-down, 'trial' version of the document was issued to take effect in April 2012, incorporating a mere 285 'standards' (Walker, 2012).[1] Nonetheless, there was a clear change in tone. Whilst the underlying 'principal aim' of preventing offending was clearly restated, the document appeared much more concerned with 'safeguarding' young people supervised by youth justice providers, and ensuring that they would be 'fairly punished and ... supported to reform their lives' (ibid.: 3).

There appears to be some evidence that this version of the standards does reflect the change of direction signalled by *Breaking the Cycle* (Ministry of Justice, 2010). Not only is there a (partially successful) attempt to reduce the level of 'prescription', but the document also demonstrates a commitment to minimise intervention in some respects: 'The overall aim of the remand strategy is to reduce the inappropriate use of remand at the earliest stage in the criminal justice process' (Walker, 2012: 9). In addition, there are a number of references to '[S]afeguarding and child protection policies' (ibid.: 4), 'support' for children and families (ibid.: 6), enabling them to access 'universal and specialist services as appropriate' (ibid.: 7), and ensuring that young people are aware of their 'rights' as well as their 'responsibilities' under court orders (ibid.: 26). Whilst their parents should 'receive appropriate information and support' throughout the duration of any order (ibid.: 26).

Perhaps surprising is the omission from this document of any significant commitment to restorative principles, and it is also noteworthy that National Standards appear to operate in something of a policy 'silo', with only very limited reference to other legislation relevant to child welfare or key instruments such as the United Nations (UN) Convention on the Rights of the

Child, which are both of central relevance to the treatment of children by state agencies and the secure estate (Smith, 2010).

Considered in detail, National Standards incorporate a range of different (and potentially competing) objectives, including broad aspirational aims, such as preventing 'children and young people from becoming involved in crime', whilst also promoting 'support' for children and their families, and involving 'young people and their parents/carers in the design and review of individual programmes' (Walker, 2012: 6) – perhaps the first hint of a commitment by government to young people's participation in youth justice. On the one hand, this does suggest some scope within the youth justice framework for the promotion of issues to do with young people's broader well-being; on the other hand, however, the revised standards continue to reflect a concern with control and compliance (Walker, 2012: 28), which necessarily shape practice and ultimately define the relationship between practitioners and young people. The National Standards documents in all their iterations have been disappointing, because, despite acknowledging the rights and needs of children and young people, and despite the persistent evidence of the need for stronger protections (Standing Conference for Youth Justice, 2010), they have not provided a strong basis for pursuing entitlements already identified in a range of human rights instruments already available (such as the Race Relations Act 1976 and the Human Rights Act 1998), or international conventions such as the afore-mentioned UN Convention on the Rights of the Child (United Nations, 1989) or the 'Beijing Rules' on the administration of juvenile justice (United Nations, 1985).

The Youth Justice Board: mouthpiece or mediator?

As the originator of the various iterations of the National Standards documents, a role it had taken over from the Home Office, and in many other aspects of its work the Youth Justice Board's role and relationships most become open to scrutiny. Fundamentally, the question is posed as to whether it has acted consistently as an effective 'mouthpiece' for government, acting as the uncritical disseminator of official policy, or whether it has adopted a more open and even-handed approach to its various functions. Has it, in this sense, acted more as a 'mediator', offering a vehicle for developing and sharing knowledge and expertise amongst those actively involved in youth justice, and between them and government? Has the YJB acted as a 'critical friend' to those with legislative responsibilities, or has it bent with the wind, and taken the line of least resistance?

Under the heading 'Partnership' in its White Paper *No More Excuses*, the incoming Labour government set out its proposals to establish an arm's-length body that would provide 'clear national leadership ... to improve the performance of the youth justice system' (Home Office, 1997b: 2). Despite Labour's professed aversion to quangos whilst in opposition, the attractions of this kind of semi-independent agency were more apparent when in power. It would allow for a concentration of expertise to oversee and bring coherence to the entire youth justice system, including the operation of the courts and the provision of secure facilities. It would be the source of authoritative advice on the setting and monitoring of standards for the delivery of services (see above). It would be well placed to 'identify and disseminate good practice' (Home Office, 1997b: 26), and it could provide independent advice to the home secretary on possible future reforms and improvements to the machinery of youth justice. This essentially advisory role was 'fudged' to the extent that the proposed body was also to be given direct operational responsibilities, significantly for 'commissioning and purchasing ... secure facilities for young offenders' (Home Office, 1997b: 26). This could be expected to pose obvious budgetary challenges in implementation to the extent that the body responsible for setting standards would also be obliged to apply commercial considerations to the allocation of public money in this context.

Despite these anomalies, the Youth Justice Board was duly established under Section 41 of the Crime and Disorder Act 1998, and it was additionally provided with grant-making powers for the purposes of developing good practice, alongside responsibility for receiving and evaluating annual youth justice plans to be submitted by local authorities (Section 40). This provision, according to Pitts (2001a), put the board in an extremely powerful position in respect of local providers of youth justice services, with the ability to determine the extent to which these plans were acceptable or consistent with national priorities. In effect, the YJB was therefore accorded very substantial influence at all levels, political, strategic and operational. It was established in such a way as to be capable of acting as a conduit for the expression of government's desired objectives, through setting the terms of reference for local service planning and target setting, whilst apparently operating as an independent and authoritative expert body. At the same time, it was put in a position of being able to exercise significant influence over key funding decisions, and it has also been able to use its authoritative position to promote change and shape practice through its public pronouncements and media initiatives.

So, how have these powerful levers (including the responsibility for National Standards discussed previously) been used by the YJB to shape the activities of agencies and practitioners? And how has its position changed?

Planning and performance management

At its inception, the YJB sought to establish tight control over the activities of local services, including provisions for sanctions to be applied where plans were deemed unsatisfactory. As a result, nationally specified objectives and performance targets were found to be reflected directly in local planning documents. So, for example, in 2001/02, the key objectives set by the board for YOTs and directly reproduced in their plans were:

1 The swift administration of justice ...
2 To confront young offenders with the consequences of their offending
3 Interventions which tackle the particular factors which put a young person at risk of offending
4 Punishment proportionate to the seriousness of offending
5 Encouraging reparation to victims by young offenders
6 Reinforcing the responsibility of parents

(Leicester YOT, 2001; Northamptonshire YOT, 2001)

Within these broad parameters, more specific performance targets were also set out centrally by the YJB, and, as a result, the aims and objectives of individual YOTs were more or less constrained to fit these overarching goals.

Initial objectives appeared to be procedurally driven, and in some respects quite inappropriate. Thus, the pre-election pledge by Labour to reduce the length of time between arrest and conviction (Straw and Michael, 1996) was reflected in the first of these, several appeared to be about holding young people responsible for their actions, and one at least (ensuring proportionate punishment) seemed to fall well outside the remit of youth offending services, lying more appropriately with the courts. In these early days of the YJB, there were significant omissions, too, from its list of priorities, including concerns with discrimination in the justice system, protecting the rights of young people, or promoting their well-being, even where welfare needs might actually be related to young people's offending behaviour. Nor was there anything here about promoting opportunities for young people, through education or other forms of activity.

These centrally determined preoccupations appear to have had a direct impact in terms of the shape and limitations of local youth justice plans at this point in time. Thus, the goal of 'speeding up' youth justice was reflected in the commitment to timely production of court reports, and the reduction of delays in identifying and processing 'persistent young offenders'. The 'provision of information to Police to execute warrants on Persistent Young Offenders' was a priority area of work for one YOT (Leicester YOT, 2001: 13).

Equally, the pressure to ensure that young people were 'confronted' with the effects of their behaviour led to a focus on the development of prescriptive reparation schemes and the establishment of bureaucratised monitoring procedures. However, even at this stage, there appears to have been some leeway for local variations. In spite of the YJB's lack of any specific reference to this issue, YOTs were able to identify diversity and discrimination as an area of concern. In one area, it was the intention that 'all minority ethnic young people in custody are referred to the Black Prisoners Support Group' (Leicester YOT, 2001: 17). In addition, the absence of any concern on the part of the YJB to address welfare issues did not prevent some YOTs from including this kind of objective in their local plans, referring, for example, to the need to promote young people's access to mental health services (Leicester YOT, 2001). This continuing concern to retain the link between justice processes and young people's needs represented a continuing recognition at the level of practice that the two could not simply be disengaged (Eadie and Canton, 2002).

Over time, the focus of the YJB's objectives and targets shifted. By 2005, and following changes at its most senior levels, the board was still acting prescriptively, directing the 156 YOTs and 38 secure establishments to address six key targets and specifying the 'levers' to be used to achieve these, subdivided under three headings:

Reducing offending and the use of custody
1 Reduce the number of first-time entrants to the youth justice system.
2 Reduce reoffending by young offenders.
3 Reduce the use of custody.

Improving outcomes for children
4 Improve the assessment of risk and need of young people who have offended, and their access to specialist and mainstream services once these have been identified.
5 Reduce local differences by ethnicity in recorded conviction rates.

Safe and appropriate use of custody
6 Accommodate all girls under 18 years of age in secure establishments that are separate from adults, and replace 250 places for boys, currently accommodated separately from adults but on sites with some shared facilities, with dedicated sites and facilities.
(Youth Justice Board, 2005b: 10)

In light of this, it seems that the principles and priorities of the YJB may have changed over the course of time. There was clearly a renewed concern with children's welfare and the provision of relevant services, and there was also now an explicit commitment to address the problem of institutional racism in youth justice (see Bowling and Phillips, 2002; Feilzer and Hood, 2004; May *et al.*, 2010).

The manner in which the YJB communicated its expectations was little changed, in that it set precise targets with which it expected YOTs to comply (a 10% reduction in the under-18 custodial population by 2008, for example), and continued to apply explicit performance measures (such as a reduction in the use of secure remands), but the content of the strategy had been modified. The shift towards a more balanced and benign approach might have been welcomed, perhaps, but the manner in which it was expressed remained heavily 'top-down' (see Muncie, 2006), leaving the board still open to accusations of centralised control and an undue willingness to compromise with the government's populist agenda.

The six key targets remained in place, and formed the basis for youth just-ice strategy until power changed hands in 2010. Consistent with their stated commitment to less prescription, the new regime's influence became apparent, with these targets being reduced to just three in 2011:

> In the youth justice system, we will end the current high level of cen-tral performance monitoring and develop a risk based monitoring programme centred on three key outcomes:
> • reducing the number of first time entrants to the youth justice system;
> • reducing reoffending; and
> • reducing custody numbers.
>
> (Ministry of Justice, 2011c: 13)

Clarifying its intentions further, the government proposed that 'The new approach will be based on the principles that youth justice services will be locally determined and driven, maximise value for money, be publicly accountable through a Minister, and be lighter-touch' (Ministry of Justice, 2011c: 13).

Youth Offending Services would therefore continue to be bound to produce annual plans as set out in the Crime and Disorder Act 1998, but these would no longer be tightly specified, while, consistent with the government's broader 'localism' agenda, and subject to demonstrating satisfactory performance, creativity and responsiveness would be encouraged.

Significantly, at this point in time, it was the intention of the new govern-ment to abolish the YJB, as part of a broader commitment to reduce the number of quangos in place. Government had applied a threefold test to all 'arm's-length bodies', concluding that the YJB did not need to 'be politically impartial' or 'act independently', and its 'oversight function' was no longer required, so its functions could be subsumed under the responsibilities of the Ministry of Justice (Justice Committee, 2011: 7). In its evidence to the com-mittee, the government specifically drew attention to the 'prescriptive' nature of the oversight exercised by the board (ibid.: 8). On reflection, however, and in response to a concerted and perhaps unanticipated (Rod Morgan, *The Guardian*, 6 December 2011) campaign of opposition, the government even-tually chose not to proceed with the YJB's abolition, but instead to realign its relationship with the Ministry of Justice, as well as with YOTs (Ministry of Justice, 2012b). The reprieve was partly attributable, it would seem, to recent improvements in performance against the 'three indicators' (reducing first-time entrants, custody numbers and proven reoffending rates), for which the board claimed largely unjustifiable credit (see earlier chapters). The YJB was to become more responsive to ministers and less prescriptive towards YOTs, building on work undertaken previously (Ministry of Justice, 2012b: 8).

At the time of writing, then, we are entering a new era in terms of the place and functions of the YJB, and the way in which it operates, both in terms of 'speaking truth to power' and in terms of supporting effective and principled practice, against the backdrop of a series of intended outcomes, which are broadly welcomed by most of those in the field. The YJB's former Chair Rod Morgan has captured very effectively the spirit of ambivalence towards the board and its new role:

> The YJB has never been allowed to express much of an independent voice and has not done so ...
>
> How long will [ministers] Clarke and Blunt last as youth unemployment and social tensions mount? And if they go, will a progressive YJB voice still be heard? ...
>
> The YJB has not exactly been a progressive guide ... and the existence of a central policy quango sits uncomfortably with a policy of localisation ...
>
> The arguments for and against abolition of the YJB are finely balanced. We must hope the close call has made it a braver rather than a weaker vessel.
>
> (Rod Morgan, *The Guardian*, 6 December 2011)

Buying influence: using money as a 'lever'

From its establishment in 1999, the YJB held responsibility for administering a range of budgets and funding programmes, on behalf of a number of government departments, but predominantly the Home Office, until that department was split in 2007, and responsibility for youth justice policy became the joint responsibility of the new Ministry of Justice and the Department for Children, Schools and Families. (On the change of government in 2010, the YJB was assigned to the Ministry of Justice.) The board also acquired responsibility for commissioning all places in the under-18 secure estate from April 2000. The way in which these very sizeable funds have been distributed is clearly an important indicator of the way in which the board seeks to influence the delivery of youth justice and promote its own priority aims.

From the outset, money was directed to almost all levels of intervention, from targeted prevention through to investments intended to improve the standards of custodial regimes. By 2002, the YJB had already been responsible for funding 70 Youth Inclusion Programmes (YIPs) and over 150 Summer Splash holiday programmes, intended to reduce the likelihood of offending by young people in high-risk areas. In order to make the case for further funding, the YJB was quick to claim success for these initiatives (Youth Justice Board, 2001).

By 2004/05, the board had secured additional investment from a range of sources including the Children's Fund, and alongside the (now) 72 YIPs there were 124 Youth Inclusion and Support Panels, 400 Safer Schools Partnerships and '125,643 at-risk children and young people participating in Positive Action for Young People' (Youth Justice Board, 2005d: 6), all of which were designed to prevent young people from becoming offenders.

For young people on the threshold of the justice system itself, the YJB made an initial three-year investment in the establishment of bail support schemes (129 by February 2002). Early in its existence, the YJB also made £5 million available for the development of the Remand Review Project (Gibbs and Hickson, 2009), with the express intention of reducing the reliance on custodial remands for young people. When responsibility for remand support was 'mainstreamed' subsequently, and dedicated funding correspondingly reduced, concerns arose about the ability to sustain consistently good practice: 'Practice is better than before the remand rescue schemes but not as good as the national remand review initiative ... at its height' (Gibbs and Hickson, 2009: 8).

In the context of direct interventions with young offenders and their families, the YJB was also active from its early days in trying to shape practice. It has, for instance, funded mentoring schemes, drug workers (Youth Justice Board, 2005c) and accommodation projects. The board also developed and evaluated new measures, such as Referral Orders, parenting programmes, 'intensive fostering' (Youth Justice Board, 2005d) and the Intensive Supervision and Surveillance Programme (ISSP). By 2005, for example, the ISSP was accounting for £32 million (8%) of the YJB budget, and nearly 5,000 young people were subject to the programme (Youth Justice Board, 2005c, 2005d).

While the YJB appeared to be committed to developing non-custodial options for young offenders (and alleged offenders pre-trial), these were often characterised by a greater degree of intrusion and surveillance than had been the case previously. For example, the use of electronic tagging became one of the vehicles by which ISSPs could be delivered, and the rationale for this was explicitly its contribution to controlling a potential threat:

> The ISSP is testimony to the fact that unprecedented levels of supervision, in the form of tagging and otherwise, does protect the public whilst the supervision element looks at the reasons for offending and challenging young people's behaviour.
>
> (Youth Justice Board press release, 26 February 2002)

Welcoming the reported achievements of the ISSP in 2004, the then chair of the YJB made it clear that the programme would remain a central plank in the board's strategy of promoting tough community sentences that would 'force' young people to face up to the consequences of their crimes (Youth Justice Board press release, 14 September 2004).

Although seeking to invest in supposed alternatives to custody, the YJB also invested heavily in the custodial estate. Its initial spending concentrated on improving provision for educational, vocational and personal development (£40 million), but it also put in motion plans to increase the number of places available in secure establishments, proposing to build an extra 400 Secure Training Centre places (Youth Justice Board, 2001). Claiming that it would thereby be able to remove young offenders under 18 from adult prisons, the board's 2002 budget proposals increased this figure to 600 places.

In fact, only 144 of these places were completed by 2005 (Youth Justice Board, 2005d: 5), but the board also claimed to have made a substantial number of improvements to the secure estate overall, such as the removal of all 15- and 16-year-old girls from Prison Service accommodation ('except in exceptional circumstances'), and improvements in educational provision and specialist after-care for young people with mental health or substance misuse 'problems'.

However, this catalogue of 'improvements' should also not mask a number of other major issues. First, and most significantly, as already observed, serious concerns persisted about the welfare and treatment of young people in custody (Goldson and Coles, 2005; Carlile, 2006). Second, apparent enhancements in secure living conditions may actually encourage sentencers to view such facilities in a positive light. Third, the level of funding demanded by secure establishments creates a massive imbalance in the spending allocated to youth justice in general – 72% of the YJB's 2005/06 budget of £411.7 million was taken up in this way, for example; and, even with the sustained reduction in the use of custody from 2009 onwards, 63% of planned expenditure (£369 million) for 2012/13 was committed to secure provision (Youth Justice Board, 2012).

It may be an over-simplification to suggest that there is any degree of consistency about the board's initial funding strategy, although it is apparent that the notion of 'targeting' and intensification of interventions does seem to represent a common theme, and these are consistent features of spending programmes across the youth justice continuum from preventive services through to community-based alternatives to custody. This might have been justifiable, in its own terms, if there were evidence of a parallel reduction in the dependence on the most restrictive sanctions, and custody in particular, but this does not appear to have been the case, with the reliance on secure regimes having remained at a consistently high level, at least until 2009.

As the policy drivers began to shift, from 2007 onwards, with the partial realignment of responsibility for youth justice policy with the ministry responsible for children's services, it is of interest to consider whether there was any clear evidence of a change in the YJB's approach to the use of funding to influence practice and outcomes, given that its previous efforts were no more than partially successful in this regard. Significantly, the early signs of a change of direction were to be found in a reduction in the funding allocated to 'prevention' (*Children & Young People Now*, 16 June 2009), which seems somewhat surprising on the face of it, given the underlying 'principal aim' of youth justice policy. It is, of course, consistent with wider trends that see that the first areas of practice to suffer cutbacks when money gets tight are usually those with no statutory basis or controversial aspects. The perversity of this development was noted subsequently by the parliamentary Public Accounts Committee:

Prevention work has had an impact on reducing the number of first time entrants to the youth justice system, but funding is being reduced. Cutting prevention funding now increases the risk of the unintended consequence that more crime could occur in the medium term, with the cost likely to outweigh any short term savings.

(Public Accounts Committee, 2011: 6)

On the other hand, there has been some evidence of a 'targeted' approach to the use of funding in recent years, with the YJB contributing to a joint-funded diversion initiative for young people with mental health, learning and communication difficulties (increasingly acknowledged as a problematic area of intervention: Bradley, 2009), thereby supporting the aim of reducing the number of 'first time entrants' to the justice system.

In addition, there was emerging evidence of a reassertion of 'welfarism' with the YJB investing in resettlement initiatives in Wales (which has also marked out its distinctive approach by retaining resettlement as a specific additional 'target' for the youth justice system; Phillips *et al.*, 2012). Additionally, the YJB has commissioned social worker posts in the secure estate, in 2005, and sustaining that investment until 2014, even in the increasingly adverse funding climate. Social workers in these roles were to focus on 'safeguarding' children in Young Offender Institutions (*Children & Young People Now*, 12 May 2011). This investment, though, might be seen as something of an anomaly, given that it was the YJB itself that was responsible for commissioning places in the secure estate for children and young people, and had not done much previously to ensure that their rights were protected in such institutions.

Indeed, the continuing irony is that the board allocates well over half its budget to the provision of secure facilities, and is therefore crucially compromised when it comes to representing children's interests in this context. As spending has become more restricted, there has been a tendency for the board to make less use of the relatively more expensive secure children's homes, and to favour custodial establishments, particularly Secure Training Centres:

[T]here has been a drop of a third in the number of children placed in secure children's homes by the YJB, while its use of STCs has risen by 19 per cent. Real concern about this trend has been expressed by virtually every specialist agency working with these children. The views of such agencies are represented by the Standing Committee for Youth Justice, which states unequivocally that the predominantly welfare-centred ethos of the secure children's homes is absolutely vital not only for the future chances and well-being of these children but for reducing reoffending. There should be no further reduction in the numbers of those beds.

(Baroness Linklater, House of Lords Debates,
7 November 2011)

In its early days, then, the YJB was able to allocate resources with a degree of freedom to try to influence services and outcomes in line with its overarching objectives. As funding has become increasingly constrained, the capacity to exercise this kind of lever explicitly has become much more limited. However, it should also be noted that 'mainstream' funding decisions and allocations themselves exert a powerful influence on the shape and the experience (for those inside it) of the justice system. Thus, continuing to fund forms of custody that are widely agreed not to meet children's best interests runs the risk of undermining both the board's own objectives and a wider commitment to the rights and interests of the children and young people for which it is directly responsible.

Using publicity to lead change?

The YJB has also taken a key role as a public 'champion' of change in youth justice, with a clear recognition of the potential value of using publicity to influence debate. This, in turn, has raised some awkward questions about its structural position and the legitimacy of its role, given that it was established ostensibly as an independent body.

In some respects, the board has acted clearly as the agent of government, in setting National Standards, for example, and in taking on responsibility for the secure estate. In constitutional terms, this might be felt to be inappropriate, and, indeed, it was this recognition that prompted the coalition government to propose the board's abolition. Repeated references in its press releases to the role of the YJB in 'spearheading' the reform programme and in implementing this 'flagship' policy (*YJB News*, March 2000) suggested that there might be some confusion over this issue within the board itself. Nonetheless, there were some signs that it was prepared to distance itself from current policy from the start, for example over the inappropriate use of custody. As its first chair pointed out, 'Short custodial sentences disrupt the lives of young people and make it more difficult to implement effective educational and behaviour changing programmes. They also waste resources' (Lord Warner, Youth Justice Board press release, 22 August 2001). Lord Warner also took this opportunity to criticise a 'wide [geographical] disparity' in sentencing practice, which 'is inherently unfair'. On the other hand, the board was paradoxically untroubled by the government's policy of increasing the number of custodial places available (or its own role in this) and by the courts' increasing eagerness to make use of them (Youth Justice Board, 2002: 15). Direct spending on expanding the custodial estate is surely more likely to have an impact on its use than countervailing press releases issued during the summer holidays. The YJB's principled position on locking up children was, and remains, conflicted and compromised.

Not withstanding these concerns, the board has shown some signs of taking a distinct position, independent of government and representing wider interests. Despite its compromised status, the chair came out increasingly strongly in favour of reducing the use of imprisonment, saying 'there are too many kids in custody' (*The Guardian*, 28 July 2002), and the YJB was also reported to be lobbying government for greater investment in alternatives to custody and crime prevention projects at around this time (White, 2002). This assertiveness on the part of the board was further emphasised by its continuing opposition to the use of short custodial sentences (Youth Justice Board press releases, 27 January 2003, 4 February 2003), and the withdrawal of sentenced young people from Ashfield Young Offenders Institution (YOI) following a highly critical inspection report (Youth Justice Board press release, 5 February 2003).

With a change at the helm, the second chair of the YJB also clearly saw it as part of his role to express an independent view when he criticised the processes of net widening and 'demonisation' associated with the use of Anti-Social Behaviour Orders (ASBOs) against young people (*The Independent*, 23 April 2006). Taken together, these might have been seen as emerging signs that the YJB was capable of exercising a degree of independence and drawing on the available evidence to promote soundly based interventions that respect the rights of children and do them no harm. However, subsequent developments saw the differences of perspective between Chair Rod Morgan and government ministers rapidly develop into a chasm. He clearly felt that his independence was under threat and left early in 2007 over concerns that the government was unwilling to do anything to address the overuse of custody (*The Guardian*, 26 January 2007).

There has been less evidence of the board acting as an independent critic of government policy since then, perhaps predictably, except in relation to the threat of abolition of the YJB itself. In this context, the YJB was very eager (perhaps understandably) to claim credit rather speculatively for developments that appear to represent a move in the right direction, including reductions in the use of formal proceedings and custody for young people.

> It is widely recognised and independently confirmed that improvements have resulted from the YJB's work, in conjunction with the dedicated work of YOTs and the secure estate. All the key indicators – first time entrants, frequency of reoffending and the unnecessary use of custody – have shown significant reductions since the YJB was established.
>
> (Youth Justice Board, 2011)

That the board had on its inception presided over an initial increase in the number of first-time entrants and the use of custody is not so readily acknowledged here.

YOTs: a turbulent voyage

The third element of the contemporary structural terrain of youth justice worthy of examination is the delivery vehicle for youth justice, namely, the

Youth Offending Team. The origins of YOTs' establishment as multi-agency constructs for the delivery of youth justice can probably be ascribed to the convergence of a number of strands in thought and practice. First, there was evidence that previous inter-agency arrangements had worked well, notably the highly regarded diversion schemes of the 1980s (Smith, 1989; Audit Commission, 1996; Bell *et al.*, 1999). The Northamptonshire model offered grounds for optimistic assumptions that good working relationships between agencies in one area could be replicated elsewhere without too much difficulty. Cautionary notes were sounded, though, by those involved, who stressed that effective partnerships have to be worked for and actively sustained: 'inter-agency strategy and working in partnership involve complex and dynamic processes which require intellectual, emotional and practical commitments' (Bell *et al.*, 1999: 101).

Others took a more cynical view of what such arrangements achieve, suggesting that they represent the emergence of a form of 'corporatism' (Davis *et al.*, 1989; Pratt, 2002). This is no accident, instead representing a:

> third model of juvenile justice ... This sociological concept refers to the tendencies to be found in advanced welfare societies whereby the capacity for conflict and disruption is reduced by means of the centralization of policy, increased government intervention, and the co-operation of various professional and interest groups into a collective whole with homogeneous aims and objectives.
>
> (Pratt, 2002: 404)

This argument is supported by broader analyses of welfare state formation (Esping-Andersen, 1990), which have suggested that corporatism is a common feature of the structure and delivery of state-provided services in general, and youth justice in particular (Smith, 2000a).

The convergence of these underlying tendencies with evidence of the effectiveness of inter-agency practice found further reinforcement in New Labour's diagnosis of social exclusion, as we have already observed, in the sense that it quickly became accepted as a truism that 'joined up problems' require 'joined up solutions'. Thus, 'in the past, governments have had policies that tried to deal with ... problems individually, but there has been little success at tackling the complicated links between them, or preventing them arising in the first place' (Social Exclusion Unit, 2000: 1). In this sense, then, the establishment of Youth Offending Teams, or something similar, was almost inevitable. They took their place alongside an array of inter-agency, inter-professional and inter-sectoral initiatives put in place from 1997 onwards, including Education Action Zones, Health Action Zones, New Deal for Communities, Neighbourhood Renewal Programmes, Sure Start, Connexions, Drug Action Teams and Crime and Disorder Reduction Partnerships.

Building YOTs

YOTs were created by the Crime and Disorder Act 1998 (Section 39), with the local authority established as the lead body, but requiring the 'cooperation' of the police and health authorities. They were required to include as members:

> at least one of each of the following, namely –
> (a) a probation officer;
> (b) a social worker of a local authority social services department;
> (c) a police officer;
> (d) a person nominated by a health authority any part of whose area lies within the local authority's area;
> (e) a person nominated by the chief education officer appointed by the local authority under section 552 of the Education Act 1996.
>   (Crime and Disorder Act 1998, Section 39(5))

Other people could also be recruited to the YOT, dependent on local circumstances. The task of the team would be to 'co-ordinate the provision of youth justice services' and to deliver the youth justice plan.

In a display of 'corporate' commitment to the principles of joint working, the guidance on their detailed operation was issued jointly by the Home Office, the Department of Health, the Welsh Office and the (then) Department for Education and Employment. It was emphasised that YOTs were 'not intended to belong exclusively to any one department or agency' (Home Office *et al.*, 1998), and that local authority chief executives should ensure that they were developed 'corporately'. The YOT manager was seen as having a key role in bringing together a disparate team, and establishing coherence of purpose and operational consistency. Where necessary, the principle of partnership could also be extended to include the voluntary sector, victims' organisations or the youth service.

Guidance also extended the legislative requirements of the YOT to include a commitment to preventive work, with a stipulation that at least 2.5% of the YOT budget should be dedicated to this purpose.

Despite the emphasis on links and shared agendas, the guidance also emphasised the distinctive nature of the YOTs' tasks in practice, with the advice that the YOT manager could be drawn from any, or none, of the participating agencies, and ought not to be '"buried" within the management structure of any of the partner agencies; it is essential that they are able to engage, as appropriate, with all the relevant local agencies' (Home Office *et al.*, 1998: 14).

Thus, a significant degree of independence from local parent agencies appears to have been vested in the YOT manager from the start, and this was reflected in their responsibility for recruitment of team members and allocation of tasks. Implicit in this is the idea that agencies should not just be able to second existing practitioners in their established roles, but that they should adapt their practice to the new structures: 'while the skills that different professionals bring to the team are likely to reflect their occupational background, rigid boundaries within the team would be inefficient and limit the benefits of joint working' (Home Office *et al.*, 1998: 21). However, it is unlikely that guidance alone can resolve the recurrent tensions to be observed in simultaneously maintaining a distinct professional identity and contributing collaboratively to a shared operation with rather different objectives. Indeed, the guidance itself incorporated some of these dilemmas by going on to specify a number of tasks that would best be carried out by specific professionals within the multi-agency team; for example, police officers were identified as best equipped to carry out victim-related tasks.

Floating YOTs

In parallel with the production of YOT guidance, pilot teams were established in nine areas (NACRO, 2001), starting in September 1998. The pilots were extensively evaluated, with one large-scale study commissioned by the Home Office (Holdaway *et al.*, 2001), and other investigations carried out independently (for example, Bailey and Williams, 2000; Burnett and Appleton, 2004). The Home Office study reported broadly positive outcomes, following some teething problems. YOTs were applauded, for example, for responding to fundamental changes in structures and working practices quickly. They were commended for overcoming initial tensions and for moving towards a collective approach to the task of delivering youth justice services: 'there was a 14% increase in the numbers of staff who, when surveyed, saw the team as having a shared view of work' (NACRO, 2001: 2). Similar findings are reported by researchers who took a case study approach to the implementation process, suggesting that, in fact, the dominance of social services staff in the early days of the YOT helped to preserve the 'welfare ethic' of practice (Burnett and Appleton, 2004: 50). According to the national survey, 'YOTs have been successful at melding the skills and expertise of members from different agencies to create the possibility of a distinctive culture for the delivery of youth justice' (Holdaway *et al.*, 2001: 113).

The pilot stage YOTs were also commended for undertaking a 'systematic approach to case management, and for drawing on 'specialist services' to tackle offending behaviour and 'criminogenic factors' in young people's lives. However, closer reading of the report suggests that criticisms could be made of certain aspects of practice. Completed assessment forms were found to be variable and subjective in content, and some aspects of intervention programmes were 'questionable' (Holdaway *et al.*, 2001: 33), a finding echoed elsewhere (Feilzer *et al.*, 2004; Wilcox, 2004). In addition, the national study found that some participants appeared uncommitted to the idea of joint working (somewhat at odds with the individual case study reported elsewhere;

Burnett and Appleton, 2004), budget disputes persisted, and service delivery was paradoxically observed to be both 'formulaic' and 'inconsistent'.

Independent research into the introduction of YOTs attributed some of their difficulties to an over-simplistic understanding of the new legislation: 'The [Crime and Disorder Act] is a complex one, capable of being interpreted in a variety of ways. In practice, this presents some difficulties for agency managers in establishing youth offending teams' (Bailey and Williams, 2000: 18). It is noted, for instance, that belief among agency managers in the diversionary potential of the new legislative framework was not widely shared; and indeed, the early evidence suggested that younger and less experienced offenders were actually being drawn into the justice system (Jennings, 2002). Differing perceptions of the likely impact of the new legislation were complemented by continuing wrangles of a more longstanding nature, such as budgetary arguments, contested access to confidential information, and the extent to which members of YOTs believed their allegiances lay with parent agencies (Souhami, 2007). Conflicts could be identified on a number of levels: organisational, professional and between practice ideologies (for example, over dealing with 'risk'). These differences of perception could also be linked to questions of professional status, organisational authority and public esteem, which are all likely sources of tension and which affect the extent to which YOT members could truly expect to work in a spirit of partnership and cooperation:

> The pressure of getting youth offending teams off the ground has meant that practitioners have largely stuck to doing what they know. Only when they have the time and resources to share their expertise and develop new skills will the real benefits of inter-agency work be seen.
>
> (Bailey and Williams, 2000: 83)

Equally, in the case study referred to above, the consensual view of YOT members was 'cautiously optimistic' (Burnett and Appleton, 2004: 51), not least because the very complexity of the new legislation enabled them to pick and choose from the array of differing principles and strategies incorporated within the legislation.

Whilst these studies indicated cautious but positive support for the initial achievements of YOTs in establishing effective working relationships, none seemed concerned about the possible limitations of a 'corporatist' strategy. Indeed, Burnett and Appleton (2004: 50) argued that this may offer opportunities to preserve a 'welfare' approach, and Smith (2000a: 129) likewise argued that 'it is at least worth considering the possibility that a more corporate approach would help to deliver [desirable] outcomes'. Reflecting again on the experiences of the 1980s, he noted that successful inter-agency projects, like the Northamptonshire Juvenile Liaison Bureaux, were 'in large measure a creation of practitioners', and that the lack of collective organisational commitment can sometimes undermine progressive interventions. We should recognise that:

The Labour government's version of corporatism is based, in large measure, on the kinds of criticism of established practice which youth justice practitioners have themselves made over the years, and it deserves, at least, a serious collective attempt to make it work in practice.

(Smith, 2000a: 142)

Against this positive portrayal of the merits of corporatism, however, we must also set the arguments of those who see it merely as an extension of centralised state control (Althusser, 1977), which restricts professional creativity and limits autonomy, enforcing a punitive straitjacket on those who deliver and those who experience youth justice interventions. For some, it was evident that uniformity and control lay at the centre of the New Labour project. The government was reported to find 'conflict uncomfortable and threatening and it therefore strives to characterise the new youth justice system it has brought into being as one in which such conflict has been "designed out"' (Pitts, 2001b: 142).

Muncie has argued that corporatism was not unique to the New Labour reform programme, but was instead a continuation of well-established trends:

By the 1990s it was already clear that traditional welfare or justice-based interventions had become peripheral to much youth justice practice. The ... setting of performance targets and the establishment of local audits does indeed suggest a depoliticization and dehumanization of the youth crime issue such that the sole purpose of youth justice becomes one of delivering a cost-effective and economic 'product'.

(Muncie, 1999b: 290)

Interestingly, then, these critics seemed to share with the New Labour government the functionalist assumption that the youth justice system can be, and has been, constructed and delivered in such a way that specific high-level policy objectives can be translated directly into the intended practice outcomes through the implementation of standardised organisational arrangements and precisely specified procedures.

YOTs on a changing tide

Certainly, as YOTs and the organisational structures within which they were based matured and took on a more permanent aspect, they began to represent a distinct new voice in the children's services arena (Fielder *et al.*, 2008). It had clearly been the YJB's intention that they should assume a distinct identity from early on (Youth Justice Board, 2004b), rather at odds with the multi-agency flavour of the enabling legislation (the Crime and Disorder Act 1998). They should 'sit between' children's services and the justice system (Youth Justice Board, 2004c: 6). Despite this intention, the turbulent nature of organisational arrangements for local government and children's services has led to a considerable degree of fluidity, and a wide range of differing models for coordination and delivery of youth offending services (Fielder *et al.*, 2008). Indeed, the ambiguities and contradictions embedded in the New Labour project itself (see earlier chapters) almost inevitably led to disparate approaches to policy implementation 'on the ground'.

As Graham (2010) observes, rapid changes of structure mirrored shifting policy agendas. In 2007, with the establishment of a joint Youth Justice Unit with shared departmental responsibility between the newly established Ministry of Justice and Department for Children, Schools and Families, it seemed that the intention was to 'bring youth justice policy closer to policy relating to children's services' (ibid.: 119). However, as he laments, the new government in 2010 immediately repositioned youth justice under the remit of the Ministry of Justice: 'The attempt to embed youth justice policy within the wider policy context of child welfare lasted less than three years' (Graham, 2010: 119).

Whilst this might indicate a reversion to more control-oriented frameworks for intervention, we have also noted that this change coincided with other developments, which, in turn, might mitigate this possibility, such as the 'localism agenda', and the incoming government's stated commitment to reduce bureaucracy and the extent of centralised diktat.

Studies of YOTs themselves suggest that some may have struggled to maintain a distinctive ethos through changing times, reflected in the cultural and occupational uncertainties identified in their early days by Souhami (2007). Others, though, noted that a distinctive 'social work ethic is alive and well in the current YOTs and that this is the case irrespective of the parent agency of the YOT officers' (Ellis and Boden, 2007: 19). The threat to professional discretion identified by Eadie and Canton (2002) was not necessarily evident to other authors, who also discerned a distinctive and collaborative identity emerging (Burnett and Appleton, 2004); Field (2007: 316), too, identified a continuing commitment to young people's welfare amongst YOT members, even if this appeared to have become more 'conditional'.

Of course, this evidence of a continuing commitment to young people's interests and well-being amongst practitioners may also be associated with the process of liberalisation from 2008 onwards, as the policy and operational climate became more supportive. Allen (2011) certainly suggests that a change in YOT behaviour was one of a number of factors to which the reduction in the use of custody from 2008–09 could be attributed. The permissive effects of changes in national targets and the reduction in centralised control may have freed space for more creative and progressive practice, in line with practitioners' default inclinations.

Note

1 Revised down again to 245 strategic and operational standards in the final version issued in 2013 (Youth Justice Bill 2013).

6 Making it happen

A tale of continuous progress?

As noted in previous chapters, recent years have witnessed extensive investment in change in the youth justice system, particularly around the turn of the century, but with significant further developments subsequently. This, it has been suggested, has seen the establishment of a sound and sustainable basis for the delivery of interventions that 'work', according to the supporting evidence (Burnett and Roberts, 2004). Youth justice has been the site of copious policy analysis (Audit Commission, 1996, 2004; Smith, 2010; Centre for Social Justice, 2012, for example), and research inquiries, including systematic reviews (Goldblatt and Lewis, 1999). Much work focused on evaluations of New Labour practice initiatives (Holdaway *et al.*, 2001; Newburn *et al.*, 2001a; Baker *et al.*, 2002; Youth Justice Board, 2005e; Gray *et al.*, 2005). This growing body of evidence has been seen essentially as providing validation for new developments in practice and procedures, and this in turn has offered reassurance to policy makers that their initiatives are on the right track. With a change in government, it is notable that much of the machinery of youth justice and the 'tools of practice' have remained substantially unaffected by political change.

On the other hand, critical perspectives have taken issue with the overwhelming sense of certainty that seems to permeate the world of 'evidence-based' practice (Loeber *et al.*, 2008, for instance). Critics have argued that this is a romanticised view of practice development, which is a convenient source of legitimacy for routinised forms of social control (Bateman and Pitts, 2005). Little professional thought is required, and instead practice can be reduced to a set of fixed and measurable processes with predictable outcomes:

> Delivery has been facilitated by encouraging standardised interventions, reflected in performance targets, to be implemented without deviation, in order, it is said, to avoid the problems of 'implementation failure' ...
>
> (Bateman and Pitts, 2005: 252)

Pitts (2001a) argued that there was a pattern to be discerned in the use of research evidence by key policy interests. Referring to one such programme, Pitts observed:

Unsurprisingly, perhaps, the evaluations of mentoring cited by the Youth Justice Board, which is funding over 100 such programmes, is remarkably upbeat ...

(Pitts, 2001a: 22)

At the same time, rather less encouraging findings were given rather less of an airing (Wilcox, 2004), and in some cases it has been suggested that findings were exaggerated or misrepresented (Green, 2004).

Indeed, there is a degree of irony here in that what appears to be an increasing reliance on rational practices based in sound evidence is not quite what it seems. When considered 'rationally' and in detail, the evidence for favourable outcomes based on routinised empirically validated interventions is 'at best, tenuous' (Goldson and Muncie, 2006a: 208). Nonetheless, the certainty afforded by such claims and the conclusiveness of the language of 'modernisation' and steady linear progress (Cohen, 1985) came to underpin a hegemonic political strategy organised around the themes of rigour, control and behaviour management (Goldson and Muncie, 2006a; Smith 2006).

Undoubtedly, the lived reality for those engaged in and experiencing youth justice is more complex, not least because behaviour is not as predictable as the 'what works' agenda might suggest. In this chapter, the aim will be to explore the developing tensions between the programmatic assumptions informing much recent practice innovation and the 'messy realities' of practice.

Processes, procedures and efficiency

Given the widely acknowledged influence of 'managerialism' (Clarke *et al.*, 2000) on New Labour, it is perhaps unsurprising that the incoming government of 1997 was preoccupied in youth justice, as elsewhere, with improving procedures and enhancing the efficiency of its processes. Indeed, speeding up youth justice was one of the five key election pledges made prior to its election. The Audit Commission (1996) had argued that delays were not just wasteful of resources, but also damaging to young people who were effectively in limbo awaiting court hearings and thus reputedly more at risk of reoffending. The White Paper *No More Excuses* concluded that delays 'impede justice, frustrate victims and bring the law into disrepute ...; they increase the risk of offending on bail and they postpone intervention to address offending behaviour' (Home Office, 1997b: 23).

Pilot schemes to put this pledge into effect were established on passage of the Crime and Disorder Act, and a guide was produced on *Speeding Up Youth Justice* (Youth Justice Board, 1999). These steps were supported explicitly by National Standards, which set limits for the completion of Pre-Sentence Reports (Youth Justice Board, 2000, 2004a) and Specific Sentence Reports (Youth Justice Board, 2004a: 42). Perhaps surprisingly, the time allowed for reports on persistent young offenders (PYOs) was 10 days, whereas for those with a less serious offending history it was 15 days. Thus, somewhat perversely, it was just those more complex cases where the time pressure for Youth Offending Team (YOT) practitioners would be greatest.

Such pressures were amplified by the advice given on behalf of the Youth Justice Board (YJB), which cited 'unnecessary adjournments between verdict and sentence as one of the five major causes of delay' (PA Consulting, 2002). In order to reduce these, requests for Pre-Sentence Reports should be made 'selectively', and these should 'only be considered where a custodial or community sentence is a serious option' (PA Consulting, 2002). Even in these cases, 'existing' reports may be acceptable to the courts, rather than taking time to request updated versions.

The concern here must be that professional issues to do with the quality, scope and thoroughness of the assessment process may be subverted by the need to hurry things along to meet externally imposed deadlines. Reviewing a number of pilot initiatives, Ernst & Young (1999) found no evidence of any impact on the 'quality of justice', although, strangely, they do not appear to have considered the implications either for the nature of assessments or sentencing decisions. On the other hand, the team reviewing the pilot Youth Offending Teams noted that:

> there is evidence from all of the pilots that the perceived need to speed up the system of youth justice is being treated as an end in itself. This is having the unintended consequence of jeopardising the attainment of other important objectives.
>
> (Holdaway *et al.*, 2001: 25)

Whilst the Audit Commission (2004) found that the targets for 'speeding up' youth justice were being met, and this was broadly welcomed, some concerns were expressed that this might have led to a greater readiness to bring 'too many minor offences' to court (ibid.: 20).

Certainly, it was not long after this when the emphasis began to change, and the notion of 'simple' and 'speedy' justice (Department for Constitutional Affairs, 2006) was reframed to incorporate out-of-court disposals, in cases 'where victims often prefer quick resolution such as a simple apology' (ibid.: 42). Inevitably, perhaps, when there is a hint of liberalisation from government, this proposal was accompanied by a stern reassurance that 'This is not about going soft on crime. A face to face apology is often quite difficult for a young person to do' (ibid.: 42).

As we have seen, this change of policy direction was associated with a subsequent reduction in the use of prosecution, hence realigning the notion of 'efficiency' with an emerging emphasis on informal, community justice. By 2012, and following a change of government, this development was underlined. This time we were promised 'Swift and Sure Justice' (Ministry of Justice, 2012c), and the White Paper thus titled claimed that, when out of court disposals 'are used appropriately, we believe that they are a simple and useful tool for dealing quickly and efficiently with minor offending by low risk offenders, particularly when they include a reparative element' (Ministry of Justice, 2012c: 37).

However, as timidly as its predecessor, the coalition government was quick to assert its unwillingness to see such disposals used 'inappropriately', and, like the previous government, it expressed support for the idea of an 'oversight' mechanism involving judicial interests such as the magistracy.

The transformation of the concrete application of the notion of speed and efficiency is indicative. It appears over a short period of time to have been utilised to justify increased volume, intensity and 'turnover' of formal proceedings in the resource-rich early years of New Labour, and yet in lean times it comes to be used equally to support measures of de-criminalisation and low-cost, community-based alternatives to prosecution. This transformation is reflected in changing patterns in approaches to alternatives to prosecution, as Bateman (2012a: 16) shows; although these processes, too, are by no means free of procedural formality, as in the case of police 'Triage' schemes (Institute for Criminal Policy Research, 2012).

Standardising practice: ASSET and beyond

The growing influence of managerialism is identifiable in other aspects of youth justice, as the various phases of intervention have become subject to more formalised and prescriptive procedures (Baker *et al.*, n.d.). This trend is epitomised by the introduction and subsequent development of ASSET, as the vehicle for assessment of young people in the justice system. As successive versions of the National Standards for youth justice have put it, in more or less the same words:

> All children and young people entering the youth justice system benefit from a structured needs assessment (using the relevant YJB-approved assessment tool) designed to identify risk and protective factors associated with offending behaviour, likelihood of reoffending and risk of serious harm to others, and to inform effective intervention programmes.
> (Walker, 2012: 17)

On its introduction, the ASSET tool was claimed to be a significant contribution to the improvement of assessing risks and needs and subsequent decision making, whilst also contributing to improved quality of management information and 'resource allocation' (Baker, 2005: 108). The principal 'function of ASSET is to help YOTs assess the needs of young people and the degree of risk they pose and then to match intervention programmes to their assessed need' (Youth Justice Board, quoted in Roberts *et al.*, 2001: 28). In this respect, ASSET and the assessment process appear to share the principles of other tools, such as the *Framework for the Assessment of Children in Need and their Families* (Department of Health, 2000) and the *Common Assessment Framework for Children and Young People* (DfES, 2006). These documents identify the importance of an integrated approach to assessing children's circumstances, well-being and needs. However, ASSET's persistent elision of risk and need and its 'actuarial' (Smith, 2006) characteristics have resulted in a rather different emphasis, which, allied with its intended uses, has become associated with a narrow and prescriptive process.

The updated ASSET form (Core Profile) itself runs to 26 pages (although there are shorter versions for specific purposes such as bail assessment and Final Warnings), incorporating basic information about the offenders, including ethnic origin, nature and circumstances of the offence, and victim details; however, significantly, it prioritises assessing the risks of further offending by the young person.

Practitioners are required to complete an offence analysis and criminal and care histories before going on to complete a detailed rating of the likelihood of further offending, based on categories such as 'living arrangements', 'education, training and employment', 'lifestyle', 'family and personal relationships' and 'motivation to change'. A section is also provided for the identification of positive factors, although these are not scored in the same way. The concluding sections focus on the 'vulnerability' of the young person and the 'risk of serious harm' to others. There is also an accompanying pro forma on which young people are invited to conduct a self-assessment: 'What do you think?' This option has been received positively by practitioners, it is reported (Roberts *et al.*, 2001), and by young people (Hart and Thompson, 2009: 24). However, despite the advice from the YJB that young people's self-assessments should 'be used routinely as part of the assessment process' (Youth Justice Board, 2008), this has not been consistently demonstrated in practice (Hart and Thompson, 2009: 17).

Despite this concession in the direction of dialogue and young people's perspectives, the general approach of ASSET can be summarised as a 'tick box' exercise, with a heavy emphasis on the negative indicators of risk of offending, which may well predispose practitioners to a narrow and unfavourable view of the young person and her/his behaviour. As a result, it is perhaps unsurprising that it has proven impossible to integrate the assessments undertaken under ASSET with those focusing on children's needs more generally under the *Common Assessment Framework* (Youth Justice Board, 2006b: para. 1.3).

From its inception, ASSET was the subject of regular evaluation and revision (Roberts *et al.*, 2001; Baker *et al.*, 2003; Baker *et al.*, 2005). An immediate dichotomy emerged in the first stage of the evaluation between ASSET as a management tool and as a flexible aid to understanding young people and their behaviour. The initial expectations of the Youth Justice Board that the form would be completed 'fully' and 'on all young people entering the justice system' (Allan, 2001) seemed to conflict with the evaluators' view that 'ASSET was not intended to be used as an inflexible interview schedule or just a checklist to run through with a young person. Whilst there appeared to be some staff using the form in this way, most recognised that this was not a helpful approach' (Roberts *et al.*, 2001: 33).

Indeed, at this point, eight different approaches to completion of ASSET were observed, with practitioners often preferring to use it as a 'framework' for interviews rather than a rigid template.

When considering the relationship between ASSET and more traditional approaches to the construction of reports for the courts, practitioners were found to express a range of opinions. Most thought there was some value in the form in that it provided a comprehensive framework to inform the preparation of Pre-Sentence Reports, although some felt that it added little to the process, and in fact oversimplified the task of providing an 'individual' picture of the young person (Roberts *et al.*, 2001: 38).

Whilst there were some concerns about the appropriateness and relevance of some of the detailed questions included in ASSET, practitioners' main worries related to the value and validity of being asked to use the form as the basis for 'rating the risk of re-offending' (Roberts *et al.*, 2001: 45). This aspect of the exercise appeared to many to be arbitrary and unreliable. It also appeared to sit rather oddly with the suggestion that the form was not intended to be used rigidly in this way, but should inform a more considered and flexible approach to information gathering and assessment:

> One police officer described how he would always give a rating of 4 [highest risk of reoffending] if a young person admitted using cannabis because this, by definition, meant that they were likely to re-offend. Other colleagues who regarded cannabis use as low risk and low priority did not accept this approach.
>
> (Roberts *et al.*, 2001: 45)

The tensions inherent in the relationship between a standardised instrument and professional judgement were strongly felt by youth justice practitioners at this point. As a result, YOT staff were found to be making limited use of completed ASSET forms to inform their subsequent interventions. While most of those responding to a questionnaire on the subject stated that they were using ASSET 'in some way' to inform their practice, in group discussions this did not appear to be borne out (Roberts *et al.*, 2001: 48) and one despairing respondent commented: 'nothing is done with completed ASSETs, so what are we doing it for?' (quoted in Roberts *et al.*, 2001: 51).

This kind of experience may have underpinned the cynical view of some staff that the main purpose of the exercise was to provide statistical information for the YJB and government. The evaluators additionally noted that their findings may have understated the depth of hostility to ASSET due to the way in which respondents were recruited (Roberts *et al.*, 2001: 61). Despite any possible reservations, however, the YJB pressed on, announcing that 'it would now make completion of the assessment tool a key condition of funding provided by the board' (Allan, 2001: 3).

Further experience of ASSET was equally mixed, with subsequent evaluations suggesting that its use had become more systematic and that this was reflected in an improvement in its ability to predict the likelihood of reoffending to 69.4% accuracy (Baker *et al.*, 2003; Baker *et al.*, 2005). However, research commissioned by the YJB appeared to be preoccupied with this aspect of ASSET:

> The results ... provide further support for the Youth Justice Board for England and Wales' (YJB) strategy of putting *Asset* at the centre of YOT practice. The data suggest that practitioners and managers can have confidence in using *Asset* as an indicator of risk of reoffending, and also therefore of the level and intensiveness of intervention required to address offending behaviour.
>
> (Baker *et al.*, 2005: 7)

However, its practical value for those working with young people remained questionable. There appeared to be no relationship between the assessment itself and intervention plans (Baker *et al.*, 2005: 6). In addition, practitioners have been found to be variable (Annison, 2005) and strategic in the way in which they have used the form (Baker, 2008), and 'YOT staff may be allocating ratings on the basis of perceived problems' (Baker *et al.*, 2005: 6). In other words, ASSET may be used as a post hoc justification for professional decisions rather than a tool to assist in making assessments. Indeed, the value of ASSET as anything other than a predictive tool was widely questioned (Birmingham Youth Offending Service, 2004), and the problems of ambivalence and inconsistent use appeared to persist (Baker, 2008: 1476).

Subsequent investigation again demonstrated a preoccupation with ASSET's predictive capabilities, and it was found that results were 'broadly consistent' with previous findings (Wilson and Hinks, 2011: 16). The same study, however, reported a very mixed picture when considering practitioner views. When asked to identify strengths or weaknesses of ASSET, respondents were slightly readier to indicate weaknesses than strengths, suggesting a continuing lack of enthusiasm for the tool amongst those responsible for administering it (Wilson and Hinks, 2011: 55).

Given the inadequacy of the assessment tools available, it should not really be surprising that a mismatch should be identified between plans and interventions, as subsequently proved to be the case (Sutherland, 2009), both in terms of intensity and content. Nor should it be surprising, perhaps, that, following impeccably the logic of Beck's (1992) *Risk Society*, the response was to develop the 'Scaled Approach', with the aim of providing a better guide to matching intervention to identified levels of risk and need (Youth Justice Board, 2010b). Within a comparatively short period of time, however, the risk-based assumptions on which the Scaled Approach was based have been demonstrated to be highly suspect in practice, as well as in theory, with no evidence of any impact on reoffending rates in areas adopting a strict risk-based approach according to one study (Matrix Evidence, 2012), and clear evidence of failure of the Scaled Approach according to another (Haines and

Case, 2012). Indeed, in the latter case, it is argued that the Youth Justice Board has been prompted by its experience to propose radically revising the approach to assessment in youth justice to re-emphasise the significance of need, alongside young people's voices and strengths (Haines and Case, 2012: 224), promising a '180-degree change in orientation from the Scaled Approach'.

Interventions: reinvention or rebranding?

The pervasive logic of risk management inevitably extended beyond assessment into the framework specified for intervention, and again this was a distinctive feature of the New Labour approach to youth justice, which also continues to exert its influence beyond the end of that government's term in power.

One of the defining characteristics of this approach was its attempt to relate finely graded interventions to the precise specifications of risk and need, which were assumed to emerge from the assessment process. Thus, for example, interventions could only be targeted at young people at specific points in their offending pathways – a strategy that sat easily both with longstanding conceptions of a sentencing tariff and with the principle of aligning intervention with finely tuned assessments of risk of future harm. Amongst these 'single use' disposals were, initially, Reprimands, Fnal Warnings and Referral Orders, whilst the encouragement of more intensive use of breach proceedings also suggested a similar approach to community orders (Bateman, 2011a). In the process, it seems, practitioners were also sensitised to the 'conditional' nature of the support they offered to young people (Field, 2007).

On the other hand, as Muncie has articulated so clearly, it would be unwise to attribute monolithic or consistent principles and objectives to policy makers or dominant interests (see also Poulantzas, 1978), just as it is also impossible simply to read off practitioner behaviour from policy intentions (Lipsky, 1980). Muncie's (2002: 156) view of the youth justice legislation of the late 1990s as an 'amalgam' of alternative and sometimes competing perspectives helpfully reminds us that the youth justice system as realised in practice is always likely to reflect an uncomfortable and unpredictable process of accommodating inconsistent aims, such as, for example, 'authoritarian populism' and 'restorative justice' alongside 'risk assessment' and 'managerialism'.

Early intervention: Final Warnings and beyond

The logic of New Labour's approach to youth justice infused all aspects of intervention, starting at the gateway to the system. In Foucaultesque fashion, interventions were to be finely graded, and aligned with the specific level and character of each individual transgression (Smith, 2001). Thus, the new arrangements for the administration of Reprimands and Final Warnings were tightly specified, with each only to be available once to a young person. Diversion was thus institutionalised and circumscribed in a way that also guarded against the accusation of being soft on crime.

Similarly, it was determined that at each level interventions would become progressively intensified. Whilst a Reprimand could be delivered in the form of a stern 'telling-off' by a police officer, a further transgression would, it was argued, necessitate a more rigorous intervention 'programme', associated with a 'Final Warning', the last chance to be offered prior to prosecution. The Youth Justice Board explicitly promoted the use of positive intervention programmes to support the administration of a Final Warning by the police, suggesting that such interventions should be made available in 80% of cases (Pragnell, 2005). These 'change programmes' would have the central aim of addressing offending behaviour, but should also meet 'the needs of victims' (Holdaway and Desborough, 2004: 24), reflecting a nod in the direction of restorative principles.

Initial findings suggested a wide variation between YOTs in their use of additional interventions alongside Final Warnings (Holdaway *et al.*, 2001: 33), suggesting in the researchers' view that the intentions of the Crime and Disorder Act were not being achieved. However, by 2004/05, 85% of Final Warnings were administered in combination with an intervention programme, following the exhortations of the YJB and government ministers.

The kind of interventions provided in this context might include restorative justice, drug counselling, letters of apology, reparation, mentoring, youth club attendance, education support, 'general offence' work and parenting support. However, there was some concern about YOTs' failure to offer programmes in some instances, and over the provision of simplistic standardised responses that might often be unsuitable:

> In some pilot areas, staff dealing with change programmes were requiring all young people to write letters of apology, irrespective of the circumstances … This is surely inappropriate in many cases and a less than satisfactory way of meeting the needs of offenders and victims.
>
> (Holdaway *et al.*, 2001: 78)

While the research team concluded with positive support for the Final Warning scheme, they raised concerns about whether YOT practice could be seen as sufficiently flexible to address the diverse range of circumstances likely to be encountered in this context. In addition, it seemed that intervention programmes were not linked in any coherent fashion to prior assessments (using ASSET), so that 'Many offenders with risk factors of relevance have not been referred to projects that could have accepted them' (Holdaway and Desborough, 2004: 26).

These concerns have been supported by other findings. Thus, one study, whilst claiming that Final Warnings were having a positive effect on reducing reconviction rates, offered no support for the argument that targeted intervention programmes could further enhance this outcome:

> There was no statistically significant difference in further criminal proceeding rates between those who the youth offending team assessed as appropriate for a 'behavioural change programme', those who were assessed

as not appropriate, and those who were not seen by the youth offending team. This result calls into question the nature and role of assessment procedures and the programme delivered as part of a final warning during the pilot period.

(Hine and Celnick, 2001: 1)

Other evidence suggested that YOT staff resented the highly prescriptive nature of the process and of its inhibiting effect on professional discretion to intervene as and when necessary (Keightley-Smith and Francis, 2007).

This framework has remained in place until 2013, with a graded and progressive response being prescribed by law and policy. Although this was modified by the introduction of the Youth Restorative Disposal in 2008, the essentially progressive nature of early intervention arrangements remained in place until the Legal Aid, Sentencing and Punishment of Offenders (LASPO) Act 2012 came into effect. At this point, though, a different rationale for early disposals appeared to become operational, with a modification of the pre-court tariff, and a shift of emphasis onto the offence rather than the offender. Under this framework, the options of community resolution, youth caution and youth conditional caution need not be seen as progressive, and it would be possible to apply each disposal more than once depending on the 'severity and impact' of the offence, and taking account of the victim's views. With echoes of the attempt by the then government to modify the sentencing tariff in the early 1990s, this seems to indicate a significant shift in the organisation of informal justice for young people, with increased discretion, the capacity to deviate from a strict tariff both at this point and in respect of the Referral Order, and a renewed emphasis on minimum intervention and welfare need (Walker and Harvey-Messina, 2012).

In practice, of course, the legislation represents a form of codification of existing tendencies, with the greater use of informal disposals having been established over a period of years prior to the LASPO legislation. As is quite common in the justice sphere, official policy appears to be following, rather than leading substantive change in the field.

New orders: a foothold for restorative practice?

In light of the increasing scope for the use of restorative or reintegrative disposals at the pre-court stage, it is interesting to reflect on the emergence and subsequent development of the Referral Order as an element in the array of disposals available to the courts.

Although it was only introduced in 1999, by the Youth Justice and Criminal Evidence Act,[1] the Referral Order quickly became a central element in the reshaped terrain of youth justice. Like other reforms of that period, the new order was extensively piloted and evaluated before its full implementation in April 2002 (Newburn *et al.*, 2001a; Newburn *et al.*, 2001b; Newburn *et al.*, 2002; Earle and Newburn, 2002; Crawford and Newburn, 2003).

The place and significance of the order was established by its initial location at a specific point in the sentencing tariff. On a first conviction, courts would be required to make a Referral Order on a young offender, except where a custodial sentence was being considered.

The Referral Order transfers responsibility for any intervention to a Youth Offender Panel, consisting of a YOT member and two independent people. The task of the panel is to agree and then oversee a 'contract' with the young person, specifying a programme of requirements to be met during the period of the order (3–12 months). Like the Action Plan Order introduced in 1998, the Referral Order 'may include' one or more of a by now familiar list of requirements: reparation; mediation; community service; school/work attendance; 'specified activities'; attendance at specified times and places; avoidance of specified places or people; and compliance monitoring (Sec 23, Powers of Criminal Courts (Sentencing) Act 2000).

The supporting guidance (Home Office, 2001c) emphasised the centrality of the victim to the process, and made it clear that her/his involvement would be expected: 'it is essential that all victims be given the *opportunity* to become involved in the referral order process, and to facilitate their involvement where they do wish it' (Home Office, 2001c: 22). Victims should be enabled to attend Youth Offender Panel meetings, so that they can express their views about the offence and their expectations of the offender. The guidance suggested that a contract should be agreed at this meeting, and that this would 'always include an element of reparation' (Home Office, 2001c: 35). Other elements of the agreed programme would depend on factors 'leading to the offending behaviour'. In this, context specific it appears that the 'principal' aim of the youth justice system, the prevention of youth crime, had been subsumed under more restorative objectives (Haines and O'Mahony, 2006).

Evaluation of the Referral Order in the initial implementation phase was broadly favourable. Thus, key features such as the Youth Offender Panels gained a positive welcome:

> possibly the most encouraging result to date is the fact that within a year YOPs appear to have established themselves as deliberative and partici-patory forums in which to address a young person's offending behaviour.
> (Newburn *et al.*, 2001b: x)

Because of the way in which the legislation was framed, many orders appear to have been made for traffic offences, and it has been suggested that up to 16% of cases coming to the panel could be classified as 'minor' (Crawford and Newburn, 2003: 111).

In terms of the panels' operation, researchers found that offenders complied with the requirement to attend in virtually every case examined, but that victim involvement at panel meetings was quite low (13%), and in only 28% of cases was any victim involvement observed (Crawford and Newburn, 2003: 185). Thus, a central plank of this new disposal appears not to have been put into place effectively in these early stages. By 2004, there was little sign of any increase, with under 9% of victims attending initial panel meetings in Leeds (Crawford and Burden, 2005: 35); National Standards were blamed for imposing unrealistic deadlines.

Despite this drawback, panels were reported to be agreeing contracts with young offenders in nearly all cases (97%), with some form of reparative activity being the most common element of the programmes agreed (41%). Most contracts had a relatively limited number of stipulations, so there were fewer instances of requirements appearing such as 'addressing educational issues' (8%), 'exploring career options' (7%) and addressing offending behaviour (7%). Of the distinctively reparative measures identified, community reparation and letters of apology figured most prominently, underpinning the very limited evidence of direct victim participation. Panels seem to have been fairly successful in obtaining expressions of regret from young people, with around two-fifths offering apologies in the course of panel meetings (Newburn *et al.*, 2001b: 29).

The implementation of programmes agreed with the panel was to be supervised by the YOT, subject to reports to 'progress panels', convened to assess compliance and to consider any need for contract variation, to refer young people back to court in cases of unsatisfactory progress, or to agree that the contract has been fulfilled. The initial evaluation found a non-completion rate of 26%, with non-compliance or reoffending being the main reasons for this (Newburn *et al.*, 2001b: 12). Subsequent investigation revised this figure slightly (to 25%, Crawford and Newburn, 2003: 139), although it was also clear that success rates were much higher for shorter orders and for 'less serious offences' (Crawford and Newburn, 2003: 140). In terms of other conventional measures of success, the one-year reoffending rate[2] for young people subject to Referral Orders has been put at 44.7% (Whiting and Cuppleditch, 2006: 18), higher than for pre-court disposals, and lower than for other disposals by the court. It is hard to say, however, whether this reflects anything other than 'differences in the characteristics of offenders given each disposal' (Whiting and Cuppleditch, 2006: 8).

The overall picture of the early experiences of the Referral Order was therefore rather uneven. Early studies suggested a considerable degree of enthusiasm for the new disposal (Newburn *et al.*, 2002), and a willingness to incorporate a victim perspective and 'restorative' aims into practice (Crawford and Burden, 2005). However, a number of concerns also emerged fairly quickly. It seemed (Smith, 2002a) that the formal requirements of Referral Order contracts often reflected rather familiar forms of intervention, with only a relatively limited use of a wider reparative repertoire (Crawford and Burden, 2005: 37). Much of the activity undertaken took the form of 'community reparation' (44% of cases, in one study; Holdaway *et al.*, 2001), which is not necessarily clearly or closely linked to the offence committed and seems more consistent with the long-established Community Service Order, in practice. The use of the order as a standardised response has apparently continued to cause concern, with fears being repeatedly expressed that neither victims' nor offenders' interests have been well served by a 'sausage machine' approach to restorative practice (Newbury, 2011: 262).

Beyond this, concerns have been expressed in several quarters that the new disposal both displaced other sentencing options and resulted in interventions 'disproportionate' to the original offence. The Audit Commission (2004: 20) suggested that one in four Referral Orders were made for minor offences, and Burnett and Appleton (2004: 54) also reported examples of orders being made for minor infringements when the young person concerned had not even been subject to an earlier warning. By 2004/05, Referral Orders had largely displaced other 'first tier' court disposals (Youth Justice Board, 2006a). According to one YOT member:

> This is processing young people when a conditional discharge would have been sufficient … Intensive supervision with over-loaded contracts to address lots of issues which are resource intensive should be reserved for higher risk offenders, in line with 'what works' principles, not low-risk one-time offenders.
>
> (Quoted in Newburn *et al.*, 2001b: 61)

Further complications are introduced when clear-cut distinctions between victim and offender are blurred, and yet the Referral Order process operates within a judicial framework that seeks to apportion blame entirely on one side of a dispute (Newbury, 2011: 259).

It is noteworthy that the further reforms introduced by the LASPO legislation both reinstate the Conditional Discharge as a standard disposal available to the courts, and at the same time allow for the repeated use of a Referral Order, allowing interventions to be more closely aligned to the circumstances of the offence (Hart 2012: 6). Equally, these moves represent a significant shift away from reliance on an offender-based tariff, and back towards the offence-based approach to sentencing of the early 1990s. This, in turn, poses challenges to the embedded rationale underlying assessment tools and processes that are strongly offender-focused and remain preoccupied with measuring levels of risk and need associated with the individual concerned.

From action to rehabilitation: reframing intervention?

The Action Plan Order was a central element in the New Labour reform programme. The intention was to create a short-term intervention that would allow for 'individually tailored' programmes to be provided for young offenders 'at an early stage', with the aim of tackling the causes of their offending (Home Office, 1997a). The order would purportedly offer a flexible framework, within which a range of more or less specific requirements could be incorporated, such as compliance with 'educational arrangements', reparation, participation in specified activities, or avoidance of certain areas (Home Office, 1997a). The

Action Plan Order was intended not to replace, but to supplement other sentences, but even at this point there seems to have been some confusion as to the relationship between the Action Plan Order and the sentencing tariff. Whilst Holdaway and colleagues (Holdaway *et al.*, 2001) believed that there was no intention to locate the order at a particular point in the tariff, this was clearly at odds with the Crime and Disorder Act guidance:

> The action plan order is ... intended to be imposed for relatively serious offending, but it is also intended to offer an early opportunity for targeted intervention to help prevent further offending. Courts may wish to consider the action plan order when a young person has *first* been convicted of an offence serious enough for a community sentence.
>
> (Home Office, 2000: 4)

The Action Plan Order was well received by courts and youth justice staff alike. Courts appreciated the opportunity to specify programme content as well as the duration and type of order. In addition, it was reported that young offenders and their parents/carers also welcomed the structure and clarity offered (Holdaway *et al.*, 2001: 41). By 2004/05, Action Plan Orders were made on 5,318 occasions by the courts, and the possibility of extending their use was also being considered.

In delivering the Action Plan Order, the approach taken by YOTs was to offer a 'core programme', with other elements added as appropriate to the circumstances. The typical core programme included elements that appear under other orders, such as the attendance centre requirement, addressing the consequences of offending behaviour, victim issues and work on family and relationships. Additional requirements that might be added included mentoring, reparation and involvement with motor projects.

The overlap with other parts of the repertoire of disposals is particularly noticeable in the context of reparation, with the same form of activity potentially available to young offenders subject to Final Warnings, Reparation Orders, Action Plan Orders, Supervision Orders and Referral Orders. This congruence was associated with the growing interest in restorative interventions, it has been suggested (Crawford and Newburn, 2003: 17).

The distinctive programme elements of the Action Plan Order were combined to form an overall package, involving about 25 hours of input from the YOT (Holdaway *et al.*, 2001: 42), although there was also found to be considerable variation in the content and delivery of the order.

The response from participants was found to be generally positive, except where victims felt that they were not being well served. The evaluation team was critical of the approach observed in some areas, which was attributed to staff with prior youth offending experience bringing 'old ways of working' with them, and turning Action Plan Orders into 'mini-supervision orders' (Holdaway *et al.*, 2001: 42), which was not what the legislation was believed to have intended. On the other hand, it could equally be argued that both the 'menu' of activities and the individualised ('tailored') nature of the programme were reminiscent of the content of conventional interventions such as Supervision Orders stretching back over a considerable period (see, for example, The Children's Society, 1988, 1993; Audit Commission, 1996). In this sense, aspects of the new order could still be characterised as essentially 'correctional', in the same way as previous disposals had been, despite the emergence of a stronger insistence on reparative activity in law and guidance.

Although, the order came under criticism for being 'mechanistic' (Williams, 2005: 214), observation of the work of YOTs also suggests that there remained a strong 'welfare' element in much of what was undertaken under the terms of an Action Plan Order. It could, in fact, be construed as a compressed attempt to deliver some of the needs-based interventions associated with Supervision Orders, including family support, assistance with accommodation, or addressing the problems arising from school exclusion (Smith, 2002a). However, this flexible approach did appear to sit awkwardly with the facility for courts to be highly prescriptive in specifying the content of orders.

As early as 2003, the Home Office had announced a plan to replace the nine juvenile non-custodial sentences with 'just one, a broader Action Plan Order' (Home Office, 2003b: 6), following the emerging logic of providing a wide 'menu' from which specific options could be chosen to suit the individual circumstances of offenders and their offences. This change was proposed purely as a means of 'simplification' (ibid.: 5) of the range of disposal options, and presumably in order to avoid the risk of compressing the sentencing tariff, it was also stated at this point that 'this sentence could be used on successive occasions, with different combinations of interventions ... courts would be required to consider different interventions available within the same as well as any different sentence' (ibid.: 7). On the other hand, one consequence of such a change might be to establish a much clearer sense of what the tariff of disposals would look like, with a more limited number of steps between first appearance and the pinnacle of the sentencing structure – that is, custody.

By 2008, following *Every Child Matters* (DfES, 2003) and the associated debates over the relationship between the youth justice system and broader child welfare services, this proposal was reprised in the *Youth Crime Action Plan 2008* (HM Government, 2008) in the form of the Youth Rehabilitation Order, subsequently brought into law by the Criminal Justice and Immigration Act 2008 and implemented from 30 November 2009. Most significantly, with the language of rehabilitation re-emerging in this context, it appeared that some of the behavioural, risk-oriented flavour of the previous community-based sentencing framework was being modified. The 'rehabilitation revolution' of the incoming coalition government in 2010 had, in fact, been anticipated by its predecessor, complicating that government's technocratic, micro-managing image, too. Contradictorily, though, the change of 'label' was not accompanied by a substantive change of content, and the different elements of the new disposal retained a substantial degree of continuity with the previous array of options and conditional requirements associated with community-based sentences. Is this just another case of 'old wine, new bottles'?

A measure of control: intensive supervision and surveillance

For those young offenders whose infractions appear most problematic, there has been a continuing discourse around the need to provide credible 'alternatives to custody' over a considerable period of time (Haines and Drakeford, 1998). That is to say, at the point where community interventions are deemed to have failed, and the logic of punitiveness reasserts itself, it has often been felt necessary to make a special case for non-custodial measures which are none-theless tough and demanding. New Labour's variation on this theme was the Intensive Supervision and Surveillance Programme (ISSP) launched in 2001, targeted at those persistent young offenders who were estimated to be responsible for 25% of all youth crime (Graham and Bowling, 1995), and at the same time, focusing on those police areas 'worst affected by street crime' (Youth Justice Board press release, 30 April 2002). Like so much of this government's programme, ISSPs were to be a 'targeted' measure.

ISSPs were initially made available as attachments to Supervision Orders, Community Rehabilitation Orders, the community element of Detention and Training Orders and as part of bail supervision packages. Young people would be eligible if they were:

> ... charged with or convicted of an offence and have previously:

- Been charged, warned or convicted of offences committed on four or more separate dates within the last 12 months and received at least one community or custodial penalty;

> In addition, young offenders can also qualify for ISSP if they are at risk of custody because:

- The current charge or sentence relates to an offence which is sufficiently serious that an adult could be sentenced to 14 years or more;
- Or they have a history of repeat offending on bail and are at risk of a secure remand under section 130 of the Criminal Justice and Police Act 2001.
> (Youth Justice Board, letter to ISSP managers, 19 June 2002)

These threshold requirements were subsequently modified by the Criminal Justice and Immigration Act 2008.

The YOT was made responsible for delivering the 'intensive supervision' element of the ISSP, involving 'structured' activities of at least 25 hours per week for the first three months of the programme. Supervision was to continue at 'reduced intensity' of one hour a day during the week. Throughout the order, additional 'support' would be made available during evenings and weekends (Gray *et al.*, 2005: 23).

Programme content incorporated five core modules (education and training; restorative justice; offending behaviour; interpersonal skills; and family support), with ancillary options based on individual circumstances and local resources, including drug or alcohol work or 'constructive leisure/recreation' (Gray *et al.*, 2005: 24). In addition, those on ISSPs should also be subject to at least one form of direct surveillance, which might take the form of 'tracking', 'electronic tagging', 'voice verification' or 'intelligence-led policing' (see Chapter 3). These elements of the programme could be contracted out to private providers of security services, although overall responsibility for compliance and decisions about breach action would rest with the YOT (Home Office, 2002a: 11).

The framework and delivery requirements for the ISSP were highly prescriptive, leaving little scope for the exercise of professional discretion by practitioners. The overall aim was to provide a demanding programme that would reassure courts and the public that it represented an 'effective' alternative to custody. According to this logic, the programme should be organised around mandatory attendance of considerable intensity, certainly in its initial stages. By 2005, the ISSP had 'become recognised as the most robust and innovative community-based programme available for persistent and serious young offenders', based on 'what works' research and backed up by 'strict enforcement' (Gray *et al.*, 2005: 7).

Despite this fanfare, results reported for the programme itself were unimpressive, at best. Detailed evaluation failed to demonstrate any substantive achievements (Moore, 2004; Gray *et al.*, 2005). ISSPs, although increasingly popular with the courts, had a negligible influence on custody rates following implementation, with no difference being detected between those areas with and without ISSPs (Gray *et al.*, 2005: 8). There were concerns about 'net widening' and the displacement of less intrusive community disposals, instead. In terms of reoffending, the positive falls in frequency (39%) and seriousness (13%) of ISSP participants' subsequent offending were matched by the comparison group, suggesting nothing more than 'regression to the mean' (Gray *et al.*, 2005: 9). At the same time, reconviction rates for the ISSP were very high, 91% over the two-year follow-up period. The achievements claimed for ISSPs, instead, were based on the broadly positive view of the programme of both young people and their parents, and the improved capacity of providers to identify and focus on welfare needs, partly as a result of the intensive nature of the programme (Gray *et al.*, 2005: 125). In light of these very limited indications of success, however defined, it is unsurprising that ISSPs came in for trenchant criticism (Green, 2004).

> In short, ISSP has not: reduced predicted reoffending; ensured adequate surveillance to ensure public protection; ensured rigorous enforcement; had a positive impact upon offenders' attitudes; provided supervision sessions specific to individual needs or offender age; improved young

offenders' life chances; ensured adequate incapacitation; brought structure to young offenders' lives; provided strong boundaries and separation from damaging environments or peer groups.

(Ellis *et al.*, 2009: 408)

Indeed, the conclusion seems to be that intensive supervision and surveillance offers nothing more than an intensified version of a fairly well-established correctional approach, which may nod in the direction of recent developments such as restorative justice, but otherwise has offered nothing new, and is singularly unsuccessful even in its own terms.

Learning the lessons of practice

In the previous edition of this book, I concluded the equivalent chapter with a pessimistic account of the experiences and impacts of a technocratic approach to intervention, based on New Labour's sterile and formulaic philosophy of youth justice. This, itself, was superseded by a reappraisal, stemming from around 2007–08, and the subsequent change of government, accompanied by an economic crisis, has given added stimulus to a more open-ended, less prescriptive and indeed less punitive framework for practice. 'Risk' no longer plays such a dominant part in the formulation of policy goals and strategies, and delivery systems are less inculcated with the calculative and deterministic methodologies associated with this orientation. This is not to suggest that these influences have simply drained away, and indeed it is clear that the language and indeed the technology of micro measurement and prescriptive templates for intervention are still heavily represented in day-to-day practice. Nonetheless, the prospect of the emergence of greater space for discretion, creativity and the exercise of professional autonomy has become more real. To conclude once again with the wise words of earlier writers on this theme:

> Wherever practice is tightly prescribed, practitioners will repeatedly discover that an uncritical application of the rules would be oppressive and unfair. Reflective youth justice workers draw on their knowledge and skills, but also give expression to their values. They are guided by awareness of the constraints upon young people, and of the differential impact of 'the same' penalty on those who they supervise. They continue to offer opportunities to change even when these appear to be rejected. Throughout, they respect both substantive and procedural justice, working openly and honestly with young offenders and with their managers. If workers behave officiously or take enforcement action prematurely, this not only constitutes poor social work, but is also reductively ineffective and unjust.
>
> (Eadie and Canton, 2002: 23)

The question that remains is whether the combination of economic retrenchment and a more liberal view of youth justice and 'rehabilitation' emerging in the second decade of the twenty-first century could be said to facilitate or inhibit this form of sensitised practice (see Chapter 10).

Notes

1 It was later consolidated in the Powers of Criminal Courts (Sentencing) Act 2000.
2 In this context, 'reoffending' covers those who received a subsequent formal disposal of any kind for an offence.

7 Theorising youth justice

The art of the possible

Having spent some time considering the 'state of play' in youth justice, it will now make sense to pause and take a step back to consider the contribution to be offered by theoretical insights into the terrain. The preceding overview of contemporary developments suggests a considerable degree of movement and instability in policy and practice, with successive periods of liberalisation and reaction numbering only a few years each. Rapid change appears to be prompted by contingent events, whether these are specific to the territory of youth justice (as in the outbreak of highly dramatic incidences of crime in the early 1990s), or of more generalised impact such as the financial crisis of the late 2000s. Such change may be interpreted as a fundamental feature of the post-modern condition, on the one hand, or as rather more superficial and ephemeral, on the other, effectively distracting attention from deeper-lying and more persistent (and powerful) influences. Thus, for example, individualised assumptions about 'responsibility' and associated punitive sentiments may be modified, but remain remarkably constant as the frame through which the behaviour of young people is observed and explained. These deeper currents may be seen to constitute a contextualising force, which may not act constantly or consistently in the same direction, but nonetheless sets the terms and establishes the boundaries for ideas and, indeed, action.

Changes at the level of practice must therefore be viewed against this kind of backdrop, with sporadic gains and losses set against a background of system inertia; where successes are achieved by imaginative and persistent practitioners and managers, these are likely to arise from the congruence of a number of enabling factors, allied with their own persistence, rather than as a result of short-term policy change. Thus, for example, the managerially driven changes in policing targets from 2007 onwards signposted and facilitated recent liberalising developments, but these are driven in turn by a spirit of pragmatism rather than principle.

If we are to develop a more systematic understanding of change in youth justice and lay the basis for a more consistently progressive system, it follows that there is a task to be undertaken in terms of explaining how and why the system is constructed in the way it is, and the assumptions and ideas that inform service delivery – that is what conditions and creates the limits of 'what is thinkable' and 'what is possible'. What, in short, are the ideological under-pinnings for the prevailing climate of thought in youth justice, with its conven-tional characterisations of 'young offenders', and its recurrent preoccupations with surveillance, risk assessment, containment and punishment? At the same time, it will naturally be important to gain a detailed understanding of the ways in which these underlying beliefs are translated into the delivery system at a particular point in time; and on the basis of little substantive evidence, to become open to significant changes in direction, as if at the flick of a switch.

Answering these questions should, in turn, provide us with a basis from which we can begin to consider the question of how success is defined and how it could be defined, that is to say, what we should expect from youth justice and how we can achieve it. The aim will be to bring together this theoretical analysis with the aspirations of those engaged with the system 'on the ground' (its 'stakeholders') in order to set out what is conceivable, practicable and desirable in terms of youth justice services. We may, on this basis, be able to sketch out some of the key elements of a system that 'does what it says on the tin' – that is, delivers justice to young people (see also Goldson and Muncie, 2006a; Smith, 2011b).

The practicality of theory

For many people involved in the day-to-day construction and delivery of youth justice in practice, theory may seem irrelevant, unimportant or simply an unaffordable luxury. So, the first task here is perhaps to justify making the effort to dig deeper and seek out broad themes and principles that might provide some form of coherent understanding. On the other hand, the evidence of failure and wasted effort identified in earlier chapters clearly seems to indicate that it is necessary to unpack the question of how to achieve 'effective' inter-ventions a little more fully. Of course, this in turn poses a major challenge – just what do we mean by the idea of effectiveness in youth justice, and how do we know what is indeed 'working'? As Bateman and Pitts (2005: 251) observe, this is never a straightforward question:

> instead of asking 'what works' we probably need to ask:
>   What kind of interventions have what kind of impact upon what kinds of people under what kinds of circumstances and why?

The establishment of a single priority objective by government in 1998, that is, the 'prevention of youth offending', might appear to have offered a ready short cut to resolving the question of what we want the system to achieve, but this is far from the case, and we must try to ascertain what assumptions are built into even this deceptively straightforward aspiration. The implicit the-ories that underpin such mundane and consensual goals, and the consequent

policies and practice are no less theoretically informed '
as 'givens' and thus not articulated or laid open to c

To illustrate this point, it may be helpful to offe᷈
how to 'prevent' youth crime, both of which wou᷈
greater certainty than the strategies pursued t᷈
framework could be amended simply to decrir
children and young people – not so far-fetched ᷈
government came close to incorporating this principle ᷈
is it so remarkable if we take a wider perspective, and recog᷈
of criminal responsibility is typically much higher in other Europeɑ᷈
(Fionda, 2005).

On the other hand, we might conceive of the institution of a system oɪ
'preventive detention', which would ensure that no child or young person had
the opportunity to offend. Again, we can observe elements of this approach in
a range of crime reduction and anti-social behaviour initiatives, including the
Dispersal Order, where police officers referred to themselves as 'child catchers'
(Smithson, 2004: 17).

Finally, we could dispense with 'youth crime' by effectively eradicating the
concept of youth itself, or childhood as a phase in which differential treatment
is necessary. Likewise, we can observe aspects of this perspective in the abolition
of the rule of *doli incapax* under the Crime and Disorder Act 1998, and the
'adulteration' of young people's miscreant behaviour, as Muncie and Goldson
(2006) put it. (In theoretical terms, the criminality/childhood dichotomy
reflects a persistent and unresolved debate between conceptualisations of these
two major social constructs.)

The fact that all these ideas are to be found, to a degree, incorporated in youth
justice practices (even if not in the 'here and now') suggests that there are both a
very wide range of alternative perspectives and a substantial degree of pragmatism and complexity at play in reality, based on the dynamic interplay between a
series of beliefs about what is desirable, possible, acceptable and legitimate.

Dominelli (1998) makes the point that interventions in social welfare are
'compelled to maintain the link between theory and practice', and this is
equally true of youth justice. It is not simply a technical or managerial exercise
(Bateman and Pitts, 2005: 251) in delivering prescribed interventions, but
rather a product of multifaceted and often conflicting or contradictory ideas
and beliefs (Muncie, 2001). These underlying assumptions must, therefore, be
laid open to analysis and critical evaluation, especially if we wish to consider
the prospects for change and the potential for progressive practice in dealing
with youth offending.

In seeking to develop a plausible account of how youth justice has taken
the form that it has, it will be helpful to consider several alternative analytical
strategies. As already indicated, Harris and Webb (1987) have offered a helpful
framework, in their analysis of power in the context of 'juvenile justice'. They
characterise the 'domains' of analysis in terms of the 'macro', 'mezzo' and
'micro' (see also Chapter 5). Within this framework, the 'macro' is represented

tate and its place in determining the shape and orientation of the
ery of intervention. This over-determining institutional framework is, in
view, the origin of a series of core contradictions between the idealised
s and purposes prescribed and the experience, professional culture and
inciples of 'expert' service providers. They suggest that it is these tensions
that lie at the heart of many of the difficulties experienced by those responsible
for delivering services:

> motivations and fine feelings are heavily circumscribed by social function,
> and in the conflict between competing ideologies of state bureaucracy and
> professional autonomy lies the source of some of the frustrations regularly
> experienced by the workers themselves.
>
> (Harris and Webb, 1987: 3)

The 'mezzo' level is associated with the welfare and justice agencies that act
as mediators in the interchange between state and professional interests.
According to Harris and Webb, it is at this level that interpretation, adaptation,
negotiation and even sometimes obfuscation and deception are deployed in
order to bridge and ultimately reconcile idealised and centrally determined
demands with the diverse and challenging realities of delivery in an unpredictable and sometimes intractable environment. This process of seeking
accommodation between the ideal goal or predictable social order and messy
reality is, for them, 'in part a reflection of the practicalities of managing
people who have already proved to be unmanageable' (Harris and Webb,
1987: 102). This fits with Lipsky's (1980) insightful analysis, which, in turn,
predicts a process of 'interpreting' generalised instructions and objectives in
their application to local circumstances in any context where practitioners are
expected to apply standardised rules to a 'real-life' situation.

At the micro level, where youth justice work is actually carried out, Harris
and Webb suggest that practice appears to be disparate, disorganised and
simply incomprehensible to those who are its objects, that is, young offenders.
This is largely a consequence of the attempts at the macro and mezzo levels to
apply over-simplistic solutions to complex circumstances. Harris and Webb draw
attention to one aspect of this, 'routine individualization', whereby standardised
instruments and procedures are applied uniformly, in ways that fail to take
account of difference and diversity, leading to the creation of anomalies and
illogical outcomes. For them, this was epitomised in the indiscriminate use of
Supervision Orders, irrespective of the offender's background or the nature of
the offence. In the empirical study that informed their observations, '58 per cent
of "not serious" and 70 per cent of "serious" cases received two-year orders,
apparently as a routine disposal' (Harris and Webb, 1987: 118). Might the
developing pattern of use of the Youth Rehabilitation Order be an updated
version of the same kind of anomalous outcome?

Harris and Webb's argument is that this is part of a process by which the
'inherent instability' that characterises all aspects of youth justice is played

out in a series of ordered interactions and compromises, which produce the impression of regularity and 'fit' whilst also leading to irrational outcomes. Here the possibility of disorder and irregularity is subsumed under mechanisms for ensuring that the appearance of rationality and order is maintained, and this sustains the conditions by which 'the game itself continues' (Harris and Webb, 1987: 3) and maintains its credibility. The development and implementation of the 'Scaled Approach' might well be seen as an attempt to operationalise this kind of principle, for instance.

Cicourel's (1968) earlier work on the 'social organisation of juvenile justice' also provides a detailed account of the way in which routines and procedures make sense of and create an internal logic to account for and deal with variable and problematic circumstances.

This analysis offers some important insights into the internal mechanisms of youth justice, indicating the continuing relevance of historical evidence and analysis, but it also illustrates the value of linking theoretical insights illuminating different aspects of a generalised subject. Accordingly, three critical questions will be considered here in turn, before we turn to some of the broader emergent themes, which might suggest commonalities. First, we will consider the 'micro' question of problematic youth – why are young people in England and Wales, at least, viewed as the source of a whole range of social ills? Second, we will address the nature of justice, and why the problems of disorder and unacceptable behaviour should be seen in the way they are, particularly at the 'macro' level of the state and other powerful institutions. Finally, we will revisit the issue of the 'mezzo'-level mechanisms that link these dimensions and in the resolution of complexity and contradictions ensure that youth justice is delivered and experienced in the ways that we can observe.

Targeting the young: the source of all our ills?

Why are societal concerns about disorder and threat focused largely on the behaviour of young people? Given that the recorded incidence of criminal activity is relatively evenly distributed across the age range, and that young people are as likely to be victims as offenders, why should there be this degree of concern about children as perpetrators of crime? Why, in short, are we afraid of the young?

The highly specific and selective nature of these concerns is exemplified by the observation that much of what we know and believe about childhood and adolescence is culturally determined. Jenks (1996), for example, has argued that 'adolescence' is a peculiarly Western phenomenon, representing the playing- out of the specific social, cultural and economic determinants that are influential in modern developed societies. Anthropological evidence offers further support here, with contributors such as Benedict (1961) and Erikson (1995) identifying very wide cultural variations in the ways in which transitions from childhood to adulthood are managed and experienced. Such variations indicate that the nature of adolescence is substantially determined by the context, and by the institutions and beliefs operating in any specific social milieu:

> Undoubtedly each culture ... creates character types marked by its own mixture of defect and excess; and each culture develops rigidities and illusions which protect it against the insight that no ideal, safe, permanent state can emerge from the blueprint it has gropingly evolved.
>
> (Erikson, 1995: 168)

Adolescence does not appear to be fixed or constant and this has prompted some authors to suggest that it can only be construed as one of the products of the interplay between broader social forces. Thus, for observers such as Willis (1977) and Davies (1986), the experience of being young and growing up is fundamentally influenced by the requirement to socialise the next generation of wage earners, producers and family members. The cultural patterns and practices of young people themselves, such as 'working class counter-school culture' (Willis, 1977: 2), make sense primarily as part of a process by which 'labour power' is reproduced, and young people are socialised into a particular work ethos, coming to terms, not without struggle, with their place in the socio-economic structure. This is not necessarily a straightforward or exclusively one-way process, in that attempts by the state and other institutions to regulate and reproduce the next generation of producers is both contradictory in itself, and is mediated by the distinctive thoughts, attitudes and experiences of children and young people. MacDonald and Marsh (2005: 189) reflect helpfully on the twists and turns involved in 'changing transitions', and young people's 'complicated' relationships with drugs and crime in illustration of this important point.

Against this, though, the purposes of the powerful interests which shape interventions with young people are primarily to secure the creation of a future generation that meets the needs of and sustains existing social relations:

> Youth policies were ... designed to satisfy some powerful sectional (especially class, gender and racial) interests. As the rawest and least valuable recruits to a given social order, the young had to be socialized, schooled, trained and ultimately contained – if necessary [according to a senior civil servant] 'in terms more or less unpalatable' to them.
>
> (Davies, 1986: 116)

Corrigan (1979), too, in his study of young people 'doing nothing' in Sunderland, linked changes in the experiences of youth to parallel changes in social structures and the shifting demands of living in a 'capitalist society'. Thus, young people are to be brought up both to accept their place in the order of things, but also to be ready to adapt in response to economic and social transitions. Young people are therefore increasingly learning to be 'flexible' in order to adapt to changing jobs and work patterns over the course of their lives in and out of employment (MacDonald and Marsh, 2005). This might be related to the experience of the 1980s and 1990s, whereby they were required first to 'equip themselves with the abilities sought after in the fast-food industry and then ... get on their bikes and ... price themselves into work' (Haines and Drakeford, 1998: 8).

One aspect of their 'educative' (Gramsci, 1971) experience is provided through their interactions with criminal justice agencies. This may be one of the more explicit aspects of a broader process of socialisation whereby young people learn their proper place and the limits of what is acceptable. To them, this may have no obvious origin or justification. It just 'is':

> The power of the police is seen as virtually total by the boys ... The police, like the teachers, are a group of people with power that do some very strange and arbitrary things; their power is massive and has to be coped with, if not obeyed.
>
> (Corrigan, 1979: 137)

> The impact of police working rules, in particular the rules relating to previous form and suspiciousness (keeping the wrong company), serve to construct a population of young people viewed by the police as innately criminal and who become the objects of continual scrutiny.
>
> (McAra and McVie, 2005: 28)

Furthermore, the control that is exercised is not connected in these youths' perceptions to specific instances of wrongdoing. It is more the case that specific boundaries are being drawn around their behaviour in order to create a sense of the 'natural order' of things, and to ensure conformity. Indeed, this is part of a broader pattern of institutionalised control (Cohen, 1985). According to Jeffs (1997), these parallel developments are not purely coincidental. A range of centralised and directive education initiatives, such as home-school contracts, citizenship education and attendance league tables, serve essentially the same purpose as explicit measures of social control, such as 'tagging' and the imposition of strict parental liability:

> the role of the police and the role of the education system are parallel here, because they are both attempting to change the styles of living of people who ... are seen as threatening ...
>
> (Corrigan, 1979: 139)

The experience of the Anti-Social Behaviour Order (ASBO) can be seen as a concrete expression of this project. Young people clearly recognised that the objective was to limit their freedoms: 'They only go for the kids they don't go after the adults. They think we're easier. We're easier to target aren't we?' (young person quoted in Smithson, 2004: 13).

The machinery of criminal justice is one of a series of mechanisms that shape the experiences and expectations of young people, which are collectively geared towards creating a spirit of acceptance and compliance with social norms. However, as Muncie (1999b) reminds us, it is important to note, too, that the social roles for which young people are being prepared are mediated by other distinctions, such as class, ethnicity and gender. Webster (2006: 42), for example, discusses the specific processes of racialised 'marginalisation'.

The preoccupation with controlling and channelling the behaviour of the young is linked to a functionalist concern to ensure that they are effectively socialised to meet the requirements of the dominant social order, apparently. Jeffs (1997) has suggested that there is a 'plethora' of government policies covering education, housing, income maintenance and youth crime, which, taken together, indicate 'the resolve on the part of the government to control those identified as the underclass. In particular, they have exhibited a willingness to adopt increasingly authoritarian policies to control and manage the young poor' (Jeffs, 1997: 160).

The perceived need to provide guidance and structure partly stems from an understanding of young people as 'unfinished' – that is, going through a process of 'transition' (Walther, 2006) – and thus likely to behave inappropriately, or in ways that are 'threatening' (Davies, 1986). Indeed, the very terms 'youth' or 'adolescent' have the capacity to 'conjure up emotive and troubling images. These range from notions of uncontrolled freedom, irresponsibility, vulgarity, rebellion and dangerousness to those of deficiency, neglect, deprivation or immaturity' (Muncie, 1999b: 3).

While concerns about the behaviour and attitudes of the young arise partly because they have not yet been fully prepared for their allotted roles as responsible and productive (or reproductive) members of society, it is also the case that the socialisation process itself is inconsistent, leading to tensions and contradictions. As Willis (1977) has observed, the demands placed on young people by social institutions themselves may not always point in the same direction, and there has never been a time (a 'golden age') when youth transitions were 'really smooth and unproblematic' (Vickerstaff, 2003: 269). MacDonald (1997) argues that their own emerging personal 'survival' strategies compel young people to develop a range of responses to economic pressures and 'chronic insecurity'. Clearly, their own background and characteristics will also be a factor in this process. 'Normal' expectations may fall foul of acute exclusionary processes (Webster, 2006: 41).

Young people can thus be expected to behave in differing and conflicting ways in order to comply with a variety of social expectations within their own specific circumstances; for example, they may be encouraged to take relatively passive roles as 'consumers', sharing 'the mainstream aspirations and values of the wider society' (Webster, 2006: 41), whilst they are also encouraged to take an active and entrepreneurial role as 'producers' (Smith, 2000b), but with 'few bridges or connections' (Webster, 2006: 41) to enable them to achieve this goal.

Paradoxically, 'it is, of course, an absolute requirement for the existing social system that the same standards, ideologies and aspirations are not passed on to all' (Willis, 1977: 177). If pre-existing distributions of status, resources and power are to be maintained, young people will need to be socialised into different roles with distinctive attributes and characteristics. This, though, will lead to a series of conflicting dynamics within the processes of transition for young people. For example, the complex expectations of masculinity appear to require young males to be dynamic, competitive and ambitious on the one hand; whilst, on the other, attributes such as being challenging or aggressive are discouraged. Against this backdrop, Webster (2006: 41) suggests that a 'racialised "exaggerated masculinity" grows by way of compensation against humiliation and anticipated school "failure"'.

Young people on the margins may also be encouraged to aspire to increased spending power, with increasing material ambitions, whilst at the same time confronting the constraints of the labour market, which, as MacDonald (1997: 106) puts it, frustrates their hopes 'for sustainable family lives and respectable futures'. Transitions in such circumstances are problematic, often resulting in 'interconnected' difficulties, extending over a considerable period of time (Webster *et al.*, 2004: 35).

Recognising these conflicts and constraints can bring us closer to understanding the relationship between the sources of power and the institutional structures that represent dominant interests, on the one hand, and the behaviour of the young in response to the 'mixed messages' they receive, on the other.

Frustrated ambitions?

In seeking to account for the behaviour of young people, it may also be helpful to reflect on the insights offered by a rather older sociological source (Merton, 1957), who constructed a 'typology' to make sense of the differing ways in which individuals adapt to social norms, depending on their circumstances, influences and personal attributes.

At the heart of this model is the distinction between 'goals' and 'means', which Merton then uses to demonstrate that there are a variety of potential combinations of these factors, with differing implications for attitudes and behaviour (see Table 7.1).

Thus, for example, if an individual shares the dominant goals of a given society, and possesses and exercises the institutionalised (socially accepted)

Table 7.1 A typology of modes of individual adaptation

Mode of adaptation	Culture goals	Institutionalised means
Conformity	+	+
Innovation	+	-
Ritualism	-	+
Retreatism	-	-
Rebellion	±	±

Source: (Adapted from Merton, 1957: 140)

means to achieve these, then that person is demonstrating social conformity. However, a number of other patterns of adaptation are possible, including 'innovation'. In this mode, the individual shares the dominant goals but adopts other than institutionalised means to achieve these. Merton (writing in the USA) observed in this respect that 'contemporary American culture continues to be characterized by a heavy emphasis on wealth as a basic symbol of success, without a corresponding emphasis on the legitimate avenues on which to march towards this goal' (Merton, 1957: 139). The 'innovative' response to this contradiction might therefore be demonstrated by way of resorting to some form of acquisitive criminal activity. Merton suggested, too, that there would be a distinctive class bias to such patterns of behaviour, for obvious reasons, in that the 'lower strata' will have fewer opportunities to achieve financial success through the labour market:

> specialised areas of vice and crime constitute a 'normal' response to a situation where the cultural emphasis upon pecuniary success has been absorbed, but where there is little access to conventional and legitimate means for becoming successful.
>
> (Merton, 1957: 139)

In other words, the prior distribution of opportunity, resources and social position plays a central part in shaping young people's own processes of adaptation and strategic choice in an unequal society (see MacDonald and Marsh, 2005). Although this framework offers an explanatory account for acquisitive crimes (such as theft, fraud and shoplifting), it may be somewhat less effective in relation to other forms of criminal activity (see, for example, Soothill *et al.*, 2002). Nevertheless, it remains of considerable use in demonstrating that accepted social norms can, of themselves, act as prompts to rational forms of adaptive behaviour that are, at the same time, socially unacceptable. So, the crimes of the young can, in part, be attributed to rational choices made in a context of social inequality and unattainable aspirations. As we have seen, Webster's (2006) analysis of 'race', youth crime and justice' indicates that there remains a strong commitment to dominant and institutionalised norms amongst marginalised groups, whilst Craine's (1997) ethnographic analysis draws the conclusion that 'alternative careers' in the illicit economy should be viewed as a response to 'triple failure'. In this study, young people were found to be constructing viable but unlawful alternatives, where 'They had "failed" educationally, "failed" to secure post-school employment, "failed" to "get into" working-class adulthood through employment, even after participation in a succession of government schemes and special programmes' (Craine, 1997: 148).

Indeed, illegal alternatives might prove considerably more lucrative for some (Webster *et al.*, 2004: 20). At least some of the behaviour of young people defined as criminal might therefore be a by-product of the social pressures and conflicting expectations they encounter, and the means by which they adapt to these. Merton's framework can also offer us some insight into other routes into criminality, such as drug use ('Retreatism').

The reality of youth crime

Whilst this framework can begin to offer ways to account for specific forms of youth offending, we must also accept that this behaviour can be experienced by others as unpleasant and unacceptable. As MacDonald (1997) points out, it is a matter of concern that crimes committed by young people are likely to have an adverse impact on their own communities: 'the social and financial costs of acquisitive and more random and violent criminality ... cannot be dismissed' (MacDonald, 1997: 184). Whilst both 'youth' and 'crime and disorder' are socially constructed (Muncie, 1999b), however defined, some of the behaviour manifested by young people is problematic, anti-social or simply unpleasant. The work of the 'left realists' in criminology was instrumental in bringing this challenge to the fore. The problem of youth crime is not just a consequence of 'labelling' (Becker, 1963) or the impact of oppressive forms of social control (Lea and Young, 1984). The behaviour of young people can be genuinely damaging, oppressive in its own right, and frightening to individuals and communities that may already be disadvantaged in other ways:

> criminologists have come to realise the essentially contradictory nature of crime, economically, socially and politically ... Radical criminology ... notes quite urgently that there is a substantial element in street crime which is merely the poor taking up the individualistic, competitive ethos of capitalism itself ...
>
> (Lea and Young, 1984: 116)

In concurring with Merton, Lea and Young identify young people as a prime source of much of the offensive behaviour that gives rise to fear and hostility within neighbourhoods, and also accounts for the apparent popularity of government anti-social behaviour initiatives.

They have also controversially argued that there may be a racial dimension to this, in that young black people might be responsible for a disproportionate amount of crime, or at least certain types of crime, in effect 'compounding the oppression' of victims (Pitts, 2001b). There is some support for this claim in one self-report study (MORI, 2004: 26), but Gilroy (2002: 66) argues that this must not be allowed to generate global assumptions that 'blacks are a high crime group' (see Chapter 8) or provide any justification for racist practices in dealing with offending behaviour. As Webster (2006) points out, the processes of 'racialisation' and 'criminalisation' are complex, socially determined dynamics, and should not be taken out of context.

Nevertheless, the recognition of the impact of crime in contributing to the suffering of disadvantaged communities has had much to do with the contemporary refocusing of thinking and policy in this area, with priority being given to tackling directly the behaviour that creates problems in communities. Whilst there has been a tendency to seek simple solutions to these issues at the policy level, there has also been a corresponding move to try to account for the 'situated' nature of crime, and its antecedents. Once we accept that patterns of behaviour, including criminal activity, are differentially distributed, it then becomes possible to focus on the question of why this should be the case.

Structural accounts alone do not provide localised explanations for diversity of experience or behaviour; nor do they offer direct help in achieving specific, deliverable solutions. After all, we are reminded, not all young people who are disadvantaged become criminals:

> This more realist approach to the delinquency of young men is a useful antidote to the excessive social constructionism which has pervaded liberal criminology ... It also reiterates the importance of appreciating the way that socially constructed aspects of identity – particularly those informed by gender, class and race – help shape the cultural survival strategies of young people ... some young men, sharing apparently similar social attributes [as those who] do not attempt ... delinquent solutions ...
>
> (MacDonald, 1997: 192)

Subsequent investigation into offending pathways by MacDonald and colleagues (see Webster *et al.*, 2004) did, indeed, identify a number of situational variables that appeared to affect 'persistence' and desistance', including 'sustained employment', 'family support' and family formation.

Not only has this refocusing of concern about the crimes of the young helped to provide the basis for more nuanced explanations, but it also has substantial pragmatic value. It paved the way for a shift of thinking on the social democratic left to the effect that it is important to respond directly to public calls to 'do something' about crime and disorder; it also implies that there may be practical and immediate 'common sense' means available to achieve this, through, for example, addressing the source of problems within families, that is 'poor child-rearing practices and weak parental control' (Pitts, 2000: 10). The danger, of course, is that the pendulum swings once again, and the door is reopened to the legitimisation of routine pathologisation of young people, especially those in marginalised communities experiencing multiple forms of discrimination.

Explaining youth crime?

In light of these considerations, structural explanations of youth crime have proven relatively unattractive to policy makers and opinion formers. Much attention has been given instead to the task of specifying as precisely as possible the factors associated with[1] young people's criminal behaviour that are rooted in their experiences, circumstances and characteristics.

Farrington's work in this context is considered to be seminal. He has been at the forefront of a body of work that has identified a number of factors demonstrated to be associated with a propensity to offend by young people, including:

- low income and poor housing;
- living in 'deteriorated' inner-city areas;
- a high degree of impulsiveness and hyperactivity;
- low intelligence and low school attainment;
- poor parental supervision and harsh and erratic discipline; and
- parental conflict and broken families.

(Farrington, 1996)

Similarly, Rutter and colleagues identified a range of conditions associated with 'anti-social behaviour', including:

- Individual characteristics, such as 'hyperactivity', 'cognitive impairment', 'temperamental features', and a 'distorted style of social information processing';
- Psychosocial factors, such as the nature of parenting, family discord and parental depression; and
- Population-wide influences, such as the mass media, school ethos and behaviour, and 'area differences'.

(Rutter *et al.*, 1998)

Further work to bring together knowledge about the relationship between youth crime and contingent factors was commissioned by the Youth Justice Board (YJB) (Anderson *et al.*, 2001), and this broadly supported these findings, suggesting that factors could be grouped under family, community, school and personal headings. These meta-analyses suggest that the relationship between characteristics, circumstances and crime is complex and 'uncertain' (Anderson *et al.*, 2001: 24). They also suggest that such factors operate at a number of different levels, so that it is unwise to focus unduly on any one of these, whether individual characteristics at one end of the spectrum or socio-economic factors at the other. Nevertheless, because a number of distinct relationships can be evidenced, it is possible to draw out implications for policy and practice.

Whilst in these examples factors beyond the young person are identified as significant, such as social deprivation and inadequate schooling – redolent of Bourdieu's (1990: 55) notion of 'habitus' and the conditions that shape it – the policy messages taken from this work focus mainly on changing young people themselves rather than the social conditions that contextualise their lives and frame their choices. It is at this point that confused and sometimes misplaced causal assumptions begin to reassert themselves implicitly.

Farrington (2002), for example, argues for the development of initiatives directed at securing behavioural change at the individual level, school improvement programmes, parental education and 'enriched' services for the early years. He also argues more broadly for 'community-based programmes against crime' following the *Communities that Care* model (France and Crow, 2002). Rutter and colleagues also share the enthusiasm for early prevention initiatives such as the Perry Pre-School Project, 'parenting enhancement', school-wide interventions and the 'early treatment' of problem behaviour (Rutter *et al.*, 1998). They caution, however, that 'focusing on high-risk samples will miss a substantial number of offenders' (ibid.: 24), a conclusion echoed by Anderson and colleagues (Anderson *et al.*, 2001: 25), raising questions about aspects of the 'preventive' approaches represented by selective strategies such as the Youth Inclusion and Support Programme.

Whilst the analyses behind these proposals are of considerable value, and demonstrate the importance of empirical research in criminal justice (if properly used), they have also been the source of considerable subsequent confusion, notably over the necessary distinctions between 'predictors', 'risk factors', 'antecedents' and 'causes'. Identifying a relationship between certain indicators and offending behaviour is not the same as demonstrating that there is a specific uni-directional causal relationship between them: 'even the most elaborate predictors of individual offending devised by criminologists have always over-predicted the incidence of crime alarmingly' (Pitts, 2001b: 82). Indeed, some proponents of meta-analyses concur with this point:

> There are methodological as well as ethical difficulties attached to using current knowledge of risk factors to target individual children 'at risk'. Multi-factor 'prediction' instruments may be relatively accurate but only apply to a small number of children, missing most of those who go on to commit offences. Those that use a narrower range of factors have been apt to identify significant numbers of children as 'high risk' who do not go on to commit offences.
>
> (Anderson *et al.*, 2001: 25)

However, the desire for simplification and certainty is apparent in the over-interpretation of this kind of study by 'politicians, policy wonks, "opinion formers" and some youth justice managers and professionals', who draw lazy conclusions about the use of predictive instruments to 'target, and then eradicate, youth crime' (Pitts, 2001b: 82). Evidence of this elision has been observed in the work of bodies such as the Social Exclusion Unit, which made the mistake of attributing causal status to a number of essentially individualised factors:

> Most juvenile prisoners have experienced a range of social exclusion factors, which may have contributed to their offending behaviour. These include:
>
> • low educational attainment;
> • disrupted family backgrounds;

- coming from a black or minority ethnic background;
- behavioural and mental health problems; and
- problems of alcohol and/or drug misuse.

(Social Exclusion Unit, 2002: para. D6)

Attempts to generate a comprehensive empirical account of the factors associated with criminal behaviour are important, not least because they have formed the basis for much recent thinking on the part of government and opinion formers, including influential think tanks such as the Centre for Social Justice (2012: 29).

However, the evidence has often been drawn on selectively. Muncie suggests, for example, that the government's preoccupation with improving the quality of parenting stems from the links identified between the nature and quality of family life and the likelihood of offending by young people. As a consequence, policies and intervention strategies are explicitly designed to address these 'presenting' problems:

> New Labour's acceptance that crime runs in certain families and that anti-social behaviour in childhood is a predictor of later criminality has opened the door to a range of legislative initiatives which target 'disorderly' as well as criminal behaviour.
>
> (Muncie, 2000: 23)

Significantly, this line of reasoning shows a considerable degree of continuity between administrations (and their advisers), with the coalition government relying on the pronouncements of organisations such as the Centre for Social Justice to inform major policy programmes such as the 2012 'Troubled Families' initiative. Similarly, the justification for the introduction of measures to tackle anti-social behaviour is provided by the evidence of the prevalence of behavioural problems such as 'impulsiveness and hyperactivity'. Indeed, the selectiveness of the policy perspective adopted has been further reinforced by the emphasis on behavioural interventions across the range of youth justice interventions emerging from the Youth Justice Board (2002). Despite the YJB's initial enthusiasm, however, implementation of a range of projects focused on behavioural change produced little evidence to justify this strategy (Feilzer, 2004).

As Muncie has pointed out, a shift of focus, which would be supported by the evidence from meta-analyses, to include 'social' factors such as poor housing and unemployment, might lead to a rather different emphasis in policy and practice. Despite this, the primary foci of youth justice interventions remain the individual and the family (parents):

> Parental training and a range of behavioural and cognitive interventions are considered to be most effective ... In such ways the targets of social crime prevention have invariably become individualised and behavioural.

Primary attention is given to responding to the symptoms, rather than the causes of young people's disaffection and dislocation.

(Muncie, 2000: 26)

On the other hand, more measured consideration of the evidence from detailed empirical studies suggests that the range of factors associated with youth crime are connected in various ways, and as a consequence that we should not overlook the part that social and structural factors play. Leonard (1984: 116) has articulated the link between social forces and individual personalities; the individual is 'moulded, inculcated or penetrated by the institutions and activities of the social order and the ideologies which inform and legitimate them', echoing Merton (1957) in many ways. The deviant behaviour of individuals must therefore be seen as the product of multifaceted, interactive and dynamic processes. Criminality emerges as the outcome of a complex interplay of social and ideological forces and personal experience: 'contradictions within and between the economy, the family and the state, connecting to the highly variable experience of specific individuals, provide space for avoidance, resistance and dissent' (Leonard, 1984: 116). Specific anti-social acts, which may be reprehensible in themselves, and which may or may not be defined as 'criminal', cannot be understood or dealt with solely in terms of their immediate manifestation. As Christie (2000) has commented, forms of 'individualised' intervention (which in fact apply 'generalised' assumptions) serve at the same time to 'depersonalise' explanations of youth crime:

A political decision to eliminate concern for the social background of the defendant involves much more than making those characteristics inappropriate for decisions on pain [punishment]. By the same token, the offender is to a large extent excluded as a person. There is no point in exploring a social background, childhood, dreams, defeats ...

(Christie, 2000: 163)

For those with direct experience of undertaking restricted and standardised assessments according to predetermined and restrictive reporting frameworks, this will no doubt strike a chord.[2] It also raises further questions about the nature of formal responses to the crimes of the young, and the extent to which these largely 'miss the point'. In order to understand the interaction between 'youth justice' and young people, we must give further consideration to the way in which institutional policies and practices are constituted and how these lead to forms of delivery that simultaneously decontextualise and problematise the behaviour of young people identified as potential or actual offenders.

The locus of power: ideologies and structures

Much attention has been given to the question of power and its relationship to ideologies of crime and disorder. The exercise of social control is a source of continuing academic fascination and debate (see Garland, 2001). Authorities such as Cohen (1985) have made major contributions in this field, and there is widespread acknowledgement that it is an important underpinning of an adequate understanding of youth justice (for example, Goldson, 1997; Scraton and Haydon, 2002; Goldson and Muncie, 2006a). The key question here is the relationship between state power, the maintenance of social and moral order and the specific machinery of the justice system itself. Clarke (2002), for example, suggests that the courts and other state institutions are constituted in such a way as to carry out aspects of this mediating function, helping to establish the legitimacy of processes that underpin a particular set of social relations. It is their ascribed status and authority that affords them the justi-fication for imposing sanctions on individuals and their families, both as a direct means of controlling their behaviour and as a way of reinforcing the legitimacy of the system of norms and rules upon which they are based. The institutions of justice therefore have a kind of self-validating quality, con-firming by their actions their right to problematise those, such as 'young offenders', who are the objects of intervention.

As we have already observed, the rationale underlying the youth justice system is probably derived from persistent concerns about the uncertainty of youth transitions and the associated threat to the maintenance and reproduction of social order. For Clarke (2002), the fear of disorder and unruly youth is endemic, having been observed in historical accounts of unrest for at least 'the past three centuries'. Pearson (1983), too, has provided evidence that modern society has been persistently troubled by fear of its young people, who become routinely vilified, often with racist overtones. Cohen's (1972) *Folk Devils and Moral Panics* graphically illustrated the way in which fears take hold, are reified and amplified, contributing to an almost constant sense of threat amongst the population in general, magnified to the extent that the very social fabric appears to be at constant risk of disintegration.

While there are grounds for recognising that the processes of transition from childhood to adulthood might generate a range of challenging behaviour, there is also considerable evidence to support the argument that the perceived threat is amplified. In other words, whatever the nature of young people's behaviour, additional forces are at play in generating more pervasive fears. The media clearly have a part to play in shaping such perceptions, and this is inevitable, given their role in creating shared meaning. However, the media are only part of a wider process of creating consensus and shared belief sys-tems: 'Social reality is experienced through language, communication and imagery. Social meaning and social difference are irretrievably tied up with representation' (McRobbie and Thornton, 2002: 76).

That is to say, there is an intelligible process in place, by means of which images of disorder are combined and utilised to generate a collective perception of 'threatening youth' (Davies, 1986). This tendency emerged once again with the 2011 riots, where, in contrast to the subsequent evidence of involvement, young people were initially targeted as the principal source of 'trouble' (Riots Communities and Victims Panel, 2012).

This proposition leads us to the notion of 'hegemony' (Gramsci, 1971). This, in essence, is the mechanism by which dominant assumptions and norms are integrated to create a shared and conventional view of the 'problem', how it arises and how it should be tackled. Thus, for example, the administration of the youth justice system does not simply reflect the routine delivery of rational processes based on established and shared social norms; it also acts, in combination with other authoritative sources (like the media), to justify and reinforce prior categorisations of acceptable and unacceptable behaviour. It is not just a matter of distinguishing between fixed and immutable categories of 'right' and 'wrong', but the exercise of judicial, organisational and professional authority also acts to legitimise this distinction, as it applies in any given social milieu. Behind this process, however, lies the question of which interests are represented in these apparently neutral and objective processes.

Gramsci (1971) observes that the key factor here is the extent to which particular forces can establish the general legitimacy of their own interests and thereby claim the authority to police these. Legitimacy has to be established, and the exercise of authority has to gain the consent of citizens in order to secure their active engagement in maintaining social control. The smooth and effective running of social institutions essentially depends on a widely shared commitment to the principles and structures on which they are based (for example, the police need the 'consent' of the community in order to be able to carry out their functions effectively; Scarman, 1982).

The authority to govern is gained in two ways, according to Gramsci: by the achievement of the 'spontaneous' consent of the population; or by the direct invocation of the 'apparatus of state coercive power', in order 'legally' to enforce discipline on those who do not conform. The latter option, though, should be seen as a kind of reserve power, only brought to bear when rule by consent has failed. It cannot become the norm because it implies at least a partial breakdown of consensual norms, and becomes increasingly difficult to sustain. The explicit use of state power in this way is in fact much less efficient or effective than the day-to-day project of earning and sustaining the consent and willing compliance of most, if not all, elements in society. In order to achieve this end, the state therefore prefers to adopt an 'educative and formative' role (Gramsci, 1971: 242). This is a specific characteristic of 'liberal democratic [governments] which make a major attempt to secure public support for state criminalisation and crime control through centralised high-profile politics of "law and order"' (Lea, 2002: 172). Here, we can see again the significance of the media as a vehicle for conveying information and securing consent, borne out by research into public attitudes (Chapman *et al.*, 2002).

The 'rule of law' aspires to create an externalised consensual objective, and purportedly neutral standard by which behaviour can be judged, and according to which the line between the law abiding and the criminal can be drawn. It is not simply a matter of creating effective machinery for crime control and the administration of official sanctions; it is also the function of 'the law' to carry out an 'educative' role in setting the terms for common standards of acceptable behaviour, and generating the only valid criteria by which compliance (or not) with these can be judged.

Althusser (1977) has developed a similar line of argument, agreeing that it is important to distinguish the ideological function of the law from its practical purposes. His useful, but over-deterministic and monolithic, characterisation of the exercise of social control depends on the notion of 'state apparatuses'. These can be subdivided into 'Repressive State Apparatuses' and 'Ideological State Apparatuses' (ISAs), which share the same objectives, but operate rather differently. In the judicial context, some bodies can be thought of as primarily repressive, such as the courts and the prisons, whilst others, including the range of community justice agencies, can be seen to perform a more specifically ideological function depending on their credibility to establish legitimacy for their interventions and gain consent for the administration of justice. In this way, 'the law belongs both to the [Repressive] State Apparatus and to the system of ISAs' (Althusser, 1977: 137).

This distinction helps us to appreciate the way in which legal institutions and judicial processes operate both directly to control certain types of behaviour by coercion, and indirectly by creating the conditions under which certain acts are defined as unlawful, and then dealt with as transgressions. The use of direct means of repression is supported by the ideological project of establishing the limits of what is acceptable.

Althusser also suggests that there is a complementary relationship between the ISAs, which support and reinforce each other in sustaining the position of dominant interests. This network includes the educational ISA, the family ISA, the communications ISA and the religious ISA. Building on this kind of argument, Garland suggests that a similar kind of relationship exists between justice agencies and other systems:

> Institutions of crime control and criminal justice have definite conditions of existence. They form part of a network of governance and social ordering that, in modern societies, includes the legal system, the labour market, and welfare state institutions. They refer to, and are supported by, other social institutions and social controls, and are grounded in specific configurations of cultural, political and economic action.
>
> (Garland, 2001: 5)

In the context of youth justice, the way in which such elements coalesce to establish and maintain an interlocking system of social control was classically illustrated by Hall and colleagues (1978). Their extensive study, based on the emergence of the phenomenon of 'mugging' in the 1970s and associated public concern, shows how perceptions of criminal behaviour can be generated and then intensified by a network of social institutions, including the media, political interests and the judiciary, intervening in public debates in such a way as to amplify fears and create an overwhelming sense of law-lessness and threat, about which something had to be done (see also Hearne, 2003). The consequence of this interactive process was, indeed, in the 1970s, a heightened level of public sensitivity to a particular form of behaviour, street robbery (or 'mugging', in its popularised form), and consequently a readiness to invoke and endorse draconian interventions by the judicial system. Thus, we can see how amplificatory spirals of this kind operate to support and strengthen ideological assumptions about the nature of offending behaviour and its perpetrators, and the way they should be dealt with – compounded in the case of 'mugging' by issues of 'race' and racism, another recurrent motif, as Garland (2001) and Hall *et al.* (2013) confirm.

A more contemporary reflection on the relationship between the repressive and ideological functions of state apparatuses might lead us to consider the example of the Youth Justice Board itself. The YJB, as previously observed, operates in a number of spheres of policy and practice, but is clearly driven by a particular set of assumptions about the offending behaviour of young people, and 'what works' in dealing with this. It is also constituted as an (apparently) independent body representing a diverse range of relevant interests. It thereby also lays claim to authority based on its collective credentials of expertise, knowledge and experience, which puts it in a privileged position to lead thinking, innovation and delivery. This standing, in turn, provides the YJB with sufficient credibility and 'clout' to be able to determine what counts as 'good practice' and what principles should underpin practitioners' activities. However, the 'ideological' function of the board in shaping our understanding of appropriate forms of intervention has been complemented by rather more 'repressive' aspects of its operation, such as the introduction of Intensive Supervision and Surveillance Programmes (ISSPs), its role in promoting excessive intervention and its acquisition of responsibility for placing children in secure facilities. The YJB's independence and professional standing will, of course, help to provide legitimacy for these activities; for instance, its claims to have made improvements in conditions and services for young people in custody (Youth Justice Board, 2005e) might help to make such an option more tolerable to those who might otherwise baulk at the idea of sending a 12 year old to prison (Pitts, 2003).

Cohen (1985) is particularly critical of the 'humanization' of apparently oppressive forms of treatment in the name of progress. He argues that this represents no more than the extension of the network of coercion, made possible precisely because of the appearance of reasonableness and solicitude. He also fears that this 'softly, softly' approach may pervade the entire criminal process:

> at the shallow end, the generation of new treatment criteria and the per-vasiveness of the social welfare and preventive structures, often ensure an erosion of traditional rights and liberties. In a system of low visibility and accountability, where a high degree of discretion is given to administrative

and professional bodies ... there is often less room for such niceties as due process and legal rights.

(Cohen, 1985: 70)

This observation may have pre-dated ASBOs, Acceptable Behaviour Contracts, Final Warnings and Referral Orders by 15 years or so, but his critique is clearly still valid, and Youth Restorative Disposals, triage and similar innovations may yet be subject to the same challenge, that they may lead to arbitrary and inequitable outcomes.

On the other hand, Cohen takes issue with the fact that 'heavy end' intensive community options (such as ISSPs) are justified largely on the grounds that they are not custody. Thus, at both ends of the spectrum, increased levels of control and coercion are imported into community disposals, whilst apparently representing liberal alternatives to repressive measures:

Meanwhile, there is no problem in finding criminologists, psychologists, social workers and others who will justify all these community alternatives as humane, kindly and even 'therapeutic' ... This is the particularly wondrous advantage ... of those programmes which use the explicit rationale of behaviourism.

(Cohen, 1985: 75)

The rationale underpinning humanitarian and personally beneficial behaviour change (anger management, for example) provides strong support for 'community corrections', whilst also sustaining the assumption that the 'problem' is located with the young person her/himself. 'Deviance must be "brought back home". Parents, peers, schools, the neighbourhood, even the police should dedicate themselves to keeping the deviant out of the formal system' (Cohen, 1985: 77). However, of course, this does not mean that nothing happens. Instead, 'the primary institutions of society', such as schools, family or neighbourhood groups, are expected to take responsibility for scrutinising and controlling the behaviour of young people who are 'at risk' of getting into trouble.

On the other hand, this kind of close attention may be counterproductive and lead to unintended consequences:

Thus, if a youth is already under the surveillance of the system – even a preventive program serving a non-offending youth from a 'high risk' neighbourhood, but particularly an offender supervised intensively – he or she is far more likely to be caught offending and sanctioned sooner, and more often.

(Kempf-Leonard and Peterson, 2002: 438)

Indicatively, the ASBO breach rate had reached 42% by 2003, and this may well be explained in part by the increased level of scrutiny associated with the order, just as 'breach' became increasingly common across the range of youth justice disposals (Bateman, 2011a).

Cohen's vision seems remarkably prescient. The language of being 'tough on crime, tough on the causes of crime', of linking 'rights' with 'responsibilities', of 'targeting' and of promoting 'parental responsibility' – in sum, the New Labour vision – fitted well with his articulation of a correctional approach extending the machinery and techniques of the justice system into the community. More recently, the parameters of intervention have changed, but it is noteworthy that the Troubled Families initiative of the coalition government incorporated many of the same assumptions. Thus, even the family becomes a 'correctional resource' (see also Donzelot, 1979), which has become a 'site for expert invasion and penetration' (Cohen, 1985: 79). Clearly, the Parenting Order is one highly explicit manifestation of this, first introduced under the Crime and Disorder Act 1998, but subsequently extended to become available in a wider range of circumstances, blurring the line between 'criminal' and merely undesirable behaviour, such as truancy and nuisance ('anti-social behaviour').

Schools and neighbourhoods are also identified as sites for the development of sophisticated methods of surveillance, supervision and correction – Cohen was perhaps anticipating the development of Pupil Referral Units, mentoring schemes (Tarling *et al.*, 2001). Youth Inclusion Projects (Eccles, 2001) and Summer Splash Schemes (Loxley *et al.*, 2002) were both explicitly targeted at 'at risk' young people in areas identified as crime 'hot spots', although their reported success in achieving reductions in crime is limited (Loxley *et al.*, 2002; Morgan Harris Burrows, 2003). As well as seeking to improve the efficacy of local social control measures, these schemes also carried out an important ideological function, focusing concern on specific young people in designated areas, and thereby shifting attention away from the wider questions of disadvantage, inequality and discrimination, and from the structural factors that, as we have seen, are equally viable explanations of the incidence of youth offending (Anderson *et al.*, 2001). Indeed, as Cohen observes, with the move towards a greater emphasis on managerial and technical solutions to the problems of crime, causes become of less importance – the logic being that 'if we can control crime, we don't really need to understand the causes', which epitomises the 'what works' philosophy (Cohen, 1985: 176). Hence, perhaps, New Labour's lack of interest in the broader 'causes of crime', which have been supplanted by a limited number of 'indicators' of social exclusion (Social Exclusion Unit, 2001a), justifying interventions targeted at specific 'at risk' populations, such as those excluded from school, workless families and 'multi-stressed families' (Day *et al.*, 2012) – a trend sustained of course by the Troubled Families initiative itself 'targeted' at the 120,000 reputedly most problematic families nationally.

In concluding this discussion, it may be helpful to recapitulate the means by which this sleight of hand is carried out. A particular and 'situated' ideology of crime and disorder is reconstituted as representing the natural order of things, which in turn necessitates a specific intervention strategy based on identifying and targeting those responsible and controlling their behaviour. Other (structural) issues are no longer viewed as relevant. However, this is just a partial view, and in reality what is defined as youth crime derives from both the actions of young people and the *ideological* process by which their behaviour is defined as criminal. This behaviour may be unacceptable, but whether or not it should be criminalised remains a matter of situated and specific human judgement, not pure fact. This is perhaps a key point for those who have been trapped in a routinised and irrational cycle of surveillance, classification and regulation of young people to no beneficial purpose.

Foucault and the techniques of justice

Following this theme, it may also be helpful to consider the extent to which contemporary youth justice practices are, indeed, essentially based on techniques of measurement, management and control, often associated with the work of Foucault. His thesis is that the modern era (late eighteenth century onwards) is characterised by a significant shift from forms of punishment based on 'spectacle' and example to an approach to intervention based on measures designed to ensure discipline and compliance. Thus, he suggests that the last 200 years have witnessed a reduction in 'penal severity' and a 'displacement in the very object of the punitive operation' (Foucault, 1979). Punishment can no longer be seen in terms of a direct physical operation inflicting pain and suffering on the body, but a more insidious activity, acting, in his words, 'on the soul'. Thus, ideas of correction and treatment have been incorporated into penal discourse, with a focus on controlling and changing behaviour.

Foucault associates these changes with a range of other transformations, such as the development of the legal concept of contract and a 'new economy'. Crime control was thus driven by a new emphasis on rationality and uniformity of treatment, based on 'new principles for regularizing, refocusing, universalizing the act of punishment. Humanize its application. Reduce its economic and political cost by increasing its effectiveness and by multiplying its circuits' (Foucault, 1979: 89). The criminal, by breaching the terms of her/his contract with the communal interest, becomes liable to punitive intervention and must accept the rational and calculated consequences that follow. Punishment will therefore be seen to be justified, reasonable and proportionate to the offence.

It follows that the machinery of justice and its coercive practices must be clearly and precisely specified and applied, rather in the manner of Weber's (1957) 'legal-rational' organisation of administrative procedures. Thus, 'the new arsenal of penalties ... must be as unarbitrary as possible' (Foucault, 1979: 104), and must be clearly calculable as the interventions merited by specific acts. This emphasis on precision and the routinisation of judicial processes suggests certain similarities between the 'scientific' strategies suggested by Foucault, and the kind of actuarial techniques (Smith, 2006) embedded in youth justice practices:

> actuarial justice presents a theoretical model of criminal justice processing in which the pursuit of efficiency and techniques that streamline case processing and offender supervision replace traditional goals of rehabilitation, punishment, deterrence and incapacitation ...
>
> (Kempf-Leonard and Peterson, 2002: 432)

'Incapacitation', though, may sometimes be dictated by scientific calculations of appropriate means of controlling behaviour, exemplified, for example, by the Youth Justice Board's development of the 'Scaled Approach' to risk management in assessment and intervention (Youth Justice Board, 2010b).

Foucault elaborates two further aspects of the technologisation of punishment that are significant: the forms and conduct of disciplinary mechanisms themselves, and the development of professional specialisms for the assessment and management of individual offenders:

> ultimately what one is trying to restore in this technique of correction is not so much the judicial subject ... but the obedient subject, the individual subjected to habits, rules, orders, and authority that is exercised continually around him and upon him ...
>
> (Foucault, 1979: 129)

Standardised procedures (such as ASSET) are applied to young people reported for offences in such a way as to discount many of the factors that are relevant or important to them:

> the defendant might as well not have been in court ... When such attributes are eliminated, a seemingly 'objective' and impersonal system is created ... in full accord with normal bureaucratic standards, and at the same time extraordinarily well-suited for power-holders.
>
> (Christie, 2000: 163)

In this way, a standardised process can be applied to produce 'tailored' interventions based on only those characteristics that are deemed relevant (the limited range of predetermined 'risk' factors already identified; Social Exclusion Unit, 2001a, 2002; Youth Justice Board, 2010b).

The kind of disciplinary techniques to be applied in Foucault's analysis include prescribed regimes for ordering and controlling the individual's day-to-day activities, thereby ensuring conformity ('tagging' is a contemporary example of this). Additionally, a 'timetable' is established in order to regulate behaviour and monitor compliance (such as the 25-hour ISSP attendance requirement). The timetable itself is a means of legitimating control over the individual concerned, as well as providing a means of micro managing her/his behaviour on a daily or even hourly basis. Every aspect of the day is structured and planned according to the logic of control.

Christie (2000: 127) suggests that such developments are predictable for other reasons, too, given wider trends towards the standardisation and commercialisation of forms of technological behaviour control and surveillance. Thus, aspects of the overall package can be parcelled up and contracted to the most appropriate provider. He offers the contemporary examples of electronic bracelets and voice verification as means by which this level of technologised coercive scrutiny can be achieved. The development of these means of behaviour management and monitoring has made possible 'the integration of a temporal, unitary, continuous, cumulative dimension in the exercise of controls and the practice of dominations' (Foucault, 1979: 160). This process culminates in the emergence of 'disciplinary networks', which involve experts in the fields of 'medicine, psychology, education, public assistance (and) social work'. These will assume quasi-judicial powers of assessment and programme delivery (as with pro-court interventions and the Referral Order), so that a wide range of professional interventions in the field of welfare will acquire the characteristics of penal and disciplinary power. As Lea (2002: 29) puts it, the establishment of a wide-ranging coalition of agencies with a crime control function (such as Youth Offending Teams) is part of a process of securing the widest possible 'collaboration in the task of regulating society'.

Donzelot (1979) takes this an important stage further by linking the development of these disciplinary structures and mechanisms with changes in the way in which intervention in the family is pursued. He suggests that similar processes can be identified in the ways in which families are pathologised and made subject to statutory interventions, especially where one (or more) family member is defined as delinquent. This is of particular relevance when we come to consider the new measures aimed at 'improving' the way in which parents bring up their children and control their behaviour, such as the Troubled Families programme. Donzelot suggests that this represents a shift in the 'modes' of social discipline, such that government *of* the family is replaced by government *through* the family:

> the modern family is not so much an institution as *mechanism* ... A wonderful mechanism since it enables the social body to deal with marginality through a near-total dispersal of private rights, and to encourage positive integration.
>
> (Donzelot, 1979: 94)

In other words, parents themselves are to be persuaded or coerced (by means such as the Parenting Order or imprisonment for allowing their children to truant) into accepting and then exercising as private obligations disciplinary techniques to ensure conformity amongst their children:

> The 'new' professional practices in the form of cognitive-behavioural treatment, reparation and mediation and mentoring all strive to make good these defects in the behaviour, beliefs and attitudes of young

offenders and their parents, and to instil in them a new, disciplined, capacity for self-regulation.

(Pitts, 2000: 10)

The limits of functionalism

Foucault's arguments have been criticised on a number of grounds, not least the functionalism that appears to run through them, incorporating monolithic visions of unified structures and machinery of state power and control. Giddens (1991), for example, suggests that Foucault over-generalises to the extent that he cannot provide a plausible explanation for the variety of state institutions and their inherent contradictions and conflicts; nor is it possible to account for change over time:

> Foucault's conception of the disciplinary world view, the *savoir* as he calls it, effectively forecloses on the possibility that the *savoir* itself was a site of contradiction, argument and conflict.
>
> (Ignatieff, 1985: 95)

Garland (1990) takes the criticism of Foucault further, suggesting that his thesis is open to challenge both on historical and sociological grounds. He, too, takes issue with Foucault's 'functionalism', which, he states, leads to a narrow view that all aspects of the penal system are determined by the pursuit and exercise of power and, in 'this sense, Foucault's conception of power is strangely apolitical. It appears as a kind of empty structure, stripped of any agents, interests or grounding, reduced to a bare technological scaffolding' (Garland, 1990: 170). This seems to imply that the ostensible purposes of custody and other penal machinery have been confused with their real and lived impact, which is much more uneven and unpredictable. Conflicts between purposes and practice are commonplace. The problem for Foucault is that the prison and other apparatuses of control do not always perform in the prescribed manner, or achieve the outcomes specified (as we have observed throughout this book). They are actually quite inefficient, and their effectiveness as direct instruments of discipline is quite limited, as we are repeatedly reminded (see Lyon *et al.*, 2000; Goldson, 2002).

Foucault himself acknowledges that the relations of power themselves generate opposing currents, distorting the patterns of social order. These 'resistances' are:

> distributed in irregular fashion: the points, knots of focuses of resistance are spread over time and space at varying densities, at times mobilizing groups or individuals in a definitive way, inflaming certain points of the body, certain moments in life, certain types of behaviour.
>
> (Foucault, 1981: 96)

In the context of the penal system, these counter-currents will manifest themselves in specific modifying effects on the delivery of justice:

the orientation of the agents involved, their ideologies, their resources or lack of them, the legal limits placed on their powers, the rights of clients and the resistance that they offer, can all moderate the extent to which the sanction's power is actualised.

(Garland, 1990: 168)

On the one hand, Foucault's analysis provides a thoroughgoing account of the means and mechanisms by which disciplinary power is organised, exercised and legitimised in order to control the behaviour of the young. On the other hand, his critics, in common with Harris and Webb (1987), demonstrate that the complex realities of intervention are much less uni-linear and predictable than these frameworks might suggest. Christie notes that legal structures should not be seen purely as rational instruments of 'utility'. Rather, law-in-practice has to elaborate and resolve competing aims, purposes and values. For example, the courts:

cannot function as instrumental tools for management without sacrificing their greatest strengths in the protection of values: spelling them out, evaluating them against each other, and also seeing to it that single-minded goals in some institutional settings are not given undue weight in the totality.

(Christie, 2000: 198)

This might, optimistically, be interpreted as a call to those populating the judicial system to act independently to resist both routinised measures of oppression and denial of the rights of children and young people, or populist calls for ever-more intense forms of surveillance and control. Power will be, and should be, modified by practice, as Kemshall (2008: 29) concludes. This leads to the relatively positive conclusion of current relevance that it is always possible to modify, resist or even transform some of the more repressive routinised and intrusive aspects of the contemporary youth justice system.

Youth justice: the value of theory

This necessary excursion into the theoretical terrain of youth crime, ideology and the machinery of youth justice has been intended to open up some alternative perspectives on what has become a rather narrowly conceived contemporary preoccupation with effective system management, which itself is nonetheless infused with ideological assumptions. In bringing together ideas about 'youth' and 'crime', theories of power and legitimacy, and accounts of the 'machinery of control', I have attempted to show that our understandings of these phenomena need to be well grounded and thorough. The interactions between these conceptual areas need to be addressed clearly and explicitly for us to develop a rounded appreciation of what is both necessary and practical in developing a progressive and responsive approach to the problems associated with youth offending.

As this chapter has illustrated, adolescent transitions are a feature of most societies, but their specific nature and the way in which the behaviour of the young is classified are contextually determined. Thus, the particular form taken by contradictory expectations, challenge and conflict (Merton, 1957) depends on the social context within which these are played out. For example, the rapid emergence of mobile-phone theft as an aspirational crime is specific to the early twenty-first century, but it is also linked to recurrent themes about culturally accepted goals and the availability (or not) of the means to achieve these.

At the same time, crime and criminalisation can be reframed in terms of the aim of dominant interests to establish hegemonic forms of control (Gramsci, 1971), which will sustain their dominance whilst legitimising disciplinary forms of intervention, exercised through the justice system. This strategy is exemplified by the establishment of structures that are able to function repressively, but are still able to secure consent by ideological means (Althusser, 1977; Cohen, 1985). Foucault's (1979) analysis elaborates this process by illustrating the way in which the state's control strategies are depoliticised and reconstituted as a managerial and technical question, essentially concerned with efficient delivery (Clarke *et al.*, 2000). Relevant and instructive research findings (Farrington, 1996; Rutter *et al.*, 1998; Anderson *et al.*, 2001) are decontextualised and cherry-picked, so that tentative 'associations' are reproduced as 'soundbite' causal explanations, reproduced as explanatory devices such as the blanket term 'poor parenting' (Muncie, 2000). In this way, the highly problematic nature of youth justice and the injustices perpetrated in its name are subsumed by what appears to be a natural, logical and scientifically grounded approach to quantifying and responding to a fixed and readily intelligible phenomenon.

However, this apparent uniformity of purpose and function also contains the seeds of its own destruction, for two reasons. First, as Foucault's critics have observed, in practice the machinery of justice is not actually very good at identifying, quantifying and dealing with youth crime – in fact, it is remarkably inefficient. Second, it may simply be unsustainable in resource terms, in light of the consequences of implementing an increasingly costly and 'top-heavy' regime for dealing with the infractions of the young, including both those that are pre-criminal and trivial matters. As early as the autumn of 2002, for example, the Treasury was expressing real concern about the costs of penal sanctions for young people (*The Guardian*, 9 October 2002), and, as we have now seen, principled and imaginative approaches to diversion have re-emerged as significant elements of youth justice in an age of austerity, just as in the 1980s.

Notes

1 Whilst such associations have been found, it is much harder to demonstrate causal connections (Anderson *et al.*, 2001), although these are sometimes assumed with tenuous justification.
2 A point belatedly recognised by policy makers, with the replacement of Asset planned for completion by 2015.

8 Measures of success and failure in youth justice

How can we judge success and failure?

As we have seen, the context is one of substantial and rapid change, which has been a recent feature of all aspects of the youth justice system, including legislation, policy guidance, national standards, strategic and operational delivery mechanisms, and front-line management and practice. Reform programmes have been driven forcefully from the centre, by government and by the Youth Justice Board (YJB). Claims of success have been articulated repeatedly (for example, Home Office *et al.*, 2002: 29; Audit Commission, 2004; National Audit Office, 2004; Public Accounts Committee, 2011), although sometimes tempered by the acknowledgement of 'mixed results' (Youth Justice Board, 2005d: 4).

Behind these observations lie further questions with which the youth justice system must engage. In particular, the reliance on a limited range of measures of overall achievement is problematic. Inevitably, the youth justice system, its processes and outcomes are about more (and less) than the rate at which young people offend. It is important, for instance, to consider the impact on a number of constituencies whose own objectives may not be equated simplistically with the patterns of youth crime as represented in official statistics and complex calculations of reoffending rates (for example, Jennings, 2002; Whiting and Cuppleditch, 2006). Thus, fear of crime and public confidence do not have a straightforward relationship with rates of crime, whether these are measured by official records or crime surveys (Home Office, 2001b; Halsey and White, 2008). The rate of offending by young people, in turn, has only a passing relationship with the youth justice system, which itself deals only with a small fraction of all offences (Audit Commission, 1996; Home Office, 2001a; Bateman, 2013). It may seem, then, that this system itself is not ideally equipped to take a leading role in preventing crime, and that caution should be exercised in making generalised claims about being responsible for achieving this. In other words, we must be very careful to distinguish between the broader phenomenon of problematic behaviour amongst young people and the policies and practices represented by the youth justice system, which plays a relatively narrow and very specific part in the context of other factors and dynamics that shape the representation and experience of 'youth crime'.

Given these observations, it may be more sensible to consider a range of aspects of the impact of youth justice practices, of which the effect on the rate of offending is but one.

In fact, the importance of wider goals and definitions of success was implicitly acknowledged by the Youth Justice Board (2000, 2004a) – for example, by including in early versions of National Standards a series of objectives that modify the principal aim of reducing offending. These included: reducing the fear of crime; providing services to children and young people, victims and communities; avoiding delay in processing young people who offend; proportionate punishment; and interventions to address risk factors, promote protective factors and reinforce parental responsibility (Youth Justice Board, 2004a: 3). In addition, it was pointed out that the rights of children should be protected and interventions delivered 'fairly, consistently and without improper discrimination, in a way that values and respects the cultural and racial diversity of the whole community' (Youth Justice Board, 2004a: 4).

In reality, maintaining the pure aim of reducing crime by young people is an impractical objective for the youth justice system. On the one hand, it does not deal with most youth crime (Audit Commission, 1996) and, on the other, additional objectives are incorporated both into the standards framework (Walker, 2012) and into the overarching goals of intervention (HM Government, 2008; Ministry of Justice, 2010), and of course there are other interests, too – families, communities and young people, whose priorities and aspirations in the context of youth crime are complex and nuanced. Thus, a wider range of interests and expectations must become part of the agenda when we come to consider the purposes and impacts of the youth justice system.

In order to develop a broader picture, this chapter will first consider the implications of the youth justice system and its practices for specific groups, and then, drawing on these observations, it will consider the wider questions of just what we mean by 'success' and its measurement.

Young black people and institutionalised discrimination

Naturally, broadening the scope of our concerns about impact and effectiveness in youth justice makes it possible to consider questions about outcomes rather differently. Are young people's rights protected, for example? What are the consequences if they are not?

As a particularly important exemplification of these questions, the issue of 'race' and discrimination has been a persistent theme, reflected in coexistent evidence of the over-representation of black young people in the justice process, and the oppressive treatment to which they may have been subjected. Indeed, it might have seemed at one point as if these problems were being addressed following the inquiry into the death of Stephen Lawrence, with the government accepting without question 56 of the 70 recommendations made (Bowling and Phillips, 2002). Notably, the inquiry had, for the first time, identified 'institutional racism' as endemic in the practices of the police and other organisations responsible for the delivery of criminal justice (Macpherson, 1999). Partly as a result, the Race Relations (Amendment) Act 2000 was introduced, applying anti-discrimination principles much more explicitly to public services than had previously been the case. For instance, some of the immunities applying to chief police officers in this regard were removed. Other legislation also appeared to support the aims of this measure, including the Human Rights Act 1998, and the earlier requirements for ethnic monitoring (introduced under Section 95 of the Criminal Justice Act 1991). These provisions were criticised for being relatively weak (Bowling and Phillips, 2002), but there was at least a greater degree of openness about discriminatory processes and outcomes (Barclay *et al.*, 2005; Home Office, 2006), following such initiatives.

It has also been argued that attempts at reform may have continued to mask the effects of deep-rooted racism and discriminatory practices, with the result that their impact has inevitably been compromised:

> Racial oppression may be real, morally repugnant, and pervasive, but when the new managerialism takes it on, it becomes little more than a dysfunctional organisational residue amenable to the kinds of administrative techniques developed to solve many other kinds of 'human resource' problems.
>
> (Pitts, 2001b: 137)

The process of transforming a major social evil into a legal-rational problem has produced limited gains in the past and, as Pitts observes, it does little to address underlying attitudes and structural influences. Thus, despite some attempts at progressive reform, there is continuing evidence of unequal treatment of young people from ethnic minorities (Feilzer and Hood, 2004; May *et al.*, 2010). One detailed study carried out on behalf of the Youth Justice Board found a series of points of concern, including:

- The higher rate of prosecution and conviction of mixed-parentage young males
- The higher proportion of prosecutions involving young black males
- The greater proportion of black and Asian males ... remanded in custody before sentence ...
- The slightly greater use of custody for Asian males
- The greater use of restrictive community penalties for Asian and mixed-parentage males ...
- The much greater proportion of mixed-parentage females who were prosecuted
- The substantial variations in outcomes between Yot [Youth Offending Team, or YOT] areas.

> (Feilzer and Hood, 2004: 27)

It appears that the experiences of young black people in the justice system continue to reflect discriminatory practices and oppressive outcomes. At different stages of the youth justice system, May *et al.* (2010: vi) found that 'there may be discrimination against ethnic minorities, in that differences ... could not be accounted for by features of the offence or criminal history', and that black and mixed-race defendants were particularly prone to experience disproportionately severe treatment. We should perhaps recall that at the start identified patterns of offending are reported to be broadly similar. Despite some apparent differences, overall there appears to be no difference in the propensity of black or white males aged 10 to 25 to commit offences, it is suggested (Barclay *et al.*, 2005: 8). Self-report evidence appears to show some variation, but, on the whole, black children are less likely to offend than white children, whilst those of mixed heritage are slightly more likely to say that they have offended (Armstrong *et al.*, 2005: 19). This kind of pattern has been consistent over time, as has the finding that young people of Asian origin are much less likely to say that they have been involved in criminal activities (Graham and Bowling, 1995; Armstrong *et al.*, 2005). As a consequence, it has been concluded that 'the answer to the question as to why black (young) people are over-represented in the ... system as "subjects" is likely to lie somewhere other than with their rates of "participation in offending"' (Goldson and Chigwada-Bailey, 1999: 54), a viewpoint with which others concur (Barclay *et al.*, 2005: lv; May *et al.*, 2010: iv).

The evidence of the over-representation of young black people at each stage in the process, from first contact in the street all the way to custodial sentencing, creates the impression that discriminatory practices are embedded at the core of the justice system, producing what has been described by Goldson and Chigwada-Bailey (1999) as a 'multiplier effect', operating from the first point of contact, and persisting over time. Whilst black and ethnic minorities were five times more likely to be stopped and searched than white people in 1993–94 (Muncie, 1999b: 233), this imbalance had risen to 7:1 by 2010 (Ministry of Justice, 2011d).

Again, black people appear to be more likely to be 'approached by the police' – 28% as compared to 24% of white people, and this was especially so for young black males (where the ratio was a third as compared to a quarter). At the same time, a much smaller proportion of those from ethnic minorities were likely to report that they had been treated 'well' by the police (Clancy *et al.*, 2001), and substantial proportions of all minority ethnic populations actually expect to experience discrimination within the justice system (Barclay *et al.*, 2005: 18).

At the next stage in the process, the proportion of black people arrested for 'notifiable offences' in 1999/2000 was four times higher than for the white population (Home Office, 2001d: 19), a figure that had declined slightly to 3.3 times higher by 2010 (Ministry of Justice, 2011d: 15). By contrast, a relatively smaller proportion of black people who were arrested were subsequently dealt with by way of cautions – 11% as compared to 16% of white people. More detailed analysis of the picture relating to young offenders suggests that this pattern persists, but with important variations. Thus, 'pre-court disposals' (Reprimands or Final Warnings) appear to be much more likely to be made in cases involving young Asian people (32%) than white (24%) or black (19%) young people, or especially those of 'mixed parentage' (9.5%), resulting in 'the odds of a case involving a mixed-parentage youth being prosecuted [being] 2.7 times that of a white youth with similar case characteristics – an indicator of unfavourable treatment' (Feilzer and Hood, 2004: 17).

Decisions by the Crown Prosecution Service and the courts have been reported to 'reflect decisions made at earlier stages of the criminal justice process including charging, cautioning and also the circumstances of the offences' (Barclay and Mhlanga, 2000: 1). In this way, initial distortions are merely confirmed by apparently neutral decisions made at later stages of the process. This highlights one of the most contentious areas of debate about racism in criminal justice. On the one hand, it is suggested that the system itself does no more than reflect inequalities in the wider society, producing unequal outcomes because of the greater likelihood of black people becoming criminalised for a variety of external reasons (Muncie, 2004: 271). Barclay and Mhlanga have argued that 'the ethnic group of the suspect was not found to be a predictor of post-arrest decisions' (Barclay and Mhlanga, 2000: 2). They suggest that arrests of young (under 22) black and Asian people are less likely to lead to a conviction than those involving young white people. The over-representation of young people from ethnic minorities at the entry point to the justice system appears to be mediated by principles of due process. Barclay and Mhlanga (2000: 1) conclude that it is 'not possible' to say whether differences in outcome 'reflect the result of discrimination in the criminal justice system'.

However, others suggest that 'the disproportionality that exists at the point of entry is largely preserved throughout the system', with some modifications (May *et al.*, 2010: 91). This qualification does illustrate the potential complexity of a system-wide analysis, but evidence of unevenness in the processes applied should not detract from the broader conclusion that the system itself reveals discriminatory tendencies. The Commission for Racial Equality initially found that decisions to prosecute are weighted against young black people (Goldson and Chigwada-Bailey, 1999: 65), which might account for the greater proportion of this group whose cases lead to discontinuances or acquittals (Feilzer and Hood, 2004: 17). Other findings appear to show that outcomes are weighted against certain ethnic groups. Higher proportions of black and mixed-parentage young people have been found to be remanded in secure conditions, higher proportions of these groups are sentenced to custody, and higher proportions of black young people receive longer custodial sentences (12 months or more), suggesting significant levels of unequal treatment at key decision points. Thus, it is observed that 'there were, at various points of the processes, differences that were consistent with discriminatory treatment' (Feilzer and Hood, 2004: 27).

The evidence from large-scale studies is consistent with more localised findings, too. The Manchester Youth Bail Project, for example, was able to demonstrate that black and Asian young people were progressively screened out of the programme (Moore and Smith, 2001). Of 136 referrals in the first year of the project, 29 (21%) were from ethnic minorities; of the 102 accepted for the bail support programme, 17 (17%) were from these groups; of the 52 then granted bail on condition that they attend, only 6 (12%) fell into this category. Whilst these six all went on to complete the programme successfully, this example illustrates quite well an institutionalised selection process that is constructed according to supposedly objective criteria, but which still produces discriminatory outcomes. May *et al.* (2010) report differential practices, with police in some areas adopting an 'adversarial' approach and effectively 'targeting' (ibid.: 90) some groups with particular characteristics.

Remands to custody have continued to be a particular focal point for discriminatory processes. Of the 650 referrals to the Howard League's *Troubleshooter Project* from December 1993 to June 1996, '45% were ... Black or Asian' (Ashton and Grindrod, 1999: 176). This is not an isolated finding; in 1999, '16.2% of children and young people remanded in HMP and YOI Doncaster; and 31.2% of those similarly remanded in HM YOI and RC Feltham were Black' (Goldson and Peters, 2000: 15). These findings are echoed in the survey carried out by Feilzer and Hood (2004: 78), which found that a significantly higher proportion of black young people were remanded in secure conditions.

At the point of sentencing, the position, according to research evidence, is less clear. Earlier studies are reported to have shown an independent 'race' effect on court disposals (Goldson and Chigwada-Bailey, 1999: 65), although more recent findings are more complex. In the most detailed study of its kind, 'no evidence was found that either black or mixed-parentage males were, once the characteristics of their cases had been taken into account, more likely to receive a custodial sentence than white males ... they were treated, if anything, more leniently' (Feilzer and Hood, 2004: 166). Nonetheless, there was a greater likelihood that black males would receive longer custodial sentences than white males from the Crown Court. May *et al.* (2010) have also reported that there is no evidence of discriminatory practice at the point of sentencing, although disproportionate use of custodial remands ensures that black young people are still over-represented in custody. Studies have nonetheless consistently shown that young black people in particular are disproportionately represented in the custodial population (Barclay *et al.*, 2005: 14); these figures might partly be accounted for by antecedent factors (such as the nature and circumstances of the offence), but they are also attributable to the 'amplification' effect of the justice system itself: 'The empirical evidence demonstrates the existence of both direct and indirect discrimination in the criminal justice process' (Bowling and Phillips, 2002: 241).

Against this backdrop of unequal treatment, we must also acknowledge the evidence of racism and mistreatment experienced by black young people once they are detained in custody (Wilson, 2006), graphically underlined by the inquiry into the death of Zahid Mubarek (Keith, 2006).

To many communities, this is just 'business as usual'. Research into the lived experiences of young black people in and around the justice system seems to confirm this (Palmer and Pitts, 2006). The system is seen as routinely hostile:

> They [police] just stop you all the time – sometimes two or three times a day. They just make up a reason, usually it's drugs, sometimes stealing.
>
> (Male, 16, quoted in Sharp, 2006: 8)

> If they were more positive with us, we might be more positive with them. If they're always on our backs, we'll keep on their backs.
>
> (Girl, quoted in May *et al.*, 2010: 64)

The result is a pervasive sense of unfairness and unequal treatment:

> British black and Asian people feel angry, unsafe and insecure. The 'double whammy' faced by these communities is that they are widely seen by the police and prison services as problematic, suspicious and, sometimes, simply criminal.
>
> (Bowling and Phillips, 2002: 255)

Against this bleak backdrop, the limited initiatives taken by the Youth Justice Board seem relatively insignificant. The development of specialist mentoring schemes, for example, may reflect a genuine attempt to address concerns about discriminatory treatment (see, for example, Leicester YOT, 2001). The YJB has also produced a 'tool kit' to assist YOTs in planning and monitoring their own efforts to avoid discriminatory practices (Youth Justice Board, 2004b). A subsequent study commissioned by the YJB (May *et al.*, 2010) also considered the question of whether or not 'specific BME [black and minority ethnic]-focused interventions were desirable or necessary' (ibid.: 104), concluding that this was a matter best decided 'at a local level'.

The need for a proactive and positive approach to challenge discrimination, whether its roots lie within or outside the justice system itself, seems clear. It should be within the scope of a body such as the Youth Justice Board to take action on this point. However, it is possible that any approach redolent of targeting of crime 'hotspots' and those 'at risk of offending' ('the fifty'; Morgan Harris Burrows, 2001) may intensify the experience of being under scrutiny, whilst the targeting of areas with relatively high minority populations for initiatives such as the Intensive Supervision and Surveillance Programme (ISSP) is also likely to have been experienced as discriminatory, given the existing propensity to subject certain groups (Asian and mixed-parentage males) to more intensive community penalties (Feilzer and Hood, 2004: 20).

'It's different for girls ...'

In order further to unpick the outward appearance of coherence and uniformity that sometimes characterises the youth justice system, it is also helpful to consider the position of girls and young women, given that this is a context dominated numerically and ideologically by masculinity (Walklate, 2004).

There has been much debate about the reasons for gender-based differential involvement in offending and criminal justice processes, without a substantial measure of agreement. To start with the question of offending behaviour, it seems that the involvement of females in crime is lower than that of males, according to both official statistics and self-report findings, in both its nature and intensity. Thus, just over a third of females report having committed an offence 'ever', as compared to rather more than half the male population (East and Campbell, 2000); equally, males are responsible for three times as many offences overall, and five times as many 'serious' offences (Graham and Bowling, 1995). In respect of young offenders, in 2004/05, males were responsible for 81.6% of offences leading to 'a disposal of some sort', compared to 18.4% committed by females (Youth Justice Board, 2005a). Although the peak age for offending is similar (MORI, 2004; Budd *et al.*, 2005: 10; Home Office, 2005a), the rate declines more quickly from this point for females (Home Office, 2001b: 101; Budd *et al.*, 2005: 11). Despite the imbalance in recorded and reported patterns of crime between males and females, it should not be overlooked that significant numbers of offences are committed by girls and young women (Youth Justice Board, 2005a: 4). In 2011/12, the proportion of offences by young people committed by females was 18% (Ministry of Justice, 2013: 28), and this figure was reported to have fluctuated between 16% and 22% over the preceding decade.

An analysis of the official pattern of offending suggests that girls and young women are more likely to be involved in certain property offences, such as theft and handling stolen goods, as a proportion of their overall offending, and less likely to commit burglary and robbery (Budd *et al.*, 2005: 14). On the other hand, it has also been found that violent offences make up 56% of the offences committed by 10–17-year-old females, as compared to 57% of offences committed by males, by their own accounts. The pattern of offending behaviour of young females appears little different to that of their male counterparts, according to this evidence, but simply of lesser intensity. On the other hand, when it comes to official processes, it appears that, whilst females are less likely than males to be proceeded against for serious offences, they are proportionately more likely to be charged with crimes of violence or theft/handling (Feilzer and Hood, 2004: 153).

Over a more extended period of time, the relative level of criminality of girls and young women appears to be on the increase. From 1981 to 1999, there was a decline in the number of 'known' young male offenders from 7,000 per 100,000 population, whilst, over the same period, the equivalent figure for females went up from 1,300 to 1,400: 'thus, although there remains a substantial decrease in the proportion of offenders among males (23%), there has been an 8% *rise* in the proportion of females found guilty or cautioned over' this period of time (East and Campbell, 2000: 22). In 1999–2004, there was a further decline in the proportion of known male offenders across the age range (10–17), whilst the rate for females stabilised or increased slightly (Home Office, 2005a). Since then, though, this relationship appears to have stabilised, with females accounting for around 20% of offences by young people over time (see above; Ministry of Justice, 2013: 28). Explanations for these variations have postulated changing patterns of behaviour amongst girls and young women, or changing attitudes (Muncie, 1999b; Worrall, 1999; Bowling and Phillips, 2002), but it is important to recognise the complexity of possible interactions between these factors and others, including the gendered nature of the construction of criminal justice (Walklate, 2004; Bateman, 2013). That is to say, we need to take account of the ways in which more general assumptions about masculinity and femininity remain embedded in both ideological assumptions and forms of practice in youth justice, as elsewhere.

It is undeniably, though, a matter of considerable interest to reflect on the way in which the youth justice system deals with identified female offenders. Again, the lessons of history suggest persistent disparities in the ways in which young males and females have been dealt with by the criminal process. For example, pre-court disposal rates have consistently differed. In 1990, 84% of 12–14-year-old boys were cautioned, as compared to 93% of girls of the same age. By 2000, the last year in which cautions were available until 2013, these figures had fallen to 68% and 86%, respectively. By 2004, with the introduction of Reprimands and Final Warnings, this position had stabilised, with 67% of boys reported for offences in this age range dealt with by these means, and 87% of girls (Home Office, 2005b; and see Bateman, 2013).

Whilst for both groups the proportions going to court have been shown to vary over time, the pattern revealed by the cautioning figures is repeated here, with females being relatively more likely to receive lesser sentences, and less likely to be sent to custody (see also Feilzer and Hood, 2004). Nonetheless, recent trends appear to indicate a relative increase in the proportion of girls amongst the custodial population. From 1994 to 2002, the number of girls in custody increased from 158 to 444 (a rise from 2.4% to 3.5% of all young people in custody; Home Office, 2005b). This trend was maintained subsequently, with an increase in 'annual receptions [to custody] of girls from 498 to 621 between 2002/03 and 2006/07' (Sharpe and Gelsthorpe, 2009: 199). Although sentencing patterns for males and females were similar, the use of custodial remands for girls appeared to account for the relative increase at this point (Arnull and Eagle, 2009: 58).

Worrall (1999) helps to provide a context for these notable variations with the ironic observation that the Conservative government's 1990 White Paper envisaged the abolition of custody for all females under 18, noting that 'the 150 or so girls in custody could be dealt with quite adequately by the "good, demanding and constructive community programmes for juvenile offenders who need intensive supervision"' (Worrall, 1999: 29). However, the increasingly punitive climate of the 1990s swept up young women as readily as their male counterparts. Indeed, she suggests, things may actually have got worse for females, because they have been seen as becoming increasingly criminal and more violent. Thus, in 1996, an intemperate newspaper editorial proclaimed this trend as fact, and Worrall argues that media responses of this kind should be seen as part of a pattern, amounting to a 'moral panic' targeted at the supposed consequences of women's liberation. In other words, the apparent increase in the criminal behaviour of young females is attributed to their rejection of traditional gender stereotypes. However, there has been little supporting evidence of a sustained increase in female offending rates, as noted above. In one sense, this may be a form of 'bifurcation' (Bottoms, 1977) in the justice system, whereby minor offences and those less likely to threaten well-established stereotypes (such as shoplifting) result in females committing this type of offence being treated relatively leniently, whilst more serious and counter-stereotypical offences might lead to more severe forms of punishment. On the other hand, it has been suggested that an increasing emphasis on 'risk' and its management has encompassed girls as it has boys, leading to a degree of 'risk-need confusion which results in girls being escalated up the sentencing tariff' (Sharpe and Gelsthorpe, 2009: 200). Bateman (2008) concurs, arguing that risk-based tools such as ASSET tend to 'over-predict' risk for girls.

Thus, because female offenders have historically been more likely to benefit from welfare-oriented interpretations of their behaviour, the increasingly 'actuarial' (Smith, 2006) orientation of criminal justice processes is likely to have a particularly dramatic impact. Coupled with increasingly dramatic media images of female delinquency (Gelsthorpe and Sharpe, 2006: 55), this has resulted in 'the abandonment of traditional welfare-oriented approaches to girls' delinquency and their replacement by an increasing desire to criminalise, punish and lock [them] up' (Gelsthorpe and Sharpe, 2006: 57).

That this is a relative rather than absolute shift of emphasis has been reflected in the treatment of girls overall, though; whatever the nature of their offending, 'females were treated more leniently than their male counterparts' (Feilzer and Hood, 2004: 168).

To what extent, then, have the developments of recent years affected the way girls and young women, in particular, are dealt with by the youth justice system? As already noted, the changes introduced in 1998 did little to stem an increasing use of harsher disposals (including custody) for young female offenders, and in this respect they appear to have been at least as vulnerable as male offenders in a punitive moral climate, and perhaps more so, for the reasons already outlined. In this context, the failings of the 'new youth justice' could partly be explained by the relative 'invisibility' of female young offenders (Walklate, 2004), with the result that their needs were simply overlooked. According to the Youth Justice Board, 'the … typical young offender [is] male, white, aged between 14–16, excluded from school and [has] committed five or more types of offence' (Youth Justice Board, 2002: 2). Targeted interventions, even those in the community such as the Youth Inclusion Programme, will by definition contain a very small proportion of females 'at risk', and, even from the point of intervention, the programmes offered are unlikely to be designed for them (Morgan Harris Burrows, 2001, 2003). Subsequent developments,

though, have been more encouraging, with gender-specific intervention programmes being developed in some areas, such as Birmingham (Sharpe and
Gelsthorpe, 2009: 201).

At the far end of the spectrum, where girls and young women are held
in custody the prisons inspectorate has been observed to express repeated
frustrations over the failure of policy to take account of their specific
circumstances. Although responsibility for the secure estate for those under
18 was transferred to the YJB in April 2000, the initial response was inadequate:

> I am … concerned about young females, including juveniles, for whom
> the YJB and the Prison Service have not yet made the same arrangements
> as they have for young males. I was appalled to find 17 year old girls on
> remand in HMP Holloway with sentenced adult women …
>
> (HM Chief Inspector of Prisons, 2001: 10)

The Youth Justice Board (2001) made a commitment to put things right in this
respect. However, concerns were only amplified subsequently. At Eastwood
Park Prison, the inspectorate considered:

> The treatment and conditions of the 12 under-18s held with 411 18–21 year
> olds in D wing. They exhibited, in acute form … chronic problems …
> This is an extremely vulnerable and disturbed group of young women: 'It
> was impossible not to be struck by the profound personality disturbance and
> mental health problems that many presented and by the inappropriateness
> of prison, or indeed any other custodial placement, for them'.
>
> (HM Chief Inspector of Prisons, 2002: 4)

In the early days of New Labour, then, girls and young women were clearly not
well served, and they were left to cope with the consequences of harsh sentences
in a hostile climate (see also Goldson, 2002, for an insight into the personal
impact of being locked up).

Futhermore, the Youth Justice Board did not meet its initial commitment to
ensure the removal of all females under the age of 17 from prison custody by
the end of 2003, continuing to rely on Secure Training Centres (Youth Justice
Board, 2005c), where mistreatment remained a problem (Carlile, 2006).

More recently, the unsuitable nature of custodial regimes for girls has been
further evidenced (All-Party Parliamentary Group on Women in the Penal
System, 2012). The type of regime provided is brought into question, given
the 'male-oriented' nature of some institutions (such as Secure Training Centres),
and this reflects a stark mismatch with the particular needs of girls who are
likely to have higher rates of mental ill health than their male counterparts,
and to have 'had deeply troubled lives' (ibid.: 5). At the same time, it is
reported that young females 'in custody are more likely to be restrained, more
likely to self-harm and more likely than boys to be placed in segregation'
(ibid.: 4).

Although there has been some recognition that youth justice provision for girls needs to be radically improved (Youth Justice Board, 2012), significant shortcomings remain clearly evident. Behind this seems to lie the challenge for a predominantly and persistently risk-oriented system of becoming more responsive to need without effectively criminalising young people (particularly females) on the basis of the very needs identified (Bateman, 2011c).

Ships in the night: victims of crime and youth justice

A third and increasingly widely acknowledged group of stakeholders in youth justice are those people who become victims of the crimes of the young (see Newburn *et al.*, 2002). They have clearly become significant in a context of heightened political interest:

> Victims of crime are a politically popular group, and an increasingly powerful one. Politicians have been quick to take account of these facts, and the balance between offenders and victims has altered correspondingly.
>
> (Williams, 2000: 176)

As noted previously, this climate has informed a considerable number of policy developments and it has clearly influenced delivery vehicles such as the National Standards for Youth Justice (Walker, 2012; Youth Justice Board, 2013). New Labour's approach to youth justice reform, for instance, incorporated an explicit aspiration to create 'a system ... which commands the confidence of victims' (Home Office, 1997b: 29), which became translated into a policy framework requiring that 'the needs of victims of crime are respected and prioritised' (Youth Justice Board, 2000: 2). In broad terms, these initiatives set the tone for a more systematic inclusion of principles of restorative justice into youth justice processes than had previously been the case.

Specific measures such as Reparation and Referral Orders were put in place to ensure that offenders were required to make amends to their victims in some way. In addition, a range of other disposals were also constructed in such a way as to facilitate similar activities, including the Final Warning, Action Plan Order and Supervision Order. The clear victim-orientation of the reformed youth justice system would be further buttressed by the requirement in the preparation of Pre-Sentence Reports for consideration to be given, in every case, to 'what is known about the impact of the offence on any victim, and assessment of the offender's awareness of the consequences to self, family and any victims' (Youth Justice Board, 2000: 16). Similarly, the ASSET form was designed specifically to draw attention to the victim's perspective.

In addition, National Standards (Youth Justice Board, 2013: 27) include an entire section on the appropriate involvement of victims. The infusion of every aspect of youth justice with an emphasis on the victim perspective has inevitably had a strong influence on the approach of Youth Offending Teams. Leicester YOT, for example, quickly engaged in a number of initiatives in this area, in conjunction with Final Warnings, including 'victim empathy sessions, letters of apology, supervising short periods of reparation [and] Restorative Justice Conferences ...' (Leicester YOT, 2001: 49). Subsequent targets included the incorporation of 'Restorative Justice Principles' in all Final Warnings, to be reflected in increased victim involvement and measured by enhanced levels of victim satisfaction with the outcomes of any intervention.

This is one early example that is representative of broader developments, with the Youth Justice Board undertaking a substantial additional investment in establishing a series of 46 'totally new restorative justice projects'. These projects worked with over 6,800 young people, 63% of whom were referred as part of a Final Warning or Referral Order programme (Wilcox, 2004: 5). Whilst it is important to avoid conflating 'restorative justice' solely with support for victims, there is no doubt that victim participation was a key aim of this initiative. Given that this 'reframing' of youth justice represents a significant departure from previous constructions of its principles and purposes, and given that it sits in a degree of tension with the 'principal aim' of reducing offending by young people, it is reasonable to consider what has been achieved through the drive to place victims at the centre of the process.

The evidence suggests that the level of victim involvement in youth justice practice has been variable, and this is partly because of the range of local arrangements put in place. Indeed, it is fair to say that diversity was encouraged in the initial stages, in order to promote innovation and improved practice (Wilcox, 2004: 15). Nonetheless, the most common form of intervention identified in the YJB's restorative projects was 'community reparation (35%)', and, although over half (53%) of victims participated 'to some extent', this usually amounted to no more than agreeing to 'their views being made known to the offender, ... to receive a letter of apology, or [making] some suggestion as to the kind of reparative activity the offender could undertake' (Wilcox, 2004: 7). Even though the YJB itself proclaimed this as evidence of a significant advance (in contrast to the rather more measured view of the evaluators; Wilcox, 2003: 31), this was not borne out to any great extent by the work of those evaluating the Referral Order, who found that:

> The involvement of victims and in particular their attendance at panel meetings across the pilot areas has been both lower than was originally anticipated and significantly lower than comparative experiences from restorative justice initiatives around the world.
>
> (Newburn *et al.*, 2002: 41)

In only 28% of cases where there was 'potential' for victim involvement were they found to have contributed to the process in any way at all, and victims attended Youth Offender Panel meetings in only 13% of possible cases (see Chapter 6). The researchers observed that 'in the absence of significant victim attendance there are obvious concerns that victims' issues are insufficiently represented' (Newburn *et al.*, 2002: 43).

The key issue here is that a system with the primary purpose to process young people who are found to have offended will almost inevitably struggle to find appropriate ways of involving other interests, especially those of victims, although some have taken a rather more positive view of developments in this area (Williams, 2005).

For those victims who do get involved, there may be positives to be gained from the experience. They are reported to have found YOP meetings generally helpful, and feelings of 'hurt' and fear can be addressed through these forums. On the other hand, subsequent follow-up was not always regarded as favourably, with a 'significant' number of victims disappointed not to receive any expression of apology or remorse by the young offender at any point in the process. Evaluators of the pilot schemes took the view that these problems were largely technical and administrative problems that could be resolved over time. They based this argument on the underlying goodwill and commitment to the Referral Order expressed throughout the youth justice system, from magistrates to youth justice staff, to community panel members and victims, and even to parents and young offenders themselves (Newburn *et al.*, 2002: 62; Crawford and Newburn, 2003: 178). Their conclusions were positive:

> The issue of victim involvement is, in essence, a problem of implementation rather than a problem of principle. Indeed, the majority of the general principles underlying referral orders appear both to be capable of being operationalised in practice and to receive high levels of approval from all the major participants. In a short period of time referral orders have gone from being an interesting set of proposals to a genuinely robust set of working practices that, notwithstanding some of the tensions identified ..., look set to have a considerable impact on the youth justice system in England and Wales.
>
> (Newburn *et al.*, 2002: 63)

This is perhaps a surprising conclusion. As Haines (2000) observed, despite the general enthusiasm for measures such as compensation, community service and other means of 'making amends', formal and highly structured mechanisms such as the YOPs had not been particularly successful in the past. Formal and structured arrangements, located 'in the shadow' of the coercive justice process, constrain offender and victim alike, whilst inevitably encroaching on the capacity for either participant to express genuine feelings of remorse, empathy or understanding (Smith, 2011a). The potential mismatch between the expectations of victims and the willingness or capacity of young people to make restitution will render the formal panel setting a particularly difficult site to resolve such tensions. For example, victims' demands for compensation may be impossible to meet in full for young people who simply cannot afford what is being sought, and indeed this is echoed in the findings of research on Youth Offender Panels (Newburn *et al.*, 2002: 46). Both the quality of practice and the low level of victim participation are a matter of continuing concern (Sherman and Strang, 2008; Victim Support, 2013), and this may partly be associated with the inflexibility of the 'criminal justice establishment' when it comes to implementing more victim-oriented policies (Crawford and Newburn, 2003: 214). Integrating victims into the process presents both practical challenges and real questions about 'what kinds of victims, under what circumstances, are more likely to benefit from active participation in restorative programmes and how best to facilitate this' (Crawford and Newburn, 2003: 241).

Other models have been tried in the past with a degree of success, and it may be worth reminding ourselves of their distinctive characteristics. Evaluations of the Northamptonshire Juvenile Liaison Bureaux in the 1980s found a valid place for reparative interventions, based on a flexible and negotiated response (Smith, 2011a). In these terms, there was no over-bearing pressure to apply 'restorative' solutions where they were unsuitable:

> the Bureaux ... have come to use reparation only in situations where all parties are able to benefit rather than where it merely responds to social pressures to treat (or punish) delinquent behaviour.
>
> (Blagg *et al.*, 1986: 135)

In relation to this, it is interesting to observe the additional constraint imposed by the timetable for interventions set by National Standards (see Youth Justice Board, 2013: 10), with which Youth Offending Teams may find it difficult to comply (Newburn *et al.*, 2002: vi). As Williams (2000) observed earlier, the emerging pressure to deal with young offenders increasingly quickly created further obstacles to the principle of prioritising victims' needs.

Williams sees this as part of a tendency for victims' interests to be subsumed under the wider demands of youth justice processes (see also Victim Support, 2013). He contrasts the approach in England and Wales to that of New Zealand, for example:

> A youth justice system based on conflict between the prosecution and the defence remains substantially unaffected by the additions of reparation as an extra sentencing option. In New Zealand, the formal criminal justice system is largely by-passed by restorative processes which replace court hearings. In England and Wales, however, these processes are 'bolted on' to an otherwise unchanged retributive sentencing system.
>
> (Williams, 2000: 189)

According to this analysis, reparation merely becomes part of the sentencing tariff, representing an imposed forfeit, as opposed to an agreed settlement, whereby the young offender really 'means' her/his apology or gesture of compensation. Victims' interests may be exploited 'cynically', according to this line of argument, simply 'to improve the presentation of punitive criminal justice policies' (Williams, 2000: 189). As Victim Support (2013) has subsequently noted, the incoming government in 2010 made 'positive' noises about restorative justice, but offered little by way of detail about how it would be implemented and how victims' interests would be recognised.

Haines and Drakeford (1998) have suggested that 'victim-oriented' restorative actions need to be distinguished from 'offender-oriented' restorative practices, and dealt with outside the constraints of the youth justice system itself, which should focus on reintegrative work with the young offender rather than 'work which is carried out for the benefit of the victim' (Haines and Drakeford, 1998: 234). In their view, an undue emphasis on the victim will distort the purpose of youth justice processes. At the very least, 'A primary requirement of any restorative approach or practice that aimed to be child-appropriate ... would be that it put the child first' (Haines and O'Mahony, 2006: 121).

As restorative practice became a more familiar feature of the landscape following implementation of the New Labour reforms, attitudes softened to some extent. Williams (2005) subsequently expressed rather more positive views about the influence of the reform programme, suggesting that a 'greater sensitivity' and 'awareness' (ibid.: 215) of victims' needs and interests was becoming evident. On the other hand, he noted that progress had been 'patchy' and there remained cause for concern that the new restorative measures may have resulted in 'net-widening' and 'up-tariffing' of young people who had offended.

Williams argued for a clearer distinction between the treatment of offenders and victims, although he did not reject the notion of reparation, arguing instead that it must be relocated at the 'front end' of the justice process (see also Sherman and Strang, 2008: 30). It should be based on a 'fundamental' change of attitudes towards victims, marginalising courts and other penal processes, and it should provide time and space for the development of consensual 'restorative solutions' to the problems created by young people's offending behaviour (Williams, 2000: 190).

In general, despite the greater recognition of victims' issues in youth justice, there remain serious concerns (Smith, 2011a). We should accept that it may not be reasonable to expect a process that is about dealing with those young people brought to justice also to be geared effectively to meet the interests of another overlapping constituency. In view of this, it must remain questionable to seek to engage victims routinely to contrive apparently successful outcomes, as the YJB initially set out to do (Sherman and Strang, 2008: 12). Whilst it is clear that for *some* victims, where the process works effectively, outcomes are broadly positive, this cannot be extrapolated to suggest that victims' interests in general are well served (Crawford and Newburn, 2003: 12). One study has concluded that 'Much reparation appeared to relate more clearly to the needs or desires of the young person rather than the nature of the offences or the involvement of the victim' (Crawford and Burden, 2005: 37). Others report young people complying 'just to get it over with' (Keightley-Smith and Francis, 2007: 7).

It is perhaps also worth reminding ourselves of the bigger picture: the vast majority of victims of crime are simply not touched by the justice system.

Considerably less than half of all crimes are reported to the police (Bateman, 2013), and just over half of this number are recorded by police as crimes (Mirrlees-Black *et al.*, 1998). Of this subset, in 1999–2000, only 14% resulted in a caution or conviction (Home Office, 2001b). It thus appears at best that a victim is matched with her/his offender in no more than 3.5% of all cases. As we have also observed, even when cases come before the Youth Offender Panel, there is often no real engagement between offender and victim, where they are 'matched'. Taking these observations into account, if we are to make any claims about the efficacy of youth justice in serving the interests of victims, we must therefore be very modest indeed:

> Restorative justice, which emphasises restitution and other forms of reparation from the offender to the victim, seems ... to have nothing much to offer the majority of crime victims. It shares this limitation with every other criminal justice intervention. Hence, it might be argued that, if our priority when a crime is committed is really to restore the victim, we should not waste our energy trying to reform the criminal justice system. What is needed is not so much an alternative form of criminal justice, but an alternative to criminal justice.
>
> (Johnstone, 2002: 78)

Changing perceptions and changing the experience of victims in the context of youth justice will therefore require far wider reforms than the introduction of the Referral Order (Crawford and Newburn, 2003: 212), or warm words of encouragement (Ministry of Justice, 2010).

Claiming success: a cautionary tale

Having identified some of the ways in which youth justice reforms have failed to meet the needs of some key interests, it may now be helpful to set these shortcomings against wider claims of progress and success (see Cohen, 1985). In being critical of the limits of reform, I do not want to belittle the continuing enthusiasm and achievements evident in the work of youth justice practitioners, who continue to strive to make the system work. For example, in more than one local authority area with which I am familiar, informal diversionary practices have been sustained outside the prescriptive framework set down in law and guidance.

On the other hand, we must be critical of the New Labour reform programme, not least because some of the claims made following its initial implementation in 2000 were substantially overstated and, at the same time, politically exploited (see, for example, Youth Justice Board, 2002), creating an unfortunate state of system malfuncture that sustained a highly punitive model of practice for a considerable period of time. Before addressing the question of what sort of 'youth justice' has emerged in the present, it will be worth reflecting on the question of what was achieved in an era of excessive target setting and inflated claims of success (Home Office, 1997b; Youth Justice Board, 2000).

The managerial flavour of the New Labour enterprise was classically illustrated by its 1997 election pledge to halve the time between arrest and final disposal for 'persistent' young offenders from 142 to 71 days. Amid much fanfare, this was reported to have been achieved by August 2001, with a figure of 65 days being reached by March 2002 (Youth Justice Board, 2002).

However, there are other questions to ask about the 'unintended consequences' of an initiative such as the reduction of delay. Early evaluations appeared to be quite relaxed about the consequences for the quality of justice delivered (Ernst & Young, 1999), but others appear to have been more critical (Holdaway *et al.*, 2001; Shapland *et al.*, 2001; Kemp *et al.*, 2002). Concerns were expressed, for example, by YOT members in response to the stricter deadlines for the submission of reports regarding the effect on standards of practice (Shapland *et al.*, 2001: 67). Others found a greater likelihood of prosecution because of the effect of limited timescales in constraining police discretion (Kemp *et al.*, 2002: 13). The pressure to complete cases might also, as already noted, mean that less attention was paid to the interests of victims, especially in complex cases (Holdaway *et al.*, 2001: 27). By becoming an 'unyielding end in its own right' (Dignan, 2000: 3), fast-tracking young offenders was therefore threatening to compromise a number of other key principles.

Aside from the impact of speeding up youth justice, wider claims of efficacy were made for other aspects of the reform programme (Hine and Celnick, 2001; Jennings, 2002; Youth Justice Board, 2002; Whiting and Cuppleditch, 2006). It has been claimed, for example, that Final Warnings had a significant impact on reducing the level of reconvictions (Hine and Celnick, 2001). Thus, 'on a like with like basis', the rate of further proceedings for those subject to Final Warnings was initially reported as being 6% better than might be expected (30% compared to a predicted rate of 36%; Hine and Celnick, 2001: 1). This finding was based on a comparison of reoffending rates in 1998 under the previous cautioning regime and those for young offenders issued with warnings in the pilot areas for the youth justice reforms.

In fact, rates of both further proceedings and reconvictions were found to be higher than previously for those subject to Final Warnings (Hine and Celnick, 2001: 16, 20), but this was attributed to the combined impact of the cessation of repeat cautioning and the changing characteristics of the Final Warning subgroup (a greater number of males, older age profile, more previous proceedings). Once these differences were taken into account, it was suggested that Final Warnings were more effective than previous pre-court disposals in reducing the rate at which young people were reported for further offences, especially for the 16+ age group. Further proceedings here were used as an indicator of 'programme effectiveness' (Hine and Celnick, 2001: 14). However, they were only a 'proxy' for reoffending, since the rate of further proceedings would be influenced by other factors, such as 'police, crown prosecution and court practice', as well as 'clear up and cautioning rates' (Hine and Celnick, 2001: 14). Over this initial period (1998–2001), for example, detection rates were falling, partly as a result of changes in police recording methods, and the proportion of cases discontinued by the Crown Prosecution Service was rising (Home Office, 2001b). Other potentially distorting aspects of the transition from one system to another were not explored by this study, such as the extent to which informal disposals previously used by the police might have been replaced by formal pre-court disposals (Reprimands or Final Warnings). There is some evidence to support the view that historically widespread informal responses (Evans and Ellis, 1997) were supplanted by formal procedures on the introduction of the new disposals (Kemp *et al.*, 2002), echoing much earlier observations about the effects of 'net-widening' (Thorpe *et al.*, 1980).

In addition, the evaluation found no effect on reoffending rates of intervention programmes:

> Firstly, evaluation of work with adult offenders shows that intervention with offenders with a low risk of reoffending can result in increased reconviction rates ... Secondly, reconviction studies (including this one) show that a large proportion of offenders receiving a first caution do not reoffend, suggesting that intervening too early could be a waste of resources.
>
> (Hine and Celnick, 2001: 35)

Despite this cautionary note, the Youth Justice Board took a rather different view, arguing both that the initial impact of Final Warnings was 'variable' (Warner, 2001: 1) and that 'research shows that an intervention programme at the Final Warning stage is one of the most effective ways of diverting an individual from criminality' (Youth Justice Board, 2002: 10). Unfortunately, this was just one early example of a recurrent pattern. The selective reading of the available evidence became a feature of the Youth Justice Board's pro-nouncements, both undermining its own credibility and confusing attempts to achieve a considered understanding of what was going on. This tendency led to strong complaints from some evaluators of youth justice innovations:

> It was ... of concern to find that the YJB had reported the results ... in its Annual Review in such a way as to imply that the restorative justice schemes had reduced crime ... Bearing in mind the clear caveat we had made ... such comments were not only highly selective, but could not be said to be based on reliable evidence.
>
> (Wilcox, 2003: 30)

A particularly striking example of this 'selectivity' concerns the repeated claims of dramatic falls in the levels of reoffending by young people. In the summer of 2002, the YJB claimed that 'even before full national roll-out the youth justice reforms in 2000 cut predicted reconviction rates by nearly 15%'

(Youth Justice Board press release, 9 July 2002). This claim was based on a study comparing 1997 reconviction rates with those of a cohort of young people proceeded against in July 2000. The stated reduction of 'nearly 15%' was arrived at by deducting the 'raw' reconviction rate for this cohort (26.4%) from the 'predicted' rate based on the outcomes for the 1997 sample (30.9%), and calculating the proportional difference between these figures; in other words, this was the most dramatic possible construction of these figures. By 2003, this purported reduction in reconviction rates was even higher, based on the same calculation, reaching 22.5% between 1997 and 2001 (Jennings, 2002). These remarkable figures subsequently became highlights of a number of key national policy documents (Home Office, 2003b; National Audit Office, 2004).

This is unfortunate, to the extent that it offered spurious justification for changes, the success of which is actually much more debatable. Further and more responsible consideration of these startling findings has led to rather more modest claims, in fact. Indeed, the study on which the claims were based acknowledged some methodological problems, such as the fact that the results were skewed by comparing two very different populations (pre- and post-reforms), which would make it difficult, for example, to adjust for the substantial 'increase in reprimands and final warnings which would be likely to result in lower reconviction rates' (Jennings, 2002: 9). In addition, a number of other commentators have drawn attention to further methodological shortcomings (Smith, 2003; Bateman and Pitts, 2005; Bottoms, 2005), and arbitrary assumptions, such as the exclusion of 'pseudo-reconvictions' (further proceedings related to offences committed before the first disposal taken into account – likely to have increased because of the practice of 'splitting' files; Shapland *et al.*, 2001). As Muncie sanguinely observes, 'changes in law enforcement and in what the law counts as crime preclude much meaningful discussion over whether youth crime is forever rising (or indeed falling)' (Muncie, 1999b: 17).

The picture is further confused by the evidence of what young people themselves say about their offending behaviour. According to self-report surveys, offending rates among young people have been fairly constant until recently (Anderson *et al.*, 2010: 14). Thus, 26% of young people aged 10 to 25 in mainstream education surveyed in 2004 said they had committed an offence in the previous year (Budd *et al.*, 2005: i), but only 3% had been arrested (not necessarily all offenders, of course), and just 10% of those who reported committing a 'serious offence' had been arrested, of whom half had been to court (Budd *et al.*, 2005: vi). By 2010, only 18% of this group reported offending in the previous year (Anderson *et al.*, 2010: 14). On the other hand, 64% of those in specialist Pupil Referral Units reported having offended over the same period. Of these, 82% had been caught by the police, compared to just 49% of 'mainstream' offenders. The evidence from large-scale surveys of young people tells a rather different story from conventional criminal statistics. Patterns of crime have not shifted as dramatically, according to their accounts, and the impact of sanctions is not a particularly significant factor in promoting desisting; it is rather the 'fear of being caught' or simply 'growing up/settling down' that are most likely to discourage further offending (Anderson *et al.*, 2010: 18). We can perhaps conclude that the sensationalist claims made in the early days of the post-2000 reforms about their impact on young people's offending behaviour were highly misleading, at best, and certainly missed the point. The youth justice system itself is a marginal influence set against the wider context of influences and structural factors that create the backdrop for young people's lives and the choices they make (see Chapter 7).

The Nero effect: ten wasted years

At this point, it is important to turn our attention once again to other changes in the way in which young offenders are processed by the justice system, and the wider trends that they signify.

The starting point for this discussion is the same reconviction study upon which the Youth Justice Board based its unsustainable claim of massive reductions in reoffending rates (Jennings, 2002). We are alerted to one key issue by the reported reduction in predicted reconviction rates, from 33.7% in 1997 to 30.9% in 2000 (ibid.: 5). This suggests, even allowing for changes in recording practices, that the cohort of young people dealt with as offenders immediately following the implementation of reforms was considerably less 'criminal' than its predecessors. Confirmation of this trend is also provided by the subsequent self-report survey that reported an increasing proportion of young people being caught and dealt with for offences (MORI, 2002: 21). The immediate impact of the new youth justice system seems therefore to have been an increasing criminalisation of young people. At the same time, as we have already observed, intervention programmes, at whatever level, were becoming more intrusive – as witnessed, for example, by the increase from 52% to 70% in the use of Final Warning programmes from 2000 to 2001/02 (Youth Justice Board, 2002: 11), despite the evidence questioning their value (Hine and Celnick, 2001).

At the same time, following a path mapped out by Foucault (Smith, 2001), the level and intensity of interventions at all stages of the process appeared to be increasing, with the implementation of demanding Referral Order contracts (Fionda, 2005), increasingly wide-ranging Action Plan Orders and, of course, the ISSP. Young people were accelerated up the 'tariff' by attracting the label 'persistent young offender' earlier in their offending careers, and in relation to less serious offences; evidence of failure to comply with programme requirements became subject to more rigorous breach procedures – with an associated increase in receptions to custody (Bateman, 2011a); thresholds for punitive sanctions were lowered (Goldson, 2006: 144). The consequence was, of course, a persistently high level of custody, at least until 2007/08.

In summary, the available evidence suggests a decline in the rates of offending from around 1995, on all official measures (Home Office, 2001b: 27). Whilst this is not unequivocally supported by young people's own accounts

(MORI, 2002; Budd *et al.*, 2005), Bateman (2006: 69) points out that this might still be the case over a longer timescale. While credit for reducing levels of offending was attributed to the youth justice reforms (Audit Commission, 2004), the evidence to support this is shaky – the start of the trend towards lower crime rates pre-dated the reform programme, and the published evidence in support of this claim is unconvincing (Hine and Celnick, 2001; Loxley *et al.*, 2002; Crawford and Newburn, 2003; Gray *et al.*, 2005).

What we are able to conclude is that younger, less serious offenders were being drawn into the formal justice system, which is even more noteworthy given the overall decline in the number of young people being processed as offenders – a fall of over 10% between 1998 and 2000, for example (Johnson *et al.*, 2001), a reduction that was then sustained (Home Office, 2005a). Despite this, the balance between those dealt with by relatively less severe means (out of court) and those sentenced by the courts tipped towards the more punitive end of the scale. Between 1994 and 2004, the ratio between the number of cautions and court disposals declined from 2.4: 1 to 1.3: 1 – a changing relationship that was not slowed by the transition from cautions to Reprimands and Final Warnings. Indeed, it was not intended to, given the apparent distaste of the government of the time for 'repeat cautioning' (Kemp *et al.*, 2002).

This progressive 'toughening up' of the youth justice system was also apparent at subsequent stages in the process. More lenient disposals, such as discharges and fines, were displaced from the start by 'community sentences' (Johnson *et al.*, 2001) and the Referral Order. An apparent decline in the number of custodial sentences for 15–17 year olds in 2000 was offset by an increase in sentence lengths (Johnson *et al.*, 2001: 11; Youth Justice Board, 2002: 15). As we have observed, the increase in the use of custody prior to 2000 was largely sustained for a number of years, with the April 2006 figure for those under 18 in secure facilities standing at 2,819, or 4% higher than on the comparable date in 2000. As Goldson (2006) has observed, there were increases at this time in the number of children sent to custody, in sentence lengths and in 'long-term detention'. At this point, he noted that 'greater use of penal custody for children is now made in England and Wales than in most other industrialised democratic countries' (Goldson, 2006: 145). Measures such as the ISSP signally failed to impact on these high levels, and their place as 'alternative[s] to custody' was thus put in doubt.

Despite the vast array of changes in youth justice from 1997, there was little evidence of any significant impact on young people, on the behaviour of the courts or on other key stakeholders including victims of crime over the following decade (Solomon and Garside, 2008). The available findings suggest an intensification of disposals targeted at increasingly minor and less experienced young offenders, whilst the injustices experienced by particular groups such as those from ethnic minorities (Bowling and Phillips, 2002) and the shoddy and oppressive treatment administered to those in custody continued unabated (HM Chief Inspector of Prisons, 2001, 2002; Bright, 2002; Goldson, 2002; Goldson and Coles, 2005; Carlile, 2006; Keith, 2006).

In some quarters, it might be thought that a greater level of activity and a greater intensity of intervention might simply be indicative of a more responsive and committed approach to youth justice – a sign that the crimes of the young are, indeed, being taken more seriously than in the past (Blair, 2002; Blunkett, 2002). On the other hand, serious questions must also be raised about the consequences of this intensification. There was clearly a diminution of the rights of children (Smith, 2010), with collateral evidence of harmful treatment in custody, and persistent inequalities in the way in which certain groups were treated, especially those from black and minority ethnic communities.

At the same time, the propagation of a much broader range of interventions based on those who present a 'risk', whether or not they are offenders (Smith, 2006), was both economically wasteful and inconsistent with other policy aspirations intended to promote social inclusion and a sense of community cohesion. Far from generating social solidarity, these measures cemented into place a sense of difference and 'otherness' (Garland, 2001). The price of an apparently more certain approach to dealing with unacceptable behaviour by young people became far too high, both financially and, more importantly, in human terms.

Changing direction ... again

As we have noted, these trends were reversed in subsequent years, from 2008 onwards, and reductions in the criminalisation of children at all levels have quickly gained pace. 'Success' has been redefined, with a commitment from government to targets such as a reduction in the number of 'first time entrants' to the justice system, and in the use of custody (HM Government, 2008; Ministry of Justice, 2012a); as we know, outcome measures demonstrate that these targets have been met to a great extent.

Practice has changed, too, with the increased use of out-of-court and informal disposals, and a diminished emphasis on the tariff, with the recognition of the Youth Rehabilitation Order as a disposal that can be reused when young people reoffend (Youth Justice Board, 2010a). Meanwhile, youth offending rates have continued to fall, irrespective of the significant system changes that have been in evidence. Before drawing unduly optimistic conclusions, however, we should move on to consider whether or not this new era of diversion and reduced (if not minimum) intervention is delivering uniformly 'successful' outcomes in the interests of all, and, beyond that, how progressive achievements can be built on and sustained in ways that were not achieved the last time this opportunity presented itself, towards the end of the 1980s.

9   The consumer view

What do we want from the youth justice system?

In the final stages of this book, my aim is to be forward-looking, drawing on what we have learned and understood about the youth justice system and in order to consider key questions about what we might want from it, and how it might be constituted to ensure that it operates in a way that does indeed do 'justice to young people' (Smith, 2011b).

There is no doubt that this is an aspect of the social world that is particularly susceptible to public perceptions and political manoeuvring (Jamieson, 2006), and this suggests that any chosen intervention strategy must take account of these influences:

> The dissatisfaction that people express with youth justice is real, whether or not it is grounded in the realities of current sentencing practice. There has to be *some* response to these public views.
>
> (Hough and Roberts, 2004: xi)

Whilst empirical knowledge and theory help us to understand the meaning and dynamics of young people's behaviour, the impact of social factors and the way these intersect with the machinery of youth justice, consideration of the practical steps to be taken must also address the expectations of 'stakeholders'. An exploration of some of these perspectives here will give us both a grasp of the range of viewpoints to be taken into account, and some idea of what may be seen as practical, realistic and achievable solutions to the perennial issue of what to do about young people 'in trouble'. Whilst we should not expect the youth justice system to be driven straightforwardly and uncritically by 'consumer' interests, a clearer understanding of the views and aspirations of key constituencies will shed more light on the question of 'what is to be done?'

The victim's perspective

Although we have noted previously that victims' interests have not been particularly well served by the youth justice system, they have nonetheless progressed steadily up the political and operational agenda in recent years. Indeed, concern for victims has become somewhat totemic, if at the same time rather tokenistic. Williams (2000) has already acknowledged that victims have become something of a 'political football', reflected in the publication of the *Victim's Charter* in 1996 and subsequent developments. As a result, the 'balance' between offenders and victims may indeed have shifted (Williams, 2000: 176; Williams, 2005: 215).

We have already seen evidence of the readiness of policy makers to respond to such pressures in the form of innovations such as the Referral Order, which mandates youth justice services to involve victims in formal interventions. The expectation is that victims' views and wishes will be routinely incorporated into youth justice decision making, set out in an early version of the National Standards (Youth Justice Board, 2004a: 32), and subsequently reiterated in the 2012 version, which requires Youth Offending Teams (YOTs) to 'have processes in place to ensure that victims of crime are involved, as appropriate, in a range of restorative processes that seek to put right the harm they have experienced' (Youth Justice Board, 2013: 27).

However, what does this increasing sensitivity to the needs of victims tell us about the best ways of responding to young people who offend, especially given the discouraging evidence from earlier evaluations of initiatives intended to achieve this kind of aim (see Chapter 8)? Of course, it is important to avoid falling into the trap of stereotyping victims or their views, just as we must not stereotype young offenders (Dignan, 2005: 87). The British Crime Survey now regularly reminds us that the risk of becoming a victim of crime is not evenly distributed (Kershaw *et al.*, 2001; Salisbury and Upson, 2004; Upson, 2005). Indeed, it has been observed that it is young people themselves, and especially young men, who are most at risk of becoming victims of violence (Kershaw *et al.*, 2001: 31) – a finding that is all the more significant when we consider the established link between 'violent victimisation' and offending amongst young people (Owen and Sweeting, 2007). Figures from the 2003 Crime and Justice Survey suggest that 21% of 10–15 year olds had been assaulted during a 12-month period (Wood, 2005: 3), higher than any other age category. Significantly, the interest in young people as victims of crime is comparatively recent, with official statistics on victimisation of under-16 year olds being unavailable prior to 2003.

The evidence is complicated by findings that the experiences of being a victim and a perpetrator of crime appear to overlap to a substantial degree. MORI (2002) has found that groups that are more likely to offend ('children who are excluded from school') are at the same time more likely to be victims of crime. In fact, they were more likely to be victims (82%) than offenders (64%). Wood (2005: 5) observes that the strongest predictor of 'personal crime victimisation' amongst 10–15 year olds was '[c]ommitting an offence in the previous year', with the odds being 2.5 times those for non-offenders. Smith (2004) has also explored this relationship, arguing that there is a demonstrable interaction between delinquency and victimisation, even over a three-year period, with one predicting the other. In addition, 'The more often victimization is repeated, the more strongly it predicts delinquency' (Smith, 2004: 3). Smith argues that this correlation is so strong as to suggest a possible causal link, in both directions. Thus, any simplistic assumption that opposes 'offenders' and 'victims' and their different interests is clearly neither accurate nor helpful.

The tendency to reify the idea of 'victimhood' must be avoided, although this is not to minimise the damaging and distressing consequences of being victimised. As Lea and Young (1984) demonstrated some time ago, the impact of crime on people and areas already disadvantaged in other ways is likely to have a powerful and demoralising effect. People are more worried about crime where its incidence is most often identified (Upson, 2005: 101). As Rock has pointed out, the concern for victims has represented a substantial shift in criminological thinking over a relatively short space of time: 'until the late 1970s victims were almost wholly neglected in criminology and criminal justice' (Rock, 2002: 1). While, as he notes, there is an association between this growing awareness and a strong populist tide of rhetoric, there have also emerged more thoughtful analyses:

> We know that our earlier assumptions about the impact, quantity and spread of crime have had to be replaced not only by an appreciation of its deep, persistent pervasive and often unexpected effects, but also by an awareness of its capacity to confound typifications of who the victim and offender might actually be.
>
> (Rock, 2002: 11)

As a consequence, he says, there needs to be a more sensitive appreciation of 'the victim' and what it means to her/him to be offended against and how s/he comes to terms with the experience. It is not simply a matter of following a predetermined script, despite the best efforts of some: 'What else do crime series and shows such as *Kilroy* and *Oprah* achieve if not to offer public representations of wounded sentiment' (Rock, 2002: 18)?

One implication of these reflections is that victims' perceptions of offenders' level of responsibility are likely to vary, as are their views about the best way of dealing with the offence. Their responses are not limited by conventional measures of the nature and seriousness of the crimes committed either. A further level of complication is introduced when we consider the position of 'corporate victims' who may well have a distinctive agenda, whilst they will also be seen in a rather different way by offenders (Young, 2002). (Of course, many of us are also victims, often unknowingly, of corporate crime (Dignan, 2005: 21)).

These reflections, added to the evidence that very few offenders are ever 'matched' with their victims (see Chapter 8), must lead us to express some caution about the global impact of the restorative measures that have now been integrated into the youth justice repertoire. It will, nonetheless, be helpful briefly to revisit some of the evidence on the victim perspective emerging from recent initiatives to develop a more central role for victims in youth justice processes (see Holdaway *et al.*, 2001; Hoyle, 2002; Newburn *et al.*, 2002; Young, 2002; Crawford and Newburn, 2003; Dignan, 2005).

The introduction of the Referral Order, for example, has provided a good opportunity to consider at close hand just what happens when the justice system seeks to involve victims more fully. However, it should be noted that problems arise from the outset, given that securing victims' participation at all is often problematic (Holdaway *et al.*, 2001; Crawford and Newburn, 2003). Those who reach the point of attendance at Youth Offender Panels are a relatively small fraction of an already highly selective group. Nevertheless, for those who do attend, evidence has been obtained of their underlying motivation. It is interesting, for example, that it was found to be more important to them to express their feelings or to have a direct say in how the offence was dealt with than on ensuring that they would be compensated or that a suitable punishment would be imposed (see Table 9.1).

Thus, although this is a partial view, it seems that those victims who take up the opportunity to attend panel meetings are very much concerned with engaging with the offender, and solving the problems that the offence has caused. Hoyle's study of the Thames Valley Restorative Justice project also appears to support this observation; for example: 'I just wanted to get the message across to him that if it happened to him how would he feel, basically, I mean, for him to put himself in my shoes' (victim, quoted in Hoyle, 2002: 120). Even 'helping the offender' appears to have come higher up victims' list of priorities than seeking redress (Newburn *et al.*, 2002: 45).

Exploring victims' views in more detail, researchers have found that their generally positive views of the process were sometimes tempered by the limited nature of their involvement, and their inability to secure the outcomes they required, in the form of compensation or apologies. Dignan (2005: 154), suggests that victims may be beneficially involved in restorative processes, but still be left dissatisfied with the outcomes. Victims appeared to want a greater sense of involvement in the entire process, rather than merely attending the formal panel meeting alone. In particular, they wanted to know what happened afterwards, and 'if the young person had managed to stay out of trouble. One of the most important factors for many of the victims was "has it worked?"' (Newburn *et al.*, 2002: 47).

Table 9.1 Victims' motivating factors for attending panel meetings

Motivating factor	Strength of factor			
	Not at all	*Not very*	*Somewhat*	*Very*
Expressing feelings	4%	9%	7%	78%
Offence resolution	22%	4%	28%	43%
Helping the offender	28%	13%	26%	28%
Seeking compensation	33%	13%	15%	35%
Ensuring appropriate penalty	52%	11%	20%	15%

Source: (Adapted from Newburn *et al.*, 2002: 45)

Nonetheless, the evidence seems to suggest that, for those victims who were involved in Youth Offender Panels, the process was generally viewed in very positive terms, although this was, of course, a self-selecting sample whose very involvement may have indicated a predisposition towards negotiated solutions. Thus, there may be some indication that victims of youth crime may aspire towards an approach based on offence resolution, rather than simply on retribution.

The partial nature of victim involvement is borne out by other evidence, both more generally (Dignan, 2005) and specific to the field of youth justice. Thus, Holdaway *et al.* (2001) reported 'low consent rates' for victims approached to participate in Reparation and Action Plan Orders, with only half of those asked agreeing to either direct or indirect means of making amends by the offender. Victims were much more likely to participate if they were not asked to 'opt in' to the process – that is, where they were specifically encouraged to participate, rather than being left to make up their own minds. The conclusion drawn is that there is limited enthusiasm amongst victims for more direct engagement with young offenders and, indeed, a feeling that in some cases their interests might be subsumed under those of the justice system, or even young offenders themselves (Holdaway *et al.*, 2001: 81). In some cases, too, this perception has been borne out by experience:

> The impression I got from [the facilitator] was that … he was wanting to get them off as lightly as possible … He was looking after them. It was outrageous … It was a very one-sided thing and we just had to go along with it …
>
> (Mother of victim, quoted in Burnett and Appleton, 2004: 48)

These observations are supported by other findings (Davis *et al.*, 1988; Hoyle, 2002; Dignan, 2005). For some, this is unsurprising, given that victims will necessarily have their own priorities. We should be more ready to doubt the 'often unquestioned assumption that victims want to assume a role in the state response to "their" offender … most restorative justice schemes find that by no means all victims wish to be fully involved' (Hoyle, 2002: 104). This certainly coincides with the present author's experience based originally in a juvenile diversion project during the 1980s, where the lack of pressure to involve victims meant that they could be approached on their own terms.

Victims' unwillingness to get involved clearly has a number of origins, including the fear of retaliation ('secondary victimisation'; Dignan, 2005: 85) and the belief that it is and should be the job of the police and the justice system to deal with the offence – in the same way, perhaps, as we might ask a plumber simply to come and mend a leak, rather than be 'engaged' in the process. For others, it may be that they do not have a particularly favourable view of the justice process itself: 'I have to say if I was a victim of a similar crime again … I've got a feeling I would administer my own justice and not involve the police' (quoted in Hoyle, 2002: 125).

This again, acts as a salutary reminder that we should not draw over-optimistic conclusions from positive accounts of victim involvement in restorative programmes. Hoyle concludes that to focus solely on improving restorative processes risks overlooking the more important challenge of 'empowering victims generally' (Hoyle, 2002: 130). The interests of victims can be seen to range well beyond the question of appropriate engagement in youth justice interventions to wider considerations of safety, security and community participation. Restorative justice initiatives may offer positive benefits to *some* victims, but they may be ill-suited to dealing with the much larger questions of the complex relationship between offending and victimhood – for example, where their experiences overlap or coincide, as in the experience of many young people (Owen and Sweeting, 2007). Indeed, arbitrary separations between the interests of 'victims' and 'offenders' are conceptual over-simplifications and are ultimately unhelpful in obstructing the pursuit of 'inclusive' forms of criminal and social justice (Dignan, 2005: 187).

The community: conflicting needs or common agendas?

As Dignan (2005) also points out, the interests of 'the community' may stand in a complex relationship to both victims and offenders, which may lead us in the direction of rather different models of restorative justice to that currently prevalent in England and Wales.

Following a line of argument that suggests that it is extremely difficult and, in fact, unhelpful to seek to create arbitrary distinctions between overlapping interests, it will be helpful now to move on to consider the broader concerns of neighbourhoods and communities in relation to anti-social behaviour, youth crime and youth justice. The backdrop for any such innovations, however, is not propitious. Concerns about the behaviour of young people are connected with wider and extensive fears about deteriorating standards of living, neighbourhood decay, abandonment and moral decline. There is said to be a close link between 'disorder', fear of crime and a progressive cycle of neighbourhood decline and increasing criminalisation (Hancock, 1999). There appears to be a direct and cumulative relationship between perceptions and experience, so that the sense of a community 'going downhill' is reinforced by observable events and changes in the landscape:

> There are lots of young people hanging around at weekends ... There is a *lot* of litter. People throw their litter down as they walk past. We have also had problems with broken windows. Buildings have deteriorated ... pride in the area has gone down.
>
> (Elderly resident of Edgebank, quoted in Hancock, 2001: 92)

Indeed, the elision of young people with the problem of disorder and decline appears to be commonplace, and it is often assumed that it is their anti-social behaviour that causes 'distress in neighbourhoods' irrespective of other contributing factors (Hancock, 2006: 176). This message was once again at the fore in responses of leading figures, including the prime minister, to the 2011 'riots' in parts of England; stating that something was 'seriously wrong' with society 'when you see children as young as 12 or 13 looting and laughing' (*Daily Mail*, 11 August 2011), he nonetheless chose to portray the problem as one of bad behaviour, originating in a poor upbringing, stating that 'if we want to have any hope of mending our broken society, family and parenting is where we've got to start' (Speech, 15 August 2011).

The British Crime Survey (Budd and Sims, 2001) had previously revealed a substantial degree of concern about anti-social behaviour, which appears to be linked in people's minds with 'teenagers hanging around on the streets', although we are reminded again that this is nothing new when we reflect on Corrigan's (1979) study of young people 'doing nothing' on the streets of Sunderland in the mid-1970s.

By 2000, over half those surveyed thought that young people 'hanging around' was 'very or fairly common', and 32% identified this as a problem in itself. At the same time, 31% of respondents thought that this was having a 'negative impact' on the quality of life in their neighbourhoods (Budd and Sims, 2001: 2); this was the single biggest factor mentioned in this respect. Furthermore, a fifth of those interviewed cited specific examples of 'young people being rude or abusive' to them in the previous 12 months (Budd and Sims, 2001: 4), once again, the most common example of problem behaviour cited. It should perhaps also be noted that it was people living in poorer areas, and those from black and minority ethnic groups who were more likely to report being victimised in this way. Young people thus appear to be widely associated with anti-social behaviour and they are blamed for a general sense of disturbance and unease experienced in communities. Detailed analysis of popular concerns about anti-social behaviour identifies 'teenagers hanging around' as a significant cause for concern, with 28% of the population regarding this as a 'very or fairly big problem' in their own area (Wood, 2004: 11). Although, as Hancock (2006) points out, forms of anti-social behaviour such as speeding and inconsiderate parking caused concern to the largest numbers of people, other behaviours specifically associated with young people also figured highly in the list of irritations (litter, letting off fireworks, graffiti and 'being drunk or rowdy', for example). Such findings appear to remain constant over time, with a subsequent survey of public attitudes to youth crime noting that:

> Participants talked, often at length, about the disruptive and threatening presence of groups of young people in their neighbourhoods. On occasion reference was made to 'gangs' but more often concerns were about informal groups 'hanging about' the streets or parks.
>
> (Jacobson and Kirby, 2012: 7)

Additional analysis deriving from the British Crime Survey (Mattinson and Mirrlees-Black, 2000) has shed further light on this issue. The public has been reported to overestimate substantially 'juvenile involvement in crime', with 28% of respondents believing that young people were responsible for most crime, whereas in fact 85% of detected crim is committed by adults aged 21 or over (Bateman, 2013: 10). This mismatch may, of course, partly be accounted for by different understandings of the term 'young', and by variable perceptions of what counts as 'crime', especially those offences that are not officially recorded as such. For example, one survey has suggested that as many as 40% of respondents thought that 'teenagers hanging around' and damage to property were problems in their own area:

> Respondents are likely to extrapolate from their own local experience when forming a view about the national crime picture. Certainly, those respondents who said teenagers hanging around was a big problem in their area were significantly more likely to say crime was mainly committed by juvenile offenders.
>
> (Mattinson and Mirrlees-Black, 2000: 12)

Of course, it is not inevitable that these views will feed straightforwardly into attitudes and beliefs about how to deal with the crimes of the young and with what degree of severity. However, studies have consistently shown that most people feel that the courts are 'too soft' with offenders in general (Hough and Roberts, 2004), but that they also underestimate the severity of sanctions actually administered (Hough and Mayhew, 1985; Hough and Roberts, 1998). Thus, demands for more stringent penalties, particularly greater use of custody for specific offences (Hough and Roberts, 1998), are largely based on a misconception about current sentencing practice. Those who have been victims of offences have been reported as being slightly more likely to demand harsher sentences (Hough and Roberts, 1998).

As well as having a distorted view of sentencing practice, surveys have also demonstrated repeatedly that the public holds erroneous views about trends in youth crime (Hough and Roberts, 1998; Mattinson and Mirrlees-Black, 2000), which is likely to be associated with a belief in the need for tougher sentences. Whilst perceptions of the pattern of youth crime are unbalanced, 'media portrayals of persistent juvenile offenders and the continuing influence of the James Bulger murder on the public psyche ... are the most likely cause' (Mattinson and Mirrlees-Black, 2000: 14). Of course, the 'hegemonic' role of politicians in both echoing and reinforcing public opinion is also significant (see Chapter 7), although these authors do not comment on this possibility. Further evidence of the mismatch between public perceptions and practice has been provided, and, once again, the media seem to be largely to blame:

> Three quarters of the population thought that youth crime was rising, when there was little evidence for this. They cited the media as the main source of information that led them to this belief.
>
> (Hough and Roberts, 2004: 17)

The role of the media in shaping opinions and attitudes about youth crime is supported by other research, too (Allen, 2004). The scepticism about crime levels amongst the general population may also be linked with their perception that other aspects of the youth justice system are also performing poorly. One report based on the British Crime Survey has suggested that only 14% of respondents thought that the 'juvenile courts' were doing a good job (Mattinson and Mirrlees-Black, 2000: 17), and those who had recently been victims of crime held even more negative views in this respect. This view seems also to be associated with a belief that courts are 'too lenient' – held by 76% surveyed in this study (Mattinson and Mirrlees-Black, 2000: 18) and remaining at about this level over time, according to others (Hough and Roberts, 2004: 26). Interestingly, it also seems that this belief applies much more strongly to the sentencing of young people who offend than to adults. As has been observed, there appears to be a correlation between ignorance of the justice system and a belief that courts perform poorly and are too 'soft'. There also appears to be a correlation between concerns about 'teenagers hanging around' and poor opinions of the court process:

> It may be that physical and social disorder is taken as evidence of a crime problem that is not being adequately contained. Or, perhaps, [this] reflects a belief that the police and courts remit does – or ought to – encompass dealing with such issues.
>
> (Mattinson and Mirrlees-Black, 2000: 23)

Subsequent investigation of attitudes to anti-social behaviour has confirmed the link between perceived levels of this type of behaviour and fears of crime, particularly violent crime (Wood, 2004: 38).

With the extension of the scope of curfew orders, and the introduction of ASBOs and dispersal orders, it could perhaps be argued that the remit of the justice system was indeed widened in just this way, in order to deal with 'nuisance' as well as criminal behaviour. Whether or not this will have a sustained impact on public confidence remains to be seen, although early findings were not particularly encouraging in this regard (Smithson, 2004). What is evident to researchers is that the link between poor knowledge and negative perceptions suggests the likely value of providing better and more accurate information to the public about the incidence and impact of youth crime as well as how it is dealt with (Allen, 2004; Hough and Roberts, 2004; Mackenzie *et al.*, 2010).

The British Crime Survey has also explored respondents' views about the best way to enhance courts' powers to deal with young people who offend, and it has found that there is considerable support for the idea of making parents take more responsibility for their children's actions (15%) and greater use of custody (12%); these were the two most popular options amongst those questioned. There was support also for other options such as corporal punishment, tagging or curfews, community work and restitution. Thus, it could be argued that the programme of sentencing reforms introduced from 2000 onwards did, indeed, reflect widely held and punitive public views, although the pressure in this direction appeared to be offset to some extent by a desire for greater use of restorative and welfare interventions (Mattinson and Mirrlees-Black, 2000: 24).

As noted by these researchers, this reflects a fairly consistent pattern, with previous evidence suggesting that 'increased discipline in the home' (36%) and 'tougher sentences' (20%) were consistently popular strategies for preventing and responding to delinquency (Hough and Roberts, 1998: 33). When this question was posed in a different way in 2003, harsher punishment remained the second most popular option (17%), but this time it was 'more discipline in schools' (42%) that proved the most effective option in the public mind (Hough and Roberts, 2004: 20).

Taken together, though these findings suggest that 'criminal justice' measures are favoured as solutions to the problem of crime by a relatively small proportion of the population:

> Thus although [it has been] established that lenient sentencing is a concern to the British public, four out of five people see the most effective solution to crime as lying outside the criminal justice sphere system, namely in the home, the schools and the workplace. These trends are worth noting, as they contradict the view of the public as being exclusively oriented towards punishment.
>
> (Hough and Roberts, 1998: 34)

A subsequent MORI survey demonstrated substantial support for community-based crime prevention initiatives with young people, as well as recognition of the negative impact of custody, and a desire to reduce the general level of imprisonment (MORI, 2001). Further work in this area (Hough and Roberts, 2004) has indicated that, when offences are made 'real' for people through the use of 'vignettes', they are willing to consider a variety of sentencing options, even in cases where custody might initially be indicated:

> Even in the case of a robbery committed with violence by an offender with previous convictions – where Court of Appeal guidance indicates a significant custodial sentence – half of respondents would accept a community penalty involving supervision and reparation.
>
> (Hough and Roberts, 2004: 43)

There is also a degree of continuity over time, with both earlier and later studies demonstrating a similar level of willingness amongst the public to consider more moderate sentencing options for some offenders, in specific circumstances (Jacobson and Kirby, 2012: 27). Readiness to consider non-custodial options for non-violent offenders, for example, was identified as early as 1984 (Hough and Mayhew, 1985: 45), and, over an extended period of time, similar sentiments could be observed. Indeed, it seems that the more people know about the offender, her/his circumstances and the range of disposals available, the more likely they are to support a non-custodial option (Hough and Roberts, 2004; Jacobson and Kirby, 2012).

These consistent findings have led researchers to suggest a number of policy implications, seeking to represent the collective view. They conclude that better public understanding is important; better awareness of the range of non-custodial sentencing options would be helpful; 'persistence' is a significant 'aggravating factor'; concerns about 'disorder' need to be addressed in their own right; and moves towards a more restorative approach might, by engaging both victims and the community, lead to improvements in public confidence (Mattinson and Mirrlees-Black, 2000: 45), as long as such measures are 'effectively implemented' (Jacobson and Kirby, 2012: 28).

There appears to be a notable shift of emphasis when questions about the problems and behaviour of young people are reframed (Allen, 2004). Against a generalised picture of fear and alarm and a desire for harsher punishment in the abstract, there appears to be a rather more ambivalent spirit at large when we consider young people as rounded and real individuals, and as members of their communities. In this context, concerns may be framed in terms of lack of facilities and restricted opportunities (Hancock, 1999), rather than their delinquent characteristics or their behaviour. Crime prevention initiatives that take an 'inclusive' approach might therefore be expected to find an echo within communities who simply want problem behaviour to stop (Hancock, 2006: 176; Haines and Case, 2007: 350). The relationship between young people and their community is important; young people themselves can be engaged and may be seen as active contributors to crime reduction initiatives (Crime Concern, 2001: 5, for example).

The shift of focus away from the stereotypical and demonised individual troublemaker to young people as a group and as members of the community is an important aspect of the process of changing the public mindset (Hancock, 1999). The Audit Commission (2002), for example, has argued that most people are concerned about crime, especially those who have recently been victimised; at the same time, a MORI survey conducted for the same report indicated very high levels of support for action to improve facilities for young people as a means to promote community safety and to reduce crime. Thus, there appears to be a clear contrast between a generalised caricature of the offender who is 'not one of us' and deserves to be treated with severity (Hancock, 2006: 177) and a more inclusive notion of young people as part of the community with their own concerns (including being victims of crime) and needs, which should be addressed (Case *et al.*, 2011).

Lea and Young (1984) have previously suggested that there is a dualistic view of crime and offending and that neighbourhood dynamics are complex, leading to the continual attribution of criminality 'elsewhere', even in areas with an established reputation for high levels of crime. This rather contradictory position finds echoes also in the work of Garland, who elaborates two distinct 'criminologies', which reflect these ambiguities:

There is a *criminology of the self* that characterizes offenders as normal, rational consumers, just like us; and there is a *criminology of the other*, of the threatening outcast, the fearsome stranger, the excluded and the embittered. One is invoked to routinise crime, to allay disproportionate fears, and to promote preventative action. The other functions to demonize the criminal, to act out popular fears and resentments, and to promote support for state punishment.

(Garland, 2001: 137)

Garland notes that it is the latter that predominates in public and political discourse, with the result that there is a prevailing view of offenders as representing this kind of stereotype: 'young minority males, caught up in the underclass world of crime, drugs, broken families and welfare dependency' (Garland, 2001: 136). Against this, however, should be noted the complexity and variety of perceptions and direct experiences, which influence assumptions and attitudes when young people and their behaviour are contextualised (Case *et al.*, 2011).

Youth crime and black and minority ethnic groups

It will also be helpful to consider questions of complexity and diversity further by addressing the position of those from black and minority ethnic (BME) communities, who have a particular interest in the interlinked issues of youth and crime for two fundamental reasons. They are, on the one hand, more likely to be victims of crime than the population in general and, on the other, some of them at least (notably young black men) are disproportionately likely to be processed as offenders, as we have seen (see Chapter 7).

First, in addressing the issue of 'victimisation', the British Crime Survey has repeatedly shown that certain groups are exposed to 'unequal risks' of being offended against (see, for example, Mirrlees-Black *et al.*, 1998; Kershaw *et al.*, 2001; Barclay *et al.*, 2005). Certain types of crime, such as burglary, vehicle-related theft and violent offences, are found to occur to a greater extent in 'multi-ethnic areas' (Mirrlees-Black *et al.*, 1998), and those people living in inner-city areas are likely to be at greater risk of repeat victimisation, which may also account for the higher levels of 'worry' about crime observed amongst ethnic minority groups (Barclay *et al.*, 2005: 4). Subsequent findings have confirmed these general trends, with 'the risk of being a victim of personal crime' remaining higher for 'members of all BME groups than for the White group'. Significantly, too, it has been found that BME children are 'more worried about their safety' than their white peers in certain circumstances (Ministry of Justice, 2012f: 23).

In a very specific sense, minority ethnic groups are likely to be disproportionately affected by racist crimes (Salisbury and Upson, 2004: 3). As Bowling and Phillips (2002) demonstrate, such crimes, from harassment to murder, have been evident throughout the history of black and minority ethnic communities in Britain, whilst recognition of this, from either criminological or other sources, has been slow to follow. Thus, records of 'racial incidents' have only been maintained since the 1980s, and it is only from the 1990s onwards that 'concern about racist violence' has been heightened (Bowling and Phillips, 2002: 109), initially in response to the murder of Stephen Lawrence, and more recently that of Zahid Mubarek (Keith, 2006). The report of the inquiry into the first of these deaths concluded that too little attention was paid by official bodies to 'racist incidents' (Macpherson, 1999). In response to this prompt, the number of such incidents recorded increased from 13,878 in the year ending March 1998 to 47,814 in the 12-month period to March 2000 (245%). Despite a decline in the intervening years, this figure had nonetheless risen to 51,187 by 2010/11 (Ministry of Justice, 2012f: 11).

Such statistics are, of course, an imprecise indicator of what is happening 'on the ground', but they suggest that one or more of three possible factors are in play. It may be that police and other elements of the justice system are taking such incidents more seriously; they may show that the number of racist crimes has increased significantly; or they may suggest a greater degree of awareness and confidence in the justice system amongst people from ethnic minorities, and thus a greater willingness to report incidents. Whatever the reason, though, the figures suggest that there is a very substantial level of racist crime taking place in Britain. In one local survey, around one in five of all black and Asian adults in Newham had experienced 'some form of racist victimisation' (Bowling and Phillips, 2002: 112). Perceptions about the perpetrators of such offences are similar to those for offences in general, with 'young, white males' being identified as primarily responsible (Percy, 1998: 1).

As Bowling and Phillips have observed, this evidence helps to explain why minority ethnic communities are more fearful of crime than their white counterparts:

> Although the relationship between fear, crime and victimisation is a complex one, fear of 'ordinary crime' among people from ethnic minority communities is fundamentally shaped by their *fear of racist victimisation*.
>
> (Bowling and Phillips, 2002: 113)

This is not a uniform pattern (Yarrow, 2005: 30), but nevertheless, people from ethnic minorities are more likely to be fearful of crime (Percy, 1998; Clancy *et al.*, 2001; Barclay *et al.*, 2005). Percy (1998: 29), for example, has reported 40% of people from ethnic minorities being 'very worried' about burglary compared to 21% of white people. Indeed, confirming Percy's (1998) earlier conclusions, Kautt (2008: 26) found that 'fear of crime adversely affects the quality of life significantly more for Black and Asian [British Crime Survey] respondents than White respondents'.

As the Stephen Lawrence inquiry forcefully demonstrated, black and minority ethnic groups are also often dissatisfied with the official response to crimes against them. The report of the inquiry commented on a pervasive sense of mistrust:

the atmosphere in which racist incidents and crimes are investigated must be considered since that will condition the actions and responses which may follow. That atmosphere was strongly voiced in the attitude of those who came to our hearings. In the words of David Muir, representing senior Black Church leaders 'the experience of black people over the last 30 years has been that we have been over policed and under protected'.

(Macpherson, 1999: para. 45.7)

Similar feelings have regularly been expressed in local surveys (AFFOR, 1978; Saini, 1997; Breese, 2013), revealing a widely held view amongst victims that involving the police would be pointless. Qualitative research also reveals a degree of suspicion and mistrust amongst certain groups, such as young black men who are victims of crime (Yarrow, 2005: 16), and amongst those who had been subject to specific practices such as police 'stop and searches' (Gervais, 2008: 68).

A distinction must be made, however, between levels of 'satisfaction' with the criminal justice system and the degree of 'confidence' held by particular groups, depending, it seems, on their differential experiences as community members, victims or alleged offenders. Thus, for example, 70% of the white population were reported at one point to be 'very/fairly satisfied', whilst this figure fell to 56% for Pakistani or Bangladeshi respondents (Clancy *et al.*, 2001: 3). These are persistent problems (Bowling and Phillips, 2002), related to dissatisfaction with the 'overall performance' of the police, who are found not to show sufficient interest or to be polite (Yarrow, 2005; Gervais, 2008). Such concerns about the nature of the police response are supported and reinforce more general beliefs about the unfair treatment of certain ethnic groups. The broad perception of inconsistency, lack of interest and second-class treatment by the police seems to be held fairly widely (Bowling and Phillips, 2002: 136; Home Affairs Committee, 2007).

However, there appears to be less concern about *other* aspects of the justice system. Indeed, people from minority ethnic groups have been reported as being more confident than white respondents that the system is 'effective in bringing people who commit crimes to justice' and that it 'meets the needs of victims of crime' (Mirrlees-Black, 2000: 3), and ethnicity has not been found to affect confidence in the police elsewhere (Myhill and Beak, 2008: 9). In other words, the concerns of black and minority ethnic communities about the operation of the criminal justice process do appear to reflect something more than blanket disapproval. The police and the prisons are more likely to be seen as doing a 'poor job' by respondents from these groups than from the white population, possibly because these are more routinely experienced as points of contact, and of direct mistreatment (MORI, 2004); however, courts, probation and prosecutors are more likely to be seen by them as doing a 'good job' (Mirrlees-Black, 2000: 4). The explanation for these disparities may well lie in the distinction between a principled support for a system of justice on which people might well need to call and the direct experiences of those coming into contact with that system, especially young people, which are discriminatory and oppressive (May *et al.*, 2009).

It may be that the police are a specific focus for discontent because they are the first point of contact with the judicial apparatus for many, and that this contact has often been experienced as inadequate and/or discriminatory (Yarrow, 2005): 'Stop and search was generally viewed by the young people interviewed as over-zealous and aggressive' (May *et al.*, 2009: 11).

More recently, perceptions of oppressive treatment are now apparent amongst Muslim communities, where young people also appear to be disproportionately targeted by police (Choudhury and Fenwick, 2011).

The unfair treatment of young black people who are suspected of crime results in low confidence in the police (Clancy *et al.*, 2001), and this is compounded by a perception that they do not receive a respectful or committed response when they are victims of crime (Yarrow, 2005). Unsurprisingly, therefore, the solutions favoured by this group are not technical, but involve major change. For black and minority ethnic groups, the strands of racist crime, victimisation and fear, and the experience of discriminatory treatment are intertwined, and lead to the conclusion that a systematic strategy aimed at (re)building mutual trust and respect is required (Macpherson, 1999; Lawrence Steering Group, 2004).

At a local level, a number of such initiatives can be identified; for example, the Black Community Safety Project produced its own agenda for change, focusing on the interests of victims and young people as well as the wider community (Saini, 1997). Those people surveyed on behalf of the project wanted 'more police patrolling the streets', but they also wanted police to treat them with more respect, and wanted more police officers to be recruited from ethnic minorities. They also expected the police to improve the service offered to those affected by crime and to work on improving their relations with young people. Despite such initiatives, little progress appears to have been made in improving the confidence of black communities in the police and criminal justice system (Lawrence Steering Group, 2004: 16; Allen *et al.*, 2006; Office for National Statistics, 2012).

In addition to police-specific improvements, local projects have also identified a desire to see greater emphasis on community safety and crime prevention, including prevention of racially motivated attacks. The education system, for example, should bear some responsibility for teaching respect for people and property, and promoting greater 'parental control'. The attention given to changes *within* the youth justice system may be quite limited, focusing on issues such as the need for better support for black people within the court setting (Saini, 1997: 40).

These aspirations were reflected in some of the recommendations arising from the Stephen Lawrence inquiry (for example, Recommendations 35–37 directed at the Crown Prosecution Service, and Recommendations 67–69 intended for the education system; Macpherson, 1999). Britton, too, has suggested that from the perspective of black and minority ethnic communities a holistic approach is needed: 'statutory organisations should place tackling institutionalised racism at the centre of their policy agendas ... statutory organisations should have their policies and daily practice rigorously monitored' (Britton, 2000: 108).

Bowling and Phillips (2002) have broadened this argument to include the impact of social variations and structural inequalities on criminal justice practices and procedures. Thus, for example, account should be taken of the way in which family circumstances impact on bail decisions, whereby apparently neutral rules of decision making produce inequitable outcomes, with a greater number of young black people liable to be remanded to custody. It is concluded that it is unacceptable to allow the continuation of practices that 'marginalise, criminalise and socially exclude ethnic minority communities in England' (Bowling and Phillips, 2002: 260).

In light of these findings, generalised moves towards harsher treatment of young offenders (Hough and Roberts, 2004) become highly problematic, since any unfairnesses built into the system will only result in more acute levels of discrimination. The technical and managerial preoccupations of New Labour with crime control and behaviour management thus seem to have been greatly misconceived (see Bowling and Phillips, 2002: 258), compounding rather than addressing systemic discriminatory practices. On the other hand, this is not to imply that the apparent liberalisation of youth justice from 2008 onwards can of itself be expected to resolve the problems associated with the discrimination experienced by black and other minority ethnic groups, which appears to be highly intractable.

'What about us?' Young people's views

More broadly, there is also evidence that young people in general are both 'over-policed' and 'under-protected'. The context in which young people form their views about crime and punishment is one in which they are more likely than the general population to be victimised or experience 'anti-social behaviour' (Haines and Drakeford, 1998; Budd and Sims, 2001; Kershaw et al., 2001; Armstrong et al., 2005). Many children have reported being fearful for their own safety; in one example, 42% of those surveyed reported feeling unsafe 'walking around their local area alone in the dark' (MORI, 2002), although those identified as potential offenders appeared to be rather more confident (MORI, 2004: 48). Levels of concern about becoming a victim of crime were high, with 45% of children in mainstream education reported as fearing theft, with 47% worrying about being physically assaulted, whilst 53% of 'Asian' young people and 42% of 'black young men' were fearful of experiencing racism (MORI, 2004: 49). Young people who were 'excluded' from school and therefore assumed to be more likely to offend were somewhat less worried about being victimised (23% fear theft and 26% physical assault, for example). In other studies, too, children have consistently expressed apprehension about the behaviour of older children and 'teenagers' (Hine, 2004). As children get older, perhaps unsurprisingly, they become less fearful (MORI, 2004: 48).

Their fears are not baseless, as we have seen. MORI's Youth Surveys have consistently shown high levels of victimisation, with 49% of 'mainstream' children stating that one or more offences had been committed against them in the previous year, including being threatened (26%), bullied (23%), experiencing theft (15%) or having property damaged (14%). Those who are 'excluded' are more likely to be victimised (55%) than mainstream children. Of those who had an offence committed against them, 74% of 'mainstream' and 59% of 'excluded' children reported that another young person had been responsible (MORI, 2004: 54). Where young people tell anyone about the offence, it is usually parents whom they inform, then friends or teachers, and only 13% report the matter to the police (21% for the 'excluded' group). A significant proportion try to 'sort it out' themselves (26% mainstream, 39% excluded; see also Haines and Drakeford, 1998: 22). The picture here is one of routine victimisation of young people, who at the same time place little reliance on the formal machinery of the justice system to resolve offences.

Although young people are at least as likely as adults to experience crime, their views on the justice system appear to differ somewhat. In comparing the views of adult respondents with those of 'juveniles', it may be that the determining factor for differences of attitude is age rather than offending (Mattinson and Mirrlees-Black, 2000: 20). Those aged 12–17 appear considerably less likely to believe the courts too lenient (29%) than adults in general (76%). However, even young people appear to believe that the youth justice system is too lenient overall.

A number of exercises to ascertain young people's views have tended to support the view that young people are in favour of tough punishment; thus: if 'somebody is caught [for an offence] they should be punished severely' (12-year-old boy, quoted in Children and Young People's Unit, 2001), and 'tougher penalties for young people' were also requested by young people surveyed in Greater Manchester (Greater Manchester Police Authority, 2002). On the other hand, young people do appear more likely than adults to believe that the police and courts' treatment of offenders is 'about right'. The reasons for this are not entirely clear, although it may be that young people are inevitably somewhat closer to the actual workings of youth justice, and do not therefore share the unrealistic beliefs of the adult population. Young people might also be less willing to support punitive measures, partly because they are more 'understanding' of those who commit crime: 'Some people in gangs get involved because they could have a bad life at home, and … [they're] pressured into it. That's how people join gangs, they're pressured into it. Having a lot of trouble at home and that' (quoted in Willow, 1999: 52).

However, there is no evidence that young people take a less serious view of 'delinquent acts' than the population overall (Smith *et al.*, 2001). They appear to share a common view of a continuum of criminal behaviours, from minor infringements, such as fare dodging, through to 'quite serious' acts, such as shoplifting and graffiti, and 'very serious' offences, such as housebreaking, joyriding and fire raising (see also MORI, 2002). However, there appears to be some evidence of 'neutralization' (Matza, 1964), whereby minor infringements can be viewed as acceptable. Those who have engaged in 'less serious' criminal behaviour are less likely than their law-abiding peers to see these as significant transgressions (Smith *et al.*, 2001), and Hine reports an age factor in this respect:

> The younger age groups are sure that stealing any item is wrong. The older groups presented more tolerance, and even approval of stealing minor items of little value, but when the item involved is more valuable (such as a CD player) there is general disapproval here too. Children and young people clearly have a moral code which they can articulate and apply.
>
> (Hine, 2004: 41)

The overall picture suggests that young people share many of the moral judgements and rules of behaviour of the community in general, expressing similar concerns about personal safety and the fear of crime (for example, Greater Manchester Police Authority, 2002; Hine, 2004), and holding similar views about the need for criminal sanctions and tougher punishment. This assessment finds support from wider surveys of the values and attitudes of young people, which have also found that 'young people's values did not differ significantly to those documented for adults' (Thompson *et al.*, 1999: 5). Despite this, it would appear that young people are not always well served by the formal justice system, with many offences going unreported, as we have seen, and a general sense of 'not being listened to', especially for black young people (Yarrow, 2005).

Young people in Manchester have identified a need for 'more interaction by the police with young people; serious treatment of young people when reporting a crime; treating young people with respect; not being judgemental' (Greater Manchester Police Authority, 2002: 1). These concerns about not being taken seriously are echoed elsewhere: 'I don't trust the police cos ... Like when someone stole my scooter. And he goes, "have you got it back?" And, he goes, "yes". "But can you find the person who done it?" and he goes "Sorry, sort it out yourself"' (8/9-year-old quoted in Hine, 2004: 31). Being treated with a 'lack of respect' remains a persistent concern for young people coming into contact with the police (Botley *et al.*, 2010).

The disparities between young people's beliefs and their experiences mirror those of BME groups and may account for their clearly ambivalent views about authority figures and the legitimacy of the powers they are ascribed (Thompson *et al.*, 1999). As active participants in the social world (Smith, 2002b), young people do not simply take existing structures and systems of power as given; indeed, respect and recognition must be earned:

> Traditional authority figures such as the police, religious leaders and the royal family received very little automatic respect from young people. They explained that respect must be earned, authority won and merit

proven ... While young people did not always invest teachers with moral authority, they watched them closely to see if they were worthy of it.

(Thompson *et al.*, 1999: 6)

Young people seem to be looking for certain characteristics in those who claim authority over them, in order to evaluate the legitimacy of these claims – characteristics such as 'consistency, care, the ability to listen and practical skills' (Thompson *et al.*, 1999: 6). It is important here to distinguish between the broad consensus to be found about what is appropriate behaviour and the means by which this is enforced, on the one hand, and the experience of the (mis)application of these normative understandings in practice, on the other. Young people consistently believe that their concerns are not taken seriously, and that they are treated unfairly: 'Police ... don't make us feel safe and take their time getting to the crime scene' (14-year-old girl), and 'I have had police harassment on the streets for no reason other than being young' (16-year-old male) (from Children and Young People's Unit, 2001); and 'they've got the authority, just abuse the power they've got, so they know they can do it, they know they can get away with it, there's nothing no one can do about it' (Botley *et al.*, 2010: 5). That these concerns are not new is graphically conveyed by a much earlier study: 'I fuckin' hate coppers. They've just tried to do us for robbing some fuckin' sword or something. Murky and me were walking up the hill. Up they screeched, pulls us into the back of the car and start acting hard' (quoted in Parker, 1974: 162).

This kind of perception creates some difficulties for the youth justice system in laying claim to legitimacy and the authority to impose sanctions for wrongful behaviour. Moral rectitude clearly does not lie only on one side, especially for young people who are identified as offenders. While Parker's study identified the police as the initial source of distrust and hostility, the resentment of unfairly imposed authority also extended to other aspects of the justice system, including probation and social services: 'Tank was extremely disillusioned to find that the social worker who had always helped out with his rather chaotic family had finally recommended him for a period of detention' (Parker, 1974: 173).

Moving forward in time again, it seems that legitimacy and fair treatment remain significant areas of concern for those processed as young offenders. In terms of system effectiveness alone, it is likely that rates of non-compliance and even reoffending may be influenced by their perceptions of what is 'just', but these issues also raise more fundamental questions about what sort of youth justice system we want. An important study carried out with young people in custody (aged 15 to 21) sheds some light on this (Lyon *et al.*, 2000). These young people talked first about the contextual factors relating to their criminal activities:

> They talked about growing up in bad areas, with high levels of crime and drug use; being labelled by education as a 'problem' and subsequently

being excluded; they gave explanations for beginning offending; and they were critical of the way they had been treated by the criminal justice system.

(Lyon *et al.*, 2000: 7)

Their complaints focused on the police, the courts and other players in the justice system. The police, for instance, were seen to be 'taking advantage of their power ... the majority of young people did not have respect for the police. Nor did they see them as any deterrent against becoming involved in crime' (Lyon *et al.*, 2000: 23). These views extended to the courts, where judges were seen as both racist and biased against young women; sentencers were criticised for 'not caring'. Youth justice professionals were seen as indifferent and lazy: 'The probation officer doesn't know what's going on. They should know you – they're your probation officer. They should know that you're going down again – they should know what's happening in your life shouldn't they?' (quoted in Lyon *et al.*, 2000: 27). The experience of custody itself was seen as a poor preparation for a law-abiding life outside (a finding that has been subsequently reinforced; see Summerfield, 2011). For most, 'prison was a dislocating experience ... It was a "whole other life", not connected to their everyday lives before entering custody, and often not preparing them at all well for release' (Lyon *et al.*, 2000: 29).

Despite their overwhelmingly negative experiences, the young people in this study appeared to have a real commitment to avoid offending in the future, and it was in this light that they made a number of suggestions for improving the justice system, in order to address issues both of effectiveness and legitimacy. They supported ideas for preventing crime by targeting children at risk of social exclusion; they argued for improved peer support (mentoring) programmes; they emphasised the importance of continuing education; and they identified the need for continuity and stability for those in local authority care.

Specifically in relation to the justice system, these young people argued for tougher treatment of drug dealers, improved relations between police and young people, and fairer and explicitly anti-racist practice at all stages of the judicial process. They were also supportive of ideas such as mentoring, reparation and citizenship education, which they felt might reduce reoffending. In addition, they argued for better and more consistent welfare support to enable them to be reintegrated effectively into the community. Above all, it was found, young people processed by the justice system wanted to be treated with respect, something that they felt had not been accorded to them in many cases.

The authors of this report concluded positively that:

Many of the young people's concerns about lack of professionalism are being tackled by the Government's agenda for reform of the youth justice system and the work of the Youth Justice Board ... The young people highlighted the need for complex solutions to complex problems.

Their views support the Government's joined-up approach to tackling social inequalities as a way to reduce crime.

(Lyon *et al.*, 2000: 80–81)

A subsequent and comprehensive study of young offenders' views confirmed many of these concerns, especially about their treatment by the police, discrimination, the adverse effects of custody and the need for suitable support in the community (Hazel *et al.*, 2002).

It seems to be the case that young people (offenders and non-offenders) share a detailed and nuanced understanding of youth offending, which means that simplistic responses are unlikely to be effective. Young people resent being targeted simply because of their age, and they feel that they have something to offer in constructing realistic solutions to perceived social problems (for example, the 'Young Voices' initiative in Liverpool; Hancock, 2006: 178). Interventions and policies need to be holistic and focus on the social context and the social construction of crime (and anti-social behaviour) as a problem as well as – and, arguably, to a greater extent than – its immediate manifestations. To concentrate on dealing with their behaviour in isolation and out of context is not seen as justified by young people, and seems to them to be inherently unfair and discriminatory.

The answers are complex

The perceptions and attitudes of those with an interest of one kind or another in the youth justice system, far from reflecting simplistic judgements and identifying simple solutions, provide ample evidence that the issue is multifaceted and demands careful analysis and considered action. Attitudes appear to be shaped partly in a context of limited and skewed knowledge (Mirrlees-Black and Allen, 1998; Hough and Roberts, 2004). Thus, for example, the public believes the youth justice system to be too lenient (Ashcroft, 2011), in fact, far more lenient than it actually is, and seeks tougher punishments in the light of this erroneous belief. Despite this, popular sentiment is not uncompromisingly punitive (MORI, 2001). Even among victims, there is support for approaches based on restorative principles (Mattinson and Mirrlees-Black, 2000), and more detailed information and understanding generates a less punitive response from the public at large (Hough and Roberts, 2004). Young people, including those who offend, appear to share widely held views about 'right' and 'wrong' (MORI, 2002), but they are concerned about the inadequacies and injustices of the criminal process, feeling that it does not take their wishes and needs seriously (Centre for Social Justice, 2012), and that it is a source of racist and oppressive practice (Lyon *et al.*, 2000; Bowling and Phillips, 2002; Children and Young People's Unit, 2002; Yarrow, 2005; Home Affairs Committee, 2007).

Although perceptions differ quite widely, it seems that there is a broad and enduring consensus that our approach to dealing with the problems of young people needs to be substantially rethought and revised. There is also sub-stantial support for the view that the most effective strategies must concentrate on securing wider social change outside the relatively narrow confines of the 'justice system' itself, which should not simply be treated as a 'dumping ground' for wider social issues (Centre for Social Justice, 2012: 12). There is a need for new and imaginative developments. If these are pursued explicitly and coherently, they might even incur public approval (Green, 2006):

> When public opinion is complex and multi-layered … there can be no policy justification for privileging people's unconsidered desire for tougher punishment and ignoring other dimensions to their views … there is clearly potential for building on public support for new approaches to sentencing young offenders …
>
> (Hough and Roberts, 2004: xi)

10 Making sense of it all

The future of youth justice

Another fine mess?

As we have observed in previous chapters, youth justice has experienced rapid change in recent years, partly associated with shifts in policy and structural arrangements, in turn associated with changes of government; however, at the same time, we should not discount a wider range of influences, including social and economic factors, on the one hand, and the influence of those engaged in practice, on the other. This concluding chapter will seek to re-evaluate the key issues highlighted thus far in order to sketch some ideas about how youth justice might be reconstituted to meet contemporary challenges (see also Muncie and Goldson, 2012).

We should not underestimate the scale of the task or the pressures that impact on all those involved in youth justice. It is located at a particularly uncomfortable conjuncture, where the perennial question of how to socialise or control our young people is addressed in the full glare of the media, community concerns and political interests. This will always be a controversial and hotly contested area of social practice. Ultimately, indeed, any progress made is tentative and susceptible to the complex dynamics flowing from this unstable brew of high drama and loud voices. Furthermore, the development of contemporary structures and processes in youth justice can be seen to derive from the state's objectives of achieving its policy goals in terms of maintaining social cohesion, exercising control of deviant behaviour and reproducing the existing structure of social relations (Althusser, 1977). The construction of 'youth' as the source of a range of social problems, including crime and disorder, is significant in this project, to the extent that it contributes to and sustains a consensual definition of 'the problem' (Gramsci, 1971; Hall et al., 1978). Underlying social factors associated with deviant behaviour are de-emphasised and the focal point of concern becomes the stereotypical 'threatening youth' (Davies, 1986). It would be wrong to suggest that the behaviour of young people is never problematic, but the ready criminalisation of their activities ensures that its origins, and indeed its purposes, fade into the background. An effective separation is achieved in contemporary discourse, between the 'criminal' and the causes of criminality, notwithstanding political rhetoric to the contrary (Blair, 2002; Centre for Social Justice, 2012).

It is this false distinction that lies at the heart of most of our difficulties in arriving at a clear understanding of youth offending, and the consequent failure to devise and put into practice appropriate interventions. It is debatable as to whether the separation of the problem behaviour of young people from its social context is conscious and deliberate or simply misguided. Althusser's (1977) argument that the judicial apparatus is simply a vehicle by which powerful interests impose their will is over-deterministic, whilst Foucault's (1979) characterisation of the machinery of justice as systematic and coherent attributes a greater degree of logic and consistency than is apparent to many who work within it. Thus, certain patterns and trends may have suggested a degree of consistency and even intent behind recent developments, such as the sustained increase in the use of custody from the mid-1990s onwards, or the 'demonising' effects of anti-social behaviour policies and initiatives (Squires and Stephen, 2005), but the subsequent reductions in the number of young people being formally processed and incarcerated and the rethink of anti-social behaviour legislation have called this into question.

We may gain a better insight into the complexities of current debates by considering analyses, such as Cohen's (1985), which identify competing strands of thought, and capture the sense of youth and criminal justice as contested territory where alternative views and disparate motives are played out in the construction and delivery of concrete practices. Certainly, it has been suggested elsewhere that, far from representing a unified and coherent 'system', youth justice is characterised by a 'melange' of different principles and provisions, which manifest 'fundamental contradictions' (Muncie, 2002: 156).

Cohen (1985) suggests that three main explanatory schema can be detected in the changing shape and shifting dynamics of criminal justice. First, there are those who believe that its history and development can be characterised in terms of steady, if sometimes uneven, progress. The justice system, according to this view, can be (and is) improved consistently by the application of increasingly refined 'scientific' methods of research, management and practice, which will progressively improve the 'targeting' and impact of service delivery. There will thus be a continually enhanced understanding of 'what works', reflected in increasingly effective interventions and outcomes. Thus, 'although we are not at the end of the journey in the quest to find out what works ... there is now a rapid accumulation of understanding and knowledge in this field' (Burnett and Roberts, 2004: 11). The development and revision of National Standards for Youth Justice, the implementation of performance management, the adoption and refinement of specific practice tools such as ASSET (Baker, 2005) and the implementation of the 'Scaled Approach' are all represented as part of a process of advancement and refinement of good practice. Not only is there consensus around means, but there also appears to be common ground in terms of the ends to be achieved, that is, crime reduction, pure and simple. The use of more sophisticated and intrusive means of monitoring and control, such as surveillance and tagging, is not problematic from this perspective, if it can be shown to contribute to lowering offending rates (Moore, 2004: 170). At the same time, the entire project is depoliticised, becoming simply a matter of finding the best technical solutions to a commonly agreed problem. Changes in the political sphere, in government or in key policy roles are therefore seen as of lesser significance (see, for instance, Pitts, 2001b: 42), since the continuing task for penal experts remains unchanged – that is, to improve the machinery for prediction, monitoring and managing the behaviour of those young people who are at risk of (re)offending.

Cohen's second explanatory category is characterised by the phrase 'we blew it', and this perspective views the progress of youth justice as a process of action and reaction, with each successive era offering evidence of apparently drastic attempts to put right the mistakes of the previous phase. This conceptualisation coincides quite neatly with a political context dominated by competing political parties that seek to establish a sense of distance between each other. Specific initiatives can be linked to the ascendancy of one or other of these positions. Thus, historically, the 'welfare'-led reforms of the Labour government of the late 1960s could be seen as a reaction to the oppressive, class-based institutional regime that preceded them, represented by Approved Schools and Borstals, in particular. As time progressed, however, these welfare reforms themselves generated a backlash, reflecting the views of a wide-ranging coalition of academics, politicians, sentencers and practitioners. This resulted in the 'back to justice' movement of the late 1970s/early 1980s (Morris *et al.*, 1980; Thorpe *et al.*, 1980). The 'justice model' then became the dominant paradigm of the following decade. As we have seen, however, aspects of this orthodoxy themselves generated a further reaction, notably in response to the liberalising impact associated with it, and the corresponding reduction in the use of punitive interventions, including custody.

The 1990s saw a further 'backlash', this time leading to a prioritisation of punishment and control over rights and minimum intervention, epitomised by the then home secretary's 'prison works' mantra (Howard, 1995). This shift of emphasis, politically driven rather than practice-led or indeed, evidence-based, produced a new coalition concerned with 'protecting the community', and provided legitimacy for the package of reforms introduced in the latter part of the decade.

By the middle part of the following decade (the 2000s), the position had changed again, and equally dramatically, as a new era of austerity-driven 'minimal intervention' began, based on a renewed consensus that the youth justice system had previously become over-committed to interventionism. On the face of it, then, there seems to be some support for the notion that youth justice is subject to periodic reappraisals leading to significant transformations in policy and practice, although, as we have seen, these shifts do not coincide neatly with changes in formal political power. Pitts (2002), for example, argued that at the time the recent history of juvenile/youth justice could be seen in terms of distinctive 'paradigm' shifts (Kuhn, 1970), represented by several distinct phases: welfarism, back to justice, systems management and correctionalism.

Cohen's third analytical discourse – 'it's all a con' – reflects a rather more critical position, which holds that the dynamics of change represented by the other perspectives are more or less superficial, disguising, and indeed contributing to, underlying attempts to legitimise the exercise of social control. Thus, even apparently favourable developments may be treated with suspicion. For example, Pratt's (1989) dismissal of juvenile diversion as an exercise in 'corporatist' control takes a cynical view of what had previously been hailed as an example of progressive practice. Goldson (2000), more recently, advanced a similar critique of the Referral Order, on the grounds that it establishes an illusory form of 'contract' that is merely a cipher for the expropriation of children's rights (see also Goldson, 2010).

The problem posed by this perspective for practitioners is that it offers little encouragement for working in ways that are genuinely inclusive and progressive; it may, indeed, appear virtually impossible to practise in a way that 'prefigures' positive transformations (Smith, 1989). Accordingly, within this critical perspective, two contrasting strands of thought are evident – 'radical pessimism' and 'radical optimism'. For those holding the former view, it may be better not to intervene at all than to muddy the waters by trying to act in children's interests in a hostile environment; 'radical non-intervention' (Schur, 1973) or 'abolitionism' (Mathiesen, 1974) are the preferred strategies. On the other hand, those taking a proactive view would argue for a selective approach to practice, concentrating on those areas that provide for the promotion of children's rights (Scraton and Haydon, 2002), such as diversion, remand rescue, community justice and anti-racist initiatives (for example, Right Track in Bristol). This appears to offer a progressive and practical agenda, but the challenge lies in working within and according to the requirements of an operational framework that is fundamentally misconceived and unjust (see Corrigan and Leonard, 1978).

Whilst the differing perspectives identified by Cohen can be identified as exercising variable influences on the management and practice of youth justice, the resultant composite picture is confused and contradictory. But it is the interplay of diverse viewpoints that results in the particular (and yet inherently unstable) articulation of youth justice at any given point in time.

By the early 2000s, the balance had moved in favour of those seeking to promote a routinised model of management, surveillance and control, based on assumptions of the perfectibility of the instruments and techniques for identifying risk and changing behaviour ('uneven progress'). This coincided with broader currents associated with the concept of 'managerialism' (Clarke *et al.*, 2000), and the ultimate 'infallibility of science' (Beck, 1992). This also chimed well with a political agenda attuned to the search for quick and certain solutions to meet popular demands. Thus, external pressures to produce instant results and guaranteed successful outcomes coincide with emerging practice orthodoxies, associated with a more and more detailed elaboration of 'what works'. Methods of prediction, surveillance and control are believed to be susceptible to continual improvement (see, for example, Baker, 2005), and therefore routinised measures of intrusion and coercion are justified, even *in anticipation* of any possible offence:

> what is noticeable in this gamut of management restructuring and evaluation is that all aspects of young people's lives are now potentially open to official monitoring and scrutiny.
>
> (McLaughlin and Muncie, 2000: 180)

We should note, however, that these developments were all based on the problematic and one-sided assumption that progress is uni-directional and that such improvements are both technically possible and desirable. Others might reflect that, in the absence of any substantive evidence to support this belief, what in fact emerged was a combination of oppressive and divisive measures, which ironically also failed to achieve the outcomes to which they aspired.

It should be noted here that the other positions identified by Cohen can also be identified in various aspects of youth justice policy and practice in the present era, coming more strongly into prominence as the occasion demands, it might seem. It is politically expedient, of course, for policy makers to be able to claim that each new initiative represents a radical alternative to previous failures. Thus, as late as 2006, after nine years in power, the prime minister was reported to be promising a 'rebalancing' of the justice system 'in favour of the decent, law-abiding majority who play by the rules' (*The Guardian*, 23 June 2006), perhaps tacitly acknowledging that he had 'blown it'. However, in speaking at the same time of analysing 'where the shortcomings are' and putting in place 'systems to remove them', he reverted to the language of the existing technocratic consensus, rather than setting out an agenda for radical change.

The radical perspective, on the other hand, did not exercise much influence for a considerable period of time, and did not act as an effective bulwark against the managerial tide. Part of the explanation for this may stem back to the mood of complacency associated with the successes of the 1980s (diversion, offence resolution and reduced use of custody) and co-option by an apparently 'friendly' government after 1997 (McLaughlin and Muncie, 2000); however, Pitts (2001b) has also argued that the weakness of the radical position can be linked to its historical unwillingness to be explicit about the structural factors associated with youth offending – perhaps in the arena of practice it might appear to make more sense, tactically, to avoid direct challenges to dominant assumptions. Thus, for example, court reports are not typically constructed in a way that addresses the contextual issues relating to specific offences, such as poverty and institutional discrimination; and arguments against excessively punitive sentences would be more likely to advance individual needs or 'mitigating factors'. As a result, the underlying discourses of due process, risk assessment and coercive interventions have remained dominant.

The problem for a pragmatic approach is that, even in favourable circumstances, it offers a weak base from which to develop principled and generalised arguments against either populist calls for tighter control over young people or technocratic measures aimed at generating a greater sense of certainty in tackling the threat they represent. It is this observation that underlines the necessity of articulating and advocating a much more radical set of arguments in order to build on and sustain the advances made in decarceration and liberalisation in youth justice in the new age of austerity.

Where have we been?

Before the recent change in direction, the disastrous consequences of the convergence of populist ideologies, political opportunism and technocratic management had become acutely apparent in the outputs of the youth justice system. In many ways, the retrograde trends of the late 1990s–early 2000s were both predictable and predicted (Goldson, 1999, for example). The move towards creating 'wider, stronger and different nets' (Austin and Krisberg, 2002) was complemented by steps to ensure that these were also deeper and more finely meshed. The system became increasingly efficient at processing and punishing young people, developing its own fearsome and inexorable logic (Pratt, 2000). The concrete evidence of this process is clearest at the apex of the structure, with a dramatic and sustained rise in the use of custody, which became firmly entrenched (Simes and Chads, 2002; Youth Justice Board, 2005d). Government implicitly endorsed the actions of the courts in increasing demand for custodial places through their remand and sentencing practices by taking steps to create ever-more secure provision (Home Office press release, 1 May 2002; *The Guardian*, 27 July 2006). This approach can be contrasted with other countries that maintained an active commitment to keeping the use of custody to a minimum (in Italy and Scandinavia, for example; Goldson and Muncie, 2006b; Hazel, 2008), or 'capping' its use (as in the Netherlands and Ireland; *Irish Examiner*, 21 August 2002).

The outcomes observed in England and Wales are not just the result of populist gestures to increase the availability of custody.[1] The machinery of youth justice, too, contributed to the emergent trends. Despite a static or falling crime rate (contrary to popular beliefs fanned by government rhetoric; see, for example, Blunkett, quoted in Home Office press release, 20 March 2002; *Daily Mail*, 24 June 2006), the greater resources invested and the increasingly sophisticated mechanisms of control applied produced more and more oppressive outcomes. Even before committing offences, young people were subject to ever-closer scrutiny and targeted for interventions – first through preventive programmes such as Youth Intervention Projects and Summer Splash, born out of 'fear not need', according to one commentator, and subsequently through the use of Anti-Social Behaviour Orders (ASBOs), Dispersal Orders and Curfew Orders.

As they moved into the criminal sphere, more young people were formally processed (rather than receiving informal sanctions); they were drawn into the justice system younger, for relatively more minor offences (Jennings, 2002); and they experienced formal and recordable disposals earlier in their offending careers. The loss of the option to administer second and subsequent cautions following the 1998 legislation almost certainly ensured quicker progression to court, where the option of a Conditional Discharge was effectively removed, and more demanding and intrusive programmes were imposed at an earlier stage, effectively compressing the sentencing tariff. At the same time, the opportunities for non-compliance, failure and breach action inevitably increased (Bateman, 2011a).

The principle of 'voluntarism' was squeezed out at all stages of the process, for example through the contractual nature of the Referral Order (Crawford and Newburn, 2003; Goldson, 2009), contrasting significantly with the negotiated and informal diversionary approaches of the 1980s. Failure to comply, or commission of further offences, promised to speed young people towards categorisation as 'persistent young offenders', qualifying them for yet more intrusive forms of constraint and surveillance (almost irrespective of the gravity of their actions). These developments were complemented by an array of bail conditions, which also led to an increase in the number of breaches and subsequent custodial remands (Bateman, 2011a).

Associated with the emergence of these highly developed and intrusive mechanisms of control was a preoccupation with the management of risk, reflected in the tools and strategies of youth justice. ASSET, for example, represents an ideal instrument for systematising apparently objective measures of likelihood of reoffending, based on 'actuarial' principles (Lea, 2002; Smith, 2006). Despite the rather over-stated claims for its predictive accuracy (Youth Justice Board, 2002; Baker *et al.*, 2005), the form is of little value in identifying welfare needs (Roberts *et al.*, 2001) or assisting in the construction of inclusive intervention programmes – welfare was written out of its remit (hence its incompatibility with the Common Assessment Framework; Youth Justice Board, 2006b). As youth justice practitioners have repeatedly commented, ASSET is highly unbalanced and selective. Indeed, the preoccupation with risk is almost bound to prompt a predisposition to 'see the worst in people' and to focus unduly on the potential for negative outcomes. In parallel with these developments, in the autumn of 2002, the Youth Justice Board (YJB) announced the establishment of 'pre-crime panels' for children as young as eight years old, who would be marked out as potential offenders, and therefore liable to correctional interventions. Following the 'successful' piloting of the Youth Inclusion and Support Panel aimed at 8–13 year olds, the Youth Justice Board was funded by the Home Office to invest in 122 such schemes (Home Office, 2004b).

Problematising young people in this way, and concentrating on the 'risk of failure' is certain to have a sensitising effect, creating both a greater predisposition to finding evidence of non-compliance or further deviant behaviour, along with a greater likelihood that this will be officially recorded, which in turn is liable to generate an increasingly punitive response. The lessons of 'labelling theory' (Becker, 1963) had clearly not been learnt, as the then chair of the Youth Justice Board belatedly reminded us (*The Independent*, 23 April 2006). Beck's (1992) portrayal of the consequences of a preoccupation with things going wrong in a 'risk society' appears to be borne out by this kind of development. As he has pointed out, a greater emphasis on the potential for failure will be associated with an 'actuarial' response, based on the principle of identifying the possibility of damaging events and taking action to control this. This, however, has certain associated effects, such as a heightening of public fear and a sense of loss of control, as it becomes increasingly apparent that there is no way of providing absolute guarantees of security and personal safety. Indeed, some of the measures undertaken may actually generate new risks, as a result of the creation of new forms of infringement (*The Independent*, 16 August 2006).

The final irony to be noted here is the contrast between the emphasis, in one policy strand, on promoting social inclusion and a sense of belonging and the opposing pressures emerging from the criminal justice sphere to mark out young people as different, to exclude them from mainstream activities and to isolate them in 'targeted' programmes or settings. Thus, the inclusive intent of programmes such as New Deal and Connexions, which focused on creating opportunities and building a spirit of community, was substantially undermined by the impact of parallel developments that depended for their very rationale on creating and sustaining a sense of 'the other' (Garland, 2001). This has permeated not just youth justice, but other settings such as education, where differentiation and segregation appear to be endemic. The use of techniques that classify young people and their behaviour on negative grounds and then insert them into specialised forms of intervention can only intensify their sense of rejection and separation (Berridge *et al.*, 2001), as well as confirming for the community in general that their special treatment is justified (Fionda, 2005: 266).

Where are we now?

Even as the dynamics of youth justice shifted, and patterns of intervention and outcomes changed from the mid-2000s onwards, so a process of adaptation had to be undergone by the structures and policy frameworks that con-textualise and provide a rationale for practice. As so often, it seemed, it was pragmatic change in the operation of the system that, in turn, necessitated the development of a coherent narrative and justificatory discourse to account for it. The first systematic attempt to articulate this was to be found in the Labour government's *Youth Crime Action Plan*, in the language of 'enforcement and punishment where behaviour is unacceptable, non-negotiable support and challenge where it is most needed, and better and earlier prevention' (Smith *et al.*, 2008: 1), and tentative moves in the direction of increased 'diversion' were signalled (HM Government, 2008: 23). Much of the content of this document, though, retained the established preoccupation with assessment, problem identification and targeted interventions, associated with the wholesale 'systems creep' of previous years.

It took the incoming government of 2010, and its proposals incorporated in *Breaking the Cycle* (Ministry of Justice, 2010) to signal a clear endorsement of the direction of travel already in evidence. Greater emphasis would be placed on 'out-of-court disposals', backed up by incentives for 'local partners to reduce youth offending and re-offending' (ibid.: 67) – that is, payment by results. The proposed end to 'automatic escalation' indicated a distinct move away from a tariff-based approach, accompanied by a renewed emphasis on determining 'the most appropriate response', based on local negotiation, rather than simply looking towards prosecution as the necessary consequence of reoffending. Associated with the emerging trends in practice, these aspirations do, indeed, offer some room for manoeuvre in the development of progressive forms of practice. On the other hand, the persistence of risk-based models of intervention, the resilience of punitive ideologies, and severe reductions in the level of resources available to counter the effects of impoverishment and disadvantage all represent significant obstacles to the achievement of a youth justice system that is genuinely 'just'.

Where are we going?

The recurrent problems of youth justice are evident. They are essentially derived from the intertwined challenges of addressing popular concerns about the behaviour of young people, and delivering interventions that are fair, reasonable and demonstrate an appropriate level of respect for young people themselves. This is always going to present particular challenges, especially when, it seems, there is such a degree of readiness to think the worst of them, and to rush to judgement. Of course, this is not to suggest that nothing can be done, but rather that we should be clear about the size and nature of the task. In many ways, the prospectus for radical change does not need to be reinvented, because the key elements of a just and liberal youth justice system have been elaborated often enough (see, for example, Schur, 1973; Smith, 1989; Scraton and Haydon, 2002; Fionda, 2005; Goldson and Muncie, 2006a). However, with each new development, the task of moving from 'where we are' to 'where we want to be' also becomes transformed, and the practical and political questions of achieving progressive reforms must be addressed rather differently. Nonetheless, it is important to set out certain central principles that ought to underpin the realisation of a fair and inclusive youth justice system.

Rights – not justice

This might seem a somewhat unusual distinction to make, but the underlying issue concerns the application of formal models of justice in unequal and unjust circumstances. In this sense, the administration of 'justice' actually compounds existing *injustices*, as is the case with institutional racism, for example (Bowling and Phillips, 2002).

Thus, as Williams (1997) has argued, merely setting the 'rights' of victims against the obligations of young offenders creates a false and simplistic opposition, which does not reflect wider social, community or interpersonal dynamics. For example, acknowledging the ambiguous position of young offenders who may also have been victims (MORI, 2002) is likely to have an impact on perceptions and attitudes (Smith *et al.*, 2001). The distinction between the idealised offender, on the one hand, and the victim, on the other, is (and should be) therefore blurred.

Furthermore, in the context of specific offences, moral judgements, too, may be inconsistent or conflictual. The 'offender' may not accept unqualified responsibility for an offence, even when the facts of the matter appear relatively clear cut. This, again, is the predictable consequence of the unfolding of complex social and personal relationships. Young people may well be unwilling to accept the blame, for instance, for incidents that arise out of longstanding local disputes, if these are taken out of context.

Rights, then, are not pure. Despite this, the concept is powerful, and there does appear to be some value in seeking to apply the abstract principle itself in concrete circumstances:

> In established, 'mature' democracies, the conceptualisation, definition and formulation of commonly held and institutionally applied rights would seem straightforward ... Yet rights discourses are complex – reflecting a long history of contestation. Rights can be defensive in nature proclaiming the 'right' not to be on the receiving end of the actions of others ... Also, they can be proactive or positive ... providing the right to something ...
>
> (Scraton and Haydon, 2002: 312)

It should be added here that rights are not fixed and determinate, and that they are subject to re-evaluation and modification over time. Thus, they can be seen as negotiable, and related to the specific context and networks of social relations relevant to the matter under consideration. It is thus inappropriate to think in terms of a static system of justice that invokes standardised procedures and fixed penalties to deal with all forms of problematic behaviour, which themselves originate in unique and variable circumstances. We may have to consider 'sacrificing due process', as Fionda (2005: 270) advocates, and it is at least a little encouraging to see that the notion of 'negotiated justice' has reappeared in recent government policy documents, such as *Breaking the Cycle*. Apparently rational and determinate logical frameworks for decision making and sentencing must therefore be called into question. The apparent benefits offered by standardised and logical methods of identifying, processing and dealing with offenders must be set against the unjust consequences, in terms of 'the "loss" to the offender of relevant mitigating circumstances. It is a significant loss, given the consequences inherent in the determining contexts of class, "race", gender, sexuality and age inequalities' (Scraton and Haydon, 2002: 315).

In order to deal with the problem of institutionalised unfairness, Bowling and Phillips (2002) propose a strategy of building into the decision-making process of the justice system an 'equalising' function, which adapts outcomes to take account of disadvantages that impact disproportionately on specific groups such as those from ethnic minorities. Thus, as already discussed, the uneven impact of differing family circumstances on remand decisions should be allowed for in order to avoid compounding prior social inequalities through the judicial process (Bowling and Phillips, 2002: 260).

It is clear that a sophisticated and nuanced conception of rights is required, which incorporates a recognition of prior experiences, inequalities and power imbalances. What is needed here is 'substantive' rather than 'formal' justice (Fionda, 2005). The starting point for the incorporation of this principle into youth justice is provided for us by international frameworks such as the United Nations (UN) Convention on the Rights of the Child, the Beijing Rules on the Administration of Juvenile Justice and the European Convention on Human Rights. If followed conscientiously, these should ensure that the administration of justice incorporates a recognition of the distinctive position of children, especially those who experience disadvantage or discrimination.[2] Clearly, the justice system should take the utmost care not to compound the negative and damaging experiences that some children and young people endure, and which may well be relevant factors in their offending behaviour.

Problem solving

In light of this, it is suggested that the primary focus of any form of intervention to deal with offending behaviour should adopt a 'problem-solving' approach. To some extent, this is consistent with the ideas associated with 'restorative justice' (Strang and Braithwaite, 2001; Johnstone, 2002), although it also extends more widely to incorporate the principle that any problem associated with an offence should be addressed, including those issues that might be thought of as 'welfare' needs.

Whereas the starting point is inevitably the 'trigger' incident, with a focus on 'putting right the wrong to the extent that it is possible for *both* victim and offender' (Gelsthorpe and Morris, 2002: 242), this should not be an isolated aim, but should be incorporated in a more far-reaching strategy, encapsulated in the phrase 'responsibility, restoration and reintegration'. Indeed, this kind of approach is reflected in the objectives of some recent practice developments such as Community Restorative Justice in the North of Ireland (see www. extern.org/restorative/CRJI.htm, for example), and similar initiatives are now emerging in Wales (Haines and Charles, 2010).

These objectives point towards a pragmatic and situated approach, drawing on ideas of social learning (Bandura, 1976), and they clearly call into question punitive and exclusive modes of intervention. Thus, for example, the extent to which problem-solving interventions such as family group conferences (Jackson, 1999) and restorative panels (Haines, 2000) are subsumed by the formalities of the justice system will play a substantial part in determining their efficacy. If they are seen merely as an adjunct to the criminal process, then their meaning and impact are likely to be compromised (Crawford and Newburn, 2003: 237). As a result, 'there have been questions about whether restorative justice principles can work when reparation orders are *imposed* on offenders without their consent' (Gelsthorpe and Morris, 2002: 247). Rather, to be genuinely constructive, methods of resolving the difficulties arising from the offences of young people need to ensure, as far as possible, that 'the key participants in all of this – offenders, victims and their families – actually … take charge' (Gelsthorpe and Morris, 2002: 249). The contradictory measures and conflicting signals of the Crime and Disorder Act 1998 could have been expected to compromise restorative principles in the absence of further reforms to promote mutually determined arrangements for addressing the consequences of the offence and putting things right.

A problem-solving approach will also need to be more broadly based than simply focusing on 'making amends'. The one-dimensional preoccupation with the offender *as an offender*, reflected in the restricted emphasis of instruments such as ASSET, creates an arbitrary and unsustainable separation between the young person concerned and her/his circumstances, needs and perspective.[3] The commission of an offence does not simply represent an atomised inter-action between free-standing individuals, where one is in the wrong and the other is simply wronged. It is rather the culmination of a series of inter-connected dynamics and influences, including family background, peer group expectations, cultural norms, personal experiences, educational needs and mental health, not to mention structural factors such as racism and poverty. Whether we think in broad systemic terms, or in terms of immediate con-textual influences, these are all relevant and therefore need to be addressed in any response.

Voluntarism

As youth justice has moved to progressively more prescriptive and mandatory interventions at all levels, so we are losing sight of an important principle, which follows from the previous discussion. At the heart of progressive and inclusive practice, we must seek to engage young people on their own terms, ensuring their active and explicit commitment to resolving the problems associated with their wrongdoing. It is not therefore merely a technical question as to whether restorative measures can 'work' when they are imposed rather than negotiated; it is also an important defining feature of the overall char-acter of the youth justice system. The attraction of imposing swift and certain solutions cuts across the opportunities available for achieving social inclusion and reconciliation, wherein the offender genuinely accepts responsibility.

As already observed, serious doubts must be raised about the value and meaning of measures that might claim to be restorative, but which depend for their implementation on coercion and threat. Thus, where 'the courts ... *direct* personal apologies, [this] may lead to grudging or insolent attitudes being displayed when young offenders meet their victims' (Gelsthorpe and Morris, 2002: 247). The impression gained is that reparation has not always been particularly meaningful, whether to offenders or to victims (Holdaway *et al.*, 2001), with routine and demeaning tasks being required of young offenders in the name of making good (Haines and O'Mahony, 2006), and with 'letters of apology being rehearsed by hard-pressed YOT [Youth Offending Team] workers anxious to get young people through' (Gelsthorpe and Morris, 2002: 248).

Whilst some (Masters, 2005) have suggested that young people's consent is unimportant, others (Haines and O'Mahony, 2006) take the view that their commitment to the process is crucial, both in relation to the genuineness of their efforts to make amends, and also in terms of their perceptions of the justice system and 'their wider social situation' (Haines and O'Mahony, 2006: 122).

It should perhaps be recalled from earlier chapters that, whilst most young offenders do not take issue with the need for rules and sanctions, they are often antagonistic to the manner in which these are applied (Lyon *et al.*, 2000). It may seem, on the face of things, that the consent of the young person is irrelevant in a context where their criminal behaviour means that they forfeit the right to be consulted. However, this point is implicitly conceded in the (limited) incorporation of the young person's viewpoint in the ASSET exercise; and at the same time securing compliance without commitment seems of limited value in terms of securing active consent or lasting change.

It is also important to consider the wider question of legitimacy, and the extent to which young people are encouraged or dissuaded from according this to the criminal process. As the previous chapter shows, there is a substantial degree of mistrust directed towards youth justice agencies, not just among those who offend, but among the wider population of young people – and this is felt even more acutely among specific subgroups, including young black people.[4] The problem here is that loss of trust, in broad terms, is likely to be exacerbated by an over-emphasis on coercion within the machinery of the justice system. So to ignore the need for consent is merely to compound a wider sense of injustice.

In light of this, it may be relevant to note that a range of community sentences (Probation Orders, Community Service Orders and Supervision Orders) actually required the consent of the offender before they could be imposed until quite recently. Clearly, 'consent' in these circumstances is very heavily circumscribed, but it does indicate an historic acceptance within the justice system of the need to engage with those responsible for offences and to secure their agreement to the disposals proposed, in turn suggesting a principled commitment to notions of personal responsibility and social solidarity. Assuming that at some level these aspirations remain feasible as well as desirable, they might point towards a broader refocusing of the principles of youth justice. As Lea argues, given the right social conditions, we should be entitled to expect that 'communities could take the law into their own hands again ... Relations of trust and solidarity will be enabled to replace those of risk and unpredictability. Social inclusion will enable robust communities to sort out a large proportion of their own disputes' (Lea, 2002: 189).

For this to be achieved, however, the state needs to take a lead role in promoting, rather than circumscribing, personal and social responsibility through pursuing voluntarism as a fundamental principle of youth justice.

Minimum intervention

These aspirations also help to generate a persuasive logic in favour of the principle of pursuing the least intrusive and coercive means of intervention achievable, since this is clearly consistent with the agenda of rights, problem-solving and voluntarism already set out here. Whilst the UK government has committed itself to this principle since 1991 through its adoption of the UN Convention on the Rights of the Child (Articles 37 and 40, in particular), along with other international instruments (Goldson and Muncie, 2006b), it has repeatedly been taken to task for failing to comply with this obligation (UN Committee on the Rights of the Child, 2002, 2008).

On purely pragmatic grounds, of course, it is extraordinarily wasteful to rely on expensive, ineffective and excessive machinery of control (Smith, 2001). The relatively high cost of custody as compared to community disposals has been repeatedly demonstrated (Goldson, 2006: 150). However, as community sentences, too, have become progressively 'toughened up', these will also become more expensive to administer, and it would therefore seem to make good economic sense not to use them unless stringent criteria are met.[5]

Regrettably, the expansion of available custodial options and the dilution of safeguards against its use, stemming from the mid-1990s onwards, ensured that the thresholds for the use of prison for young people were clearly lowered, as is confirmed by the statistical evidence (Simes and Chads, 2002). The sustained increases in the use of custody over a number of years (Goldson, 2006: 145) suggested a system out of control, rather than one that was rigorous and rational in setting limits to the use of extreme measures such as the deprivation of liberty.

Not only is the excessive use of measures of containment and control inefficient in economic terms, but it is also ineffective in terms of the 'principal aim' specified for the youth justice system of reducing youth crime. The evidence of the failure of custody to reduce further offending is compelling (Muncie, 1999b; Goldson, 2006); this is perhaps unsurprising, given that a period of incarceration represents a severe rupture in the lives of those who are locked up (Goldson, 2006: 147), and that the experience itself is often oppressive and demoralising (Goldson and Peters, 2000).

Of course, a rather more important consideration than the inefficiency and ineffectiveness of such measures in terms of system goals is the damage caused to young people, for which there is copious evidence (Lyon *et al.*, 2000; Goldson and Coles, 2005; Carlile, 2006). The most dramatic and severe injustices perpetrated in the name of youth justice, and its most divisive and discriminatory impact, are inevitably experienced through the needless use of custody. At a point in time when there has been a significant decrease in the use of custodial sentences for young people in England and Wales (although the rate of use remains significantly higher than in many other countries; Hazel, 2008), it is important to continue to support this development, through focusing interventions on those most clearly on the margins of incarceration. At the same time, of course, the reduced costs of custody should be expected to enable government to meet its commitments under the UN Convention by ensuring that children (including 17 year olds) who are detained are not held in prison custody but in establishments governed by the safeguards and rights embedded in children's legislation.

Inclusion

Rather than seeing historic failures compounded through ill-conceived coercive measures, the core of youth justice practices should be informed by the principle of inclusion, ironically one that has been promulgated extensively by government in recent times. It is an attractive notion, suggesting the possibility of achieving a greater sense of social solidarity and mutuality, and in this respect government's aspirations should be applauded. Garland (2001), too, provides theoretical justification for this by contrasting it with the kind of 'exclusionary' criminology to which it is opposed. As he puts it, those policies that set offenders apart, representing them as 'the other', are likely to have divisive consequences on a broader scale. They are likely to institutionalise oppressive and discriminatory practices that are both based upon and sustaining of inequality. By contrast, an inclusive approach to youth justice will seek to reintegrate those who are on the outside with their communities and the wider society, to promote their acceptance as fellow citizens, and to ensure that their offences are dealt with constructively. A forward-looking strategy based on personal and social development should therefore be emphasised.

This distinction between ways of thinking about the justice system highlights one of the central contradictions of the New Labour project, which attempted to keep a foot in both camps, adopting policies geared towards inclusion in some respects (see Chapter 3), whilst at the same time pursuing policies and practices that worked to mark out and exclude those who did not comply with normative expectations, who did not behave responsibly or who rejected the opportunities available to them.

Even within the field of youth justice these contradictions are apparent, with 'inclusive' measures borrowed from France (Pitts, 2001b), such as the Youth Inclusion Projects, competing for both resources and ideological justification with the 'exclusive' model of justice associated with the USA (electronic monitoring, surveillance and behavioural programmes). Even with a change of government, and an apparent change of ethos, questions remain about the extent, impact and justifications for the use of technologies of surveillance and control, which might appear to offer the benefits of certainty and economy, but remain a significant threat to the wider goal of 'rehabilitation' (Crook, 2013). Ultimately, these two objectives are incompatible, and the evidence we have considered here demonstrates unquestionably that the inclusive agenda must be prioritised (Hughes and Follett, 2006).

The way ahead: working at different levels

Beyond setting out the foregoing set of principles to inform future developments in youth justice, it is also important to propose some concrete suggestions by which these aspirations could be realised and sustained, or at least to suggest some practical steps along the road. In order to do so, it may be helpful to follow the structure introduced earlier (Harris and Webb, 1987) and suggest options to be pursued at each of the 'macro', 'mezzo' and 'micro' levels.

Implicit in this, of course, is an assumption about the power relationships between these levels, and the extent to which there is a hierarchy of influence stemming from the level of government and policy ('macro'), through the intermediate structures and agencies ('mezzo'), to the level of practice and first-line management ('micro'). Whilst some have suggested that this model may underestimate the extent to which 'street level bureaucrats' are able to work independently and creatively to develop good practice (Crawford and Newburn, 2003: 236), the evidence we have considered suggests that this remains an uneven relationship, as these authors also seem to acknowledge (Crawford and Newburn, 2003: 222).

Global coalitions – pie in the sky?

As globalisation becomes more of a reality, and as international frameworks become more firmly established (Goldson and Muncie, 2006a), there may be some value in beginning our exploration of the 'macro' level with a consideration of the potential for change offered by these developments. If we do not look beyond the national context, it may seem that suggestions such as the 'decriminalisation' of childhood wrongdoing are too far-fetched. However, it is possible to look to other states not too far away, to see that they may have a quite different view of crime and criminality in relation to young people (the age of criminal responsibility in Spain and Portugal is 16, and for Belgium it is 18; Goldson and Muncie, 2006a: 219).

In a rather different vein, Lea (2002) also argues that a global perspective is important, suggesting that a major restructuring of social relations is a necessary prerequisite of a fair and humane justice system:

> There must be a fundamental redistribution of economic and welfare resources to poor communities, both within advanced capitalist countries and on a global scale. This will enable the disconnection from dependence

> on criminality, violence and the violation of the rights of others like oneself as a survival necessity ... But [despite this] there will be a need for criminal justice agencies to facilitate dispute resolution by providing legal resources to track people down and bring disputants together and to furnish legal frameworks for handling disputes.
>
> (Lea, 2002: 189)

Thus, social transformation will not remove the need for criminal justice systems and processes, but these will be driven democratically by the emergence of a broad global coalition of 'social groups, political and voluntary organisations [and] non-governmental organisations' (Lea, 2002: 191), which might include those already engaged in the delivery of youth justice, with the skills and experience to develop the new problem-solving legal frameworks envisaged. So, in Lea's view, broad transformations at the global level must be mirrored by practical initiatives at the level of communities and individuals. This is an important connection to make, although it clearly leaves unexplored the intermediate steps by which such changes can be achieved.

Youth justice and social inclusion

Opportunities are provided, for example, in the political rhetoric currently being espoused, and the policy agendas being pursued. As already suggested, it is important that consistency is achieved between youth justice strategies and the broader aim of ending social exclusion and promoting a more cohesive society. It is clearly important that the specific policies and structures that underpin youth justice do not contradict or undermine these aspirations. Thus, shortcomings of policy and failures of practice will need to be addressed, not just because they are not likely to be effective in terms of reducing crime levels, but also because they are not consistent with the goal of achieving social inclusion. Thus, there is a need to bring an end to measures that set offenders apart, and create barriers between them and the wider community, such as the Anti-Social Behaviour Order, segregated education provision, and 'targeting' of potential offenders from an early age.

Curbing custody

On revisiting the first edition of this book (Smith, 2003), I recognised that it should have been stronger in its support of an 'abolitionist' approach to youth custody (Mathiesen, 1974; Fionda, 2005; Goldson and Muncie, 2006a). Given that this is still unlikely to be achieved in the short term, however, it seems reasonable to suggest interim measures that will support this goal. For example, as in other countries, a clear limit could be set for the number of secure places available for young people. The Children's Society (1988, 1993) calculated, for example, that the number of secure places required for those under 17 throughout England and Wales would be no more than 500. At the same time, building on limited progress in this direction (ADSS *et al.*, 2003), all secure settings for children and young people should be brought unequivocally under the protections, standards and operational requirements of child care legislation, such as the Children Act 1989 and the UN Convention on the Rights of the Child (see Goldson and Coles, 2005).

Minimum intervention and children's rights

Again, in terms of immediate policy objectives, it is important to re-emphasise those objectives to which national government is committed in principle, but which are not being honoured in practice, such as minimum intervention. The use of informal means of dealing with offences should be pursued more robustly (Fionda, 2005), and greater flexibility in the use of pre-court diversion utilised, as is clearly signposted by the Legal Aid, Sentencing and Punishment (LASPO) Act 2012. At the same time, it is important to revisit the longstanding argument for the raising of the age of criminal responsibility in line with international norms. Scotland and Ireland (Northern and Republic) have made recent moves in this direction (Lipscombe, 2012), and it has been considered by previous governments for England and Wales.[6]

Criticisms of the UK's performance by the UN Committee on the Rights of the Child have been stringent (Muncie, 2009; Smith, 2010), and would seem to require a full and committed response. In fact, at one point it was made clear that 'the Committee notes with serious concern that the situation of children in conflict with the law has worsened' (UN Committee on the Rights of the Child, 2002: 15). Despite subsequent gestures towards making improvements, the committee remained strongly critical in its 2008 report (Muncie, 2009), and concerns persist in key areas such as the use of physical 'restraint' in secure settings (Muncie, 2009: 207). The UK government has also shown a continuing reluctance to take the lead in committing itself to the implementation of internationally agreed guidelines on best practice in youth justice, and its wavering support for the Human Rights Act 1998 suggests, too, a lack of support for the 'social' rights of young people implicated in the justice system.

Such instruments, if incorporated enthusiastically into the judicial process, should ensure that family life is not disrupted by the imposition of intrusive and punitive orders, whether these are measures of community control or custodial sentences, only allowing children's liberty to be curtailed as a 'last resort' (UN Committee on the Rights of the Child, 2002). Likewise, these measures should ensure that punitive pre-trial restrictions (bail conditions, surveillance or curfews) would no longer be acceptable to the extent that they impose penal sanctions on young people prior to a finding of guilt.

Problem solving and policy

I suggested in the previous edition that a 'problem-solving' (restorative) approach to youth crime could complement a rights-based minimum intervention strategy quite well. Relatively small-scale legislative and policy changes would facilitate this quite substantial reorientation of the shape of youth justice. For example, removal of the arbitrary ceilings placed on the use of Reprimands and 'Final' Warnings would create space for a much more flexible approach to pre-court disposals, as would explicit approval of the use of non-recordable informal measures where appropriate. The new (2013) cautioning framework and its supporting guidance (Walker and Harvey-Messina, 2012) have been designed with just this end in mind, allowing for repeated use of the same disposal, reversal of the normal tariff-based escalation of disposals and an increased use of informal measures.

Similarly, extension of the availability of the Referral Order would ensure greater scope for mediated settlements whilst also reducing the dominance of the retributive sentencing tariff. Whilst the previous government did make some modest steps in this direction by proposing 'a limited extension to Referral Orders to allow them on a later court appearance, for example where the young person has not previously received one, or did so at least two years ago' (Home Office, 2004b: 11), it was only the incoming coalition government that ensured that repeated use of the order became a standard option for courts (Ministry of Justice, 2012d), as well as ensuring that it no longer supplanted the use of discharges, as had been the case previously.

Such approaches are also associated with the emergence of a broader range of essentially restorative interventions, which concentrate on resolving the problems associated with an offence, whether these relate to the feelings of the victim or the offender's needs (Smith, 1989; Rutherford, 1992). In Italy, a problem-based approach is embedded in youth justice practice:

> these are all youths with big problems and dealing with these must be the best way of solving the problems youths represent for the legal system.
> (Juvenile court judge, quoted in Nelken, 2006: 173)

Government is clearly in a position to initiate such moves towards a youth justice system that is inclusive, and limits the adverse potential consequences of 'labelling' (McAra and McVie, 2010); in the case of England and Wales, this would bring this aspect of its programme into line with the broader agenda of promoting children's 'well-being'. At the same time, this might also open up possibilities for the development of a greater sense of order and cohesion within communities (Haines and O'Mahony, 2006; Hancock, 2006), and give some substance to the vague notion of the 'Big Society' (Hollingsworth, 2012; Morgan, 2012).

Of course, such steps also depend on maintaining the political will to move away from the attractions of inflammatory and misleading populist rhetoric, and on recognising the need for 'joined-up' policies:

> *No More Excuses* promised that the Crime and Disorder Bill would establish prevention as a statutory aim of the youth justice system ... That is

radical and encouraging – as long as preventive policies are not seen as solely the responsibility of the youth justice system and as long as its strategies are genuinely proactive, preventive and not simply reactive in the face of emergent problems of delinquency. Crime prevention has to be a concern of all public policies.

(George and Wilding, 1999: 194)

Of course, all the available evidence (see previous chapters) suggests that the youth justice system itself is poorly placed to do much about preventing or reducing crime. Indeed, such progressive measures as the coalition government put in place in the specific context of youth justice are massively undermined in the context of its broader agenda of driving down living standards in order to meet the economic needs of crisis capitalism (Hollingsworth, 2012: 255); of course, the youth justice system itself has borne its share of the post-2010 cuts in resources. Socially inclusive crime prevention measures could, nonetheless, be much better resourced if funding were to be shifted into the community and away from the expensive and ineffective machinery for processing and punishing young offenders currently in place. Futher reducing the throughput of the system would, of course, enable this kind of constructive refocusing to take place.

Oiling the wheels: the 'mezzo' level

Naturally, change cannot be achieved simply by putting the right policies in place and then 'rolling them out' to achieve the desired outcomes, despite the sometimes rather naive assumptions of policy makers themselves:

The Government's reforms of the youth court in England and Wales will help to shape a more effective youth justice system for the next century. The approach combines the principles of restorative justice with more traditional punitive measures, which must be available to the courts to protect the public. The overall result should be a more streamlined and effective system, with a clearer focus on preventing offending.

(Home Office, 1997b: 34)

Grandstanding rhetoric was not the exclusive preserve of the former government, however, as is clear from the following extract from *Breaking the Cycle*:

Our plans represent a fundamental break with the failed and expensive policies of the past. They are about finding out what works – the methods of punishment and rehabilitation which actually reduce crime by reducing the number of criminals. I believe they constitute a bold vision for more effective punishments, more reparation, and by breaking the cycle of crime, a safer public.

(Clarke, 2010: 2)

By the same token, it should be noted that bombastic policy claims do not inevitably lead to bad practice and undesirable outcomes. The history of youth justice is, in fact, littered with misguided policies, generating unrealistic expectations, unintended consequences and unresolved contradictions. There has been therefore, a substantial and continuing challenge facing those whose responsibility is to organise and make possible the delivery of effective interventions, both practitioners and those at the 'mezzo' level responsible for interpreting and adapting policy and delivering systems and strategies, including the Youth Justice Board, local partnerships, agencies, the courts and penal institutions. At this level rests the obligation to make sense of national policy and translating it into operational guidance.

At the same time, an important responsibility for those at this intermediate level is sometimes overlooked, and that is to pass messages in the other direction as well, as Pitts (2002) reminds us. It is important that those responsible for administering youth justice also recognise their obligations to represent to the concerns of those engaged in direct practice as well as those on the receiving end – that is, those who offend or are affected by the problematic behaviour of young people (Brown, 2005: 126). This role, as a conduit for ideas, evidence, opinion and critical feedback, appears to be underplayed, except perhaps where the message is uncritically affirmative. Equally, there appears to be considerable evidence of 'selective listening' from those on the receiving end of such comment (see *YJ*, formerly *Youth Justice Board News*, as a prime example of this).

The Youth Justice Board: shameless collaborator or 'critical friend'?

Since its establishment as an arm's-length quango, the position of the Youth Justice Board has been problematic; indeed, it is wrought with tension, reflected in its ambiguous position and constantly changing approach. In its early days, it seemed to be concerned primarily with 'franchising and McDonaldising' youth justice services, and overlooking its evaluative and critical responsibilities. With a change of leadership, it appeared subsequently to show signs of taking on more diverse and responsive functions, as indeed it should if it is to serve a useful purpose. These include acting as:

- a 'buffer' between government and the field, encouraging diversity and ironing out inconsistencies in government policy;
- an 'informed adviser' to government and other policy makers on best practice, rather than purveying simplistic and erroneous assumptions;
- a 'champion of rights' of young people and their families as well as victims of crime (especially those groups that experience consistent forms of discrimination);
- a consistent 'purveyor of advice' to practitioners, the judiciary and other interests;

- a 'developer and supporter' of professional youth justice practice, rather than simply promoting a 'homogeneous, offence-oriented' culture; and
- a commissioner and disseminator of wide-ranging and independent research designed to broaden understanding rather than simply to confirm prior assumptions.

(based on Pitts, 2002)

All this suggests a shift of emphasis from a managerial perspective, based on securing routinised compliance with targets, performance indicators and specified measures of 'success', towards a more developmental approach, which encourages and builds on professional innovation and creativity, encourages debate and risk taking, funds critical and exploratory research, and acts as a 'knowledgeable friend' to those in the field.

Some signs of attempts to take up an independent position were initially apparent in tentative expressions of concern over excessive use of custody (Youth Justice Board press release, 22 August 2001, 5 September 2002), and the promotion of community alternatives. However, these were limited and muted until the board's second chair began to take a more explicitly critical view of certain aspects of government policy, such as the use of ASBOs (*The Independent*, 23 April 2006), the unnecessary 'criminalisation' of young people and the unacceptable conditions in some custodial settings (*The Guardian*, 16 August 2006).

Subsequently, the board was able to make more effective use of a favourable tide, as the mood swung back towards diversionary approaches and reduced use of custody. Indeed, with its joint letter to magistrates drawing attention to inconsistencies in sentencing practices, the YJB might even have been able to claim that it had contributed to or perhaps accelerated this process (Duff and Done, 2009), and perhaps that it had begun to deliver on the agenda set out for it by Pitts (2002).

The courts and sentencing bodies as opinion formers

Of course, the YJB is not the only 'middle-range' body with considerable power and influence in the youth justice arena. For instance, the impact of judicial pronouncements (for good or bad) was demonstrated graphically by the imposition of an 'exemplary' custodial sentence by the Lord Chief Justice for the theft of a mobile phone in 2002. The immediate consequence was a rapid sequence of copy-cat sentences around the country (for instance, a 16 year old was sentenced to a three-and-a-half-year jail term for robbery of a phone on 8 February 2002 at Sheffield Crown Court). One of the consequences, clearly, is that the specific circumstances and characteristics of the offender concerned become subsumed under the wider imperative of 'stamping out' a certain type of behaviour. Such effects are not new, as Hall and colleagues (1978) have demonstrated, and as we witnessed again with the knee-jerk reaction by courts to the 'riots' of 2011 (Roberts and Hough, 2013).

However, the courts need not simply be a source of pressure for more severe sentencing, and their direct contribution to the more lenient ethos within which 'alternatives to custody' came to live up to their name is significant. Rutherford (1992) documented the role of the local magistracy in supporting and promoting the development of one such initiative in Basingstoke, the Woodlands centre. This is a good example of the ability of local networks of agencies, sentencers and practitioners to achieve positive change, even in a punitive climate:

> There was growing despair that the juvenile court did not have local alternatives to incarcerative institutions, and a powerful determination to do something about it. The main initiative was taken by Margaret Baring, chairperson of the juvenile court. She and other magistrates, the clerk to the court and other local people wanted a programme which did more than pack young people and canoes into a mini-bus.
>
> (Rutherford, 1992: 136)

It is perhaps no coincidence that Hampshire became one of the pioneers of the 'custody-free zones', which became a feature of significant numbers of local youth justice systems throughout England and Wales in the 1980s.[7]

A more recent example of the progressive use of judicial influence was the then lord chief justice's attempt to encourage his colleagues to consider non-custodial options for first- and second-time burglars (Woolf, 2002) – somewhat ironic in view of his earlier pronouncements on mobile-phone theft. The Sentencing Guidelines Council established in 2004 may also have an increasing role in influencing practice in this respect, too, and it is of interest that this body has sought to resist what it perceives as unhelpful media influence (Phillips, 2006). The council's further elaboration of 'overarching principles' for sentencing young people also helpfully stressed the importance of taking certain welfare considerations into account, and encouraged courts not to feel bound by the assumption of a progressive tariff (Sentencing Guidelines Council, 2009).

Effective agency coalitions

Progressive developments in other aspects of the youth justice process have been identified, for example in Northamptonshire, where the achievement of consistently high levels of diversion for young offenders was attributable to close and committed inter-agency collaboration (Smith, 1989). Interestingly, the police were prime movers in this initiative. The continuing emphasis on partnership and inter-agency working that has permeated youth justice since the 1998 reforms (and through *Every Child Matters*, too) has continued to give rise to similar opportunities, such as the collaborative arrangements supporting out-of-court diversion in Durham and other local authority areas (Eshelby, 2011). However, this also depends on sustaining the ability to establish a degree of independence and meet the essential requirements of a shared vision and collective commitment. Poulantzas's (1978) notion of 'relative autonomy' provides theoretical support for the idea that specific coalitions of interest can arise, even within highly centralised frameworks of power and bureaucracy, indicating that these groups will have the capacity to set their own terms of reference and act independently. The emergence of the 'localism' agenda under the coalition government has given further practical substance to this argument. Clearly, different practices do arise in different areas given our knowledge of the substantial geographical variation in interventions and outcomes (Feilzer and Hood, 2004: 95). The task then is to share and build upon the experience of those that demonstrate a consistently progressive and principled approach in this respect.

The power of the inspectors

Other significant actors at the 'mezzo' level are the regulatory bodies, including the various inspectorates and auditing authorities that have an interest in youth justice, and the impact of which on policy and practice can be significant (Audit Commission, 1996, for example). The work of the Prison Inspectorate has been of particular interest in this respect, with a series of strongly critical reports challenging the unacceptable treatment of young people in custody, and a clear underlying commitment to promote the human rights of children who are locked up. The extent to which these criticisms will have a cumulative effect is perhaps unclear, given the other influences at play, but they have clearly affected the behaviour of individual regimes (Travis, 2002).

Further evidence of the potentially valuable contribution of the inspectors has been provided by the report of a collaborative exercise, *Safeguarding Children*, which found that:

> the welfare needs of young people who commit offences were not being adequately addressed by those services responsible for their welfare. There were no national minimum standards for the work of YOTs, and there was no regular inspection of their work. They were operating largely in isolation from other services in most areas.
>
> (Joint Chief Inspectors, 2002: 69)

Given the importance of collaboration, as set out above, and given that YOTs were established precisely to encourage joint working, this was particularly damning criticism.[8]

The report concluded that young people in custody were still seriously at risk, and that youth justice services generally were paying insufficient attention to the protection and safeguarding of children's welfare. A more proactive role for Area Child Protection Committees was recommended (see also Smith, 2002b), and the report's conclusions were at least partly responsible for the increased emphasis on collaboration reflected in the *Every Child Matters* reform agenda.

Subsequent reports, however, have still identified serious concerns about the treatment of children in custody (see Summerfield, 2011, for example), further underlining the importance of a principled approach to the inspectorial function of shining a light on hidden practices.

Campaign groups and collective interests

It is also important to acknowledge the role of a rather different kind of middle-range organisation – that is, the various representative bodies, trade unions, lobby groups and voluntary organisations that all perform an important function in casting a critical gaze over areas where change may be required. Such networks act as collective whistle-blowers, as well as a site for risk taking and innovation, which would not otherwise be sanctioned or financially supported. The role of bodies such as the National Association for Youth Justice is particularly important, for example, through its work in formulating and disseminating a clear philosophical base and manifesto for action (NAYJ, 2002, 2006).

The extent to which these alternative sources of power, knowledge and influence might lead to change over time is always unpredictable, but they do provide a focal point for critical thinking and practical opposition to prevailing norms and practices. We should not be as pessimistic as those left-wing 'functionalists' such as Althusser (1977) who saw power as flowing only in one direction. Resistance is possible, and others have suggested that 'institution building' at the local and community level is a central part of any strategy to create an inclusive and just society (George and Wilding, 1999). The experience of communities in Northern Ireland in trying to develop their own frameworks and practices to deliver youth justice is a strong case example in support of this proposition, despite the problematic aspects of these initiatives, which have also been acknowledged (Schrag, 2003; Eriksson, 2006).

Local agencies and community and professional interests, therefore, have a key role to play in generating approaches to youth crime that engage those who are affected and attract their commitment, especially in a context of effective abandonment by the state under the fig leaf of promoting 'localism' (Drew, 2012).

Following Scarman's (1982) prescription for the police, it seems that we should be pursuing active strategies to secure 'youth justice by consent'. Crawford and Newburn (2003: 236), for example, have suggested that, whatever its shortcomings, the Referral Order provides one such opportunity to engage with communities in the process of 'reworking' youth justice to promote 'the principles of "inclusivity, reciprocity, appreciation and tolerance"' – a prospect that might become more significant following the coalition government's enhancement of the order's status: 'The referral order is a unique sentence directly involving the local community, by means of the volunteer youth offender panel members, in holding the young offender to account for their actions' (Ministry of Justice, 2012d).

The search for progressive practice at the 'micro' level

It is probably right to conclude with some observations about the possibilities for working to deliver constructive and effective practice within youth justice, according to the principles outlined earlier. These ideas have been developed more fully elsewhere (see, for example, Crawford and Newburn, 2003; Bateman and Pitts, 2005), but here the aim will be to concentrate on a few areas of significant potential and certain key themes.

Informal justice

As noted previously, the principle of 'voluntarism' is crucially important, not just because it can lead to a reduction in the use of punitive measures, but also because it aims to secure the active engagement of young people rather than their passive compliance. This leads, in turn, to a renewed emphasis on promoting diversionary approaches (Goldson and Muncie, 2006a) and informal action – given that they represent a non-criminalising, quick and cheap way of resolving minor infractions. In some parts of England and Wales, it appears that informal action is promoted as a strategic option, and this perhaps represents another example of 'justice by geography'. Wherever the opportunity arises, practitioners should seek to pursue offence resolution by this means. Not only does this strategy ensure that young people's misdemeanours are dealt with outside the statutory (and criminalising) framework, but it also creates space for a more genuine engagement with young people, their families and their victims to reach mutually agreed solutions, without unnecessary pressure to contrive a 'happy ending'.

Equally, in terms of system efficiency, this approach to minimum intervention removes a substantial and needless burden from youth justice agencies, and notably the police. This would, of itself, contribute substantially to other objectives such as 'speeding up' youth justice, purely by removing large numbers of cases from the formal system – allowing more time to be devoted to other matters of public concern (such as lack of community policing and low clear-up rates). The challenge here is to resist at all points the persistent logic (Foucault, 1979) that insists that all infractions are recorded, accounted for and processed in the cause of routinised discipline and control.

Making sense of restorative practice

Given that 'restorative justice' has become the dominant discourse under which problem solving and negotiated interventions are subsumed, it is important to consider the implications for progressive practice of this development. It is clearly a contested term, and the argument here is that the quality of the process is more important than meeting prescribed targets, such as specified participation rates for victims (Masters, 2005). Interventions based on the principles of reconciliation and 'making good' are most likely to be effective when they are carefully planned and have genuine meaning for those involved – that is, the offender, victim and other interested parties (Smith, 1985; Dignan, 2005) – and where the issues to be resolved are mutually agreed and clearly understood.

In many cases, though these conditions cannot be met straight-forwardly, for example where the young person's formal 'guilt' is mediated by a history of mutual hostility between different groups within the community. The constraints of the justice system do not easily lend themselves to dealing with ambiguity and unfinished business, but restorative processes need to avoid the tendency to abstract criminal matters from their personal and social context (see Bradley *et al.*, 2006, on the New Zealand experience, too); rather, they must ensure that these are factored into the proceedings – this means ensuring that offenders and victims are able to influence the restorative 'agenda', as well as determining significant practical issues, such as where and when meetings will take place, and who should attend.

As well as being largely meaningless for offenders, contrived 'restorative' solutions are also often unsatisfactory for victims, as the initial evaluation of Referral Orders amply demonstrated (Newburn *et al.*, 2002). The position of 'corporate' (private or public sector) victims is also problematic, as are the views young people may have of such interests. Thus, for practitioners the challenge is one of thinking widely and creatively about how to achieve real-world 'restoration' free from the constraints of tightly prescribed operational parameters, such as those established by Final Warnings (until 2013), Referral Orders or Reparation Orders. In contrast to Masters (2005), I would argue that it is clear that a consultative approach is required, which relies on developing a clear understanding of participants' perspectives on the offence, and the ideas young people themselves may have about how to deal with the problems arising from it. They are, indeed, often remorseful, apologetic and willing to make amends, sometimes perhaps because of their own experiences of being victimised, but these responses cannot be extorted from them; it is a process of engagement and dialogue that may, necessarily, take time.

Managing the system and avoiding the tariff

Whilst the introduction of a range of highly prescriptive new orders appears to impose additional constraints on both young people and practitioners, it has also created possibilities for 'system management' (Smith, 2002a). The espousal of restorative principles, as well as the 'principal aim' of reducing offending, has generated support for approaches to intervention that are less tariff-based than in the immediate past. Further steps, as signposted by the Sentencing Guidelines Council and the LASPO legislation in relation to out-of-court disposals and Referral Orders, along with the earlier introduction of the youth rehabilitation order, also suggest a gradual loosening of the idea that sentencing should be progressively more intrusive and punitive.

The principle that sentencing should be 'proportionate' (Youth Justice Board, 2000), allied with the range of requirements of sentencers proposed by the Home Office (2003b: 4), and the more recent modification of the disposal 'tariff' (Walker and Harvey-Messina, 2012) indicates that the rationale for progressively more severe sentences might have been eroded somewhat. However, this sits rather oddly with the residual armoury of assessment tools and measures consistent with an 'actuarial' approach to the gradation (Foucault, 1979; Smith, 2006) of risk and seriousness, which may still influence decisions and outcomes, such as the route by which young people progress to the status of 'persistent young offender' with all the implications associated with that particular label.

Despite these tensions, the emerging recognition of the value of 'restorative' approaches does provide some support for alternatives to the narrow actuarialism that has previously pervaded the youth justice system (Kempf-Leonard and Peterson, 2002). It is important that practice reflects this orientation, and avoids the tendency to regard 'failure' (such as non-compliance with the terms of a specific order) as an automatic justification for a further escalation of the sanctions applied to any young person. Rather, we should adopt Rutherford's (1992) approach of 'holding on', showing support and commitment to young people in trouble, and offering them opportunities to 'grow out of crime'.

Refocusing: welfare and rights

An intervention strategy that is based on dealing with young people holistically, and considering the factors underlying the offence, also implies an approach to assessment, planning and intervention that is not driven by the spurious scientific accuracy offered by instruments such as ASSET (Baker *et al.*, 2005). Rather, we should reassert the importance of 'causes', and at the same time reintroduce proper concern with the 'welfare' principles that were crowded out of the youth justice system (Joint Chief Inspectors, 2002),[9] at least until the 'rehabilitation revolution' was announced (Ministry of Justice, 2010; see also, Baker, 2012).

As well as rediscovering 'welfare', we must also be driven by socially based notions of 'justice' that take proper account of factors such as inequality, poverty and discrimination. Bowling and Phillips (2002), as we have seen, argue that, to be genuinely fair, interventions must take account of prior factors such as institutional racism and disadvantage. It is not simply a matter of applying standard rules and procedures even-handedly, but of adjusting these to offset their impact on young people from particular origins. Legislative attempts to introduce equalising principles into judicial processes (such as 'day fines' under the Criminal Justice Act 1991) have not been successful, but it remains open for practitioners and provider agencies to incorporate notions of social as well as criminal justice into their work.

In line with this approach, consideration should be given to bringing 'rights' more explicitly into the practice arena, even where this might prejudice smooth running and efficiency. As young people become exposed to the risk of an ever-increasing armoury of discretionary interventions, applying at pre-trial (and even pre-criminal) stages, agencies must be concerned with the consequences in terms of net widening (and net strengthening; Austin and Krisberg,

2002). The certainty and security offered by the imposition of ever-more stringent bail conditions, tags or curfews should not be gained at the expense of 'proportionality' or basic rights, especially at the pre-trial stage where questions of guilt and responsibility have not been determined. Home visits, for example, are a better, more natural and less oppressive option than electronic tags, and they are certainly less likely to represent a breach of the UN Convention on the Rights of the Child or the Human Rights Act 1998. We must avoid contributing to the furtherance of the 'technologies of control' envisaged by Foucault (1979), and instead pursue an agenda of 'welfare rights' (Scraton and Haydon, 2002) that engages with young people, linking their offending to other aspects of their lives, establishing sensitive and effective working relationships with them and their families (Smith and Fleming, 2011).

As we have seen throughout this book, the youth justice system is poorly equipped to do many of the things it claims to address, such as preventing crime, meeting victims' needs or administering fair and effective punishment. Those of us concerned with effective practice must recognise these limitations in order to put forward alternative strategies that prioritise bridge building and solution finding rather than social division and oppression. This is not about criminalising young people who offend, but addressing the problems associated with their crimes, both individual and social, in order to find mutually beneficial ways forward.

Lessons from elsewhere

Briefly, before concluding, it will be helpful to reflect on the growing body of evidence from elsewhere, which offers some optimistic (and some less encouraging) signs (see, for example, Muncie and Goldson, 2006; Hazel, 2008). Buckland and Stevens (2001) suggest, for example, that there are 'significant differences' of approach, even amongst European countries. These differences are to be found, it seems, at the level of culture, philosophy and purpose, as much as in direct practice (see also Lappi-Seppala, 2006; Nelken, 2006), even though there is a common fear of increasing punitiveness (Muncie and Goldson, 2006).

Some fundamental variations in orientation can be identified. France is less inclined to use custody than England (Christie, 2000), as are Japan and Sweden (Hazel, 2008), although such predispositions may be periodically threatened, as in the Netherlands (Beijerse and Swaaningen, 2006; Gendrot, 2006). Pitts (2001b) has contrasted the inclusive philosophy informing youth crime policy and 'Specialised Prevention' in France, and what he calls the 'politics of blame' that have underpinned debate in England and Wales.

Spain and Belgium are identified as being strongly committed to 'welfare approaches' (Buckland and Stevens, 2001; Hazel, 2008), which have generally held firm against the punitive drift evident elsewhere (Muncie and Goldson, 2006). Diversion of children towards 'social welfare methods', as opposed to punishment, is identified as the starting position for interventions in Scandinavian countries (Goldson and Muncie, 2006b; Hazel, 2008).

Interestingly, too, there is clear evidence of increasing divergence between the countries of Britain and the Republic of Ireland, with 'diversion' remaining central to strategies in Scotland (Scottish Executive, 2002) and Ireland (Seymour, 2004; Fionda, 2005), and 'welfare' re-emerging as a central theme in Wales (Cross *et al.*, 2003), although Muncie (2011) raises a cautionary note about the true extent of such divergence under the umbrella of a common governmental framework. Nonetheless, a distinctive emphasis on community-based justice and locally supported interventions has been evident in both policy and practice in Scotland and Northern Ireland:

> We need youth justice teams to listen to the concerns of local communities to tackle youth crime and to work with communities to identify solutions to reduce crime and the fear of crime. All those who work with young people who offend will know that many young people can be diverted from crime if effective programmes are in place to tackle their behaviour.
> (Jamieson, 2002)

Under the 'unique' non-criminal children's hearings, Scotland has been able to establish a wide range of interventions to deal with youth offending outside the courts (Scottish Executive, 2004). In Northern Ireland, long experience of conflict and division has generated a greater willingness to seek communal solutions, based in notions of reconciliation (Schrag, 2003). As a result, there has been considerable impetus behind a range of imaginative community-based restorative initiatives, which have, in turn, received positive initial evaluations (Beckett *et al.*, 2005).

Whilst we must not allow ourselves to become too idealistic about positive alternative approaches in evidence elsewhere (the custody rate in Scotland was at one point the highest in Europe; Muncie and Goldson, 2006), other countries are able to demonstrate successful outcomes based on principles of diversion and informal offence resolution, just as England and Wales did in the 1980s (and may be doing again in the 2010s). In the Netherlands and Germany, there have been long-established mechanisms outside the court setting for dealing with the issues arising from young people's offences (Buckland and Stevens, 2001), associated with the higher age of criminal responsibility applying in these countries. Evaluations of such programmes have suggested that they have been successful according to a number of conventional criteria, such as reduced reoffending rates, satisfactory compliance, victim satisfaction, and reductions in the use of formal proceedings and punishment measures (Buckland and Stevens, 2001).

We must be cautious about the quality of such evidence and we must also avoid drawing lessons uncritically from elsewhere ('criminological tourism'), but this does provide international support for approaches that we also know to have been effective domestically. Such evidence offers further validation for the principles of youth justice outlined here. However, we cannot underestimate the economic, cultural and ideological influences which contextualise change:

Devolved and local youth justice remains heavily circumscribed by central government risk-based directives and targets ... The current settlement of the purpose of youth justice in a rationale of *crime prevention* has allowed multiple claims and counterclaims to hold legitimacy. The rationalities of risk, restoration, welfare and rights can all be brought to bear discursively in pursuit of either preventive or punitive goals.

(Muncie, 2011: 51)

Whilst recognising the obstacles, I have sought to set out here some creative possibilities for intervention at all levels of the justice system to promote inclusive, anti-oppressive and rights-based practice. The aim of the first edition was 'to generate some inspiration for reinventing' diversionary, problem-solving, negotiated forms of youth justice, which would act as the touchstone for all aspects of the process, and in this context I referred to the lessons of earlier years. By now, though, against a much-changed policy and practice backdrop, the agenda must be revised. The recent rediscovery of diversion and the growing emphasis on restorative, localised and negotiated forms of justice need to be nurtured, whilst the broader issues of giving young people a voice and, indeed, giving them hope in a bleak climate of austerity is at least as (and probably more) important if they are genuinely to be treated justly and afforded respect.

Notes

1 It is worth reminding ourselves here that the abolition of custody for children and young people seemed a realistic possibility as recently as the early 1990s.
2 Regrettably, successive reports by the UN Committee on the Rights of the Child suggest that the UK government has still to meet all of its obligations in relation to youth justice under the UN Convention (Smith, 2010).
3 The 'What do you think?' section in the revised ASSET represents little more than an afterthought in this respect.
4 We might expect, too, that increased attention directed by justice agencies recently towards young Muslims will be a matter of concern in this respect (see www.ihrc.org.uk/show.php?id=1149).
5 Indeed, in 2005, the criteria for admission to the Intensive Supervision and Surveillance Programme (ISSP) were strengthened somewhat.
6 In fact, the Children and Young Persons Act 1969 included provisions that would have effectively raised the age of criminal responsibility to 14, but these were never implemented.
7 It is also worthy of note that the Audit Commission (2004: 34) identified a positive relationship between courts' level of confidence in local youth justice services and low use of custodial sentences.
8 Despite these critical comments, it was perhaps surprising that YOTs were applauded for their collaborative practice only a short while later by the Chief Inspector of Probation (Bridges, 2004).
9 An important point of divergence was the *All Wales Youth Offending Strategy* issued jointly by the Welsh Assembly Government and the Youth Justice Board in 2004, which was much more welfare-oriented than anything comparable in England at the time.

References

Abel, R. (1982) 'The Contradictions of Informal Justice', in R. Abel (ed.) *The Politics of Informal Justice, Vol. 1*, London: Academic Press, 267–320.

ADSS (Association of Directors of Social Services), Local Government Association and Youth Justice Board (2003) *The Application of the Children Act 1989 to Children in Young Offender Institutions*, London: ADSS.

AFFOR (1978) *Talking Blues*, Birmingham: AFFOR.

Allan, R. (2001) 'Why ASSET Must be a Real Asset for YOTs', *Youth Justice Board News*, June, 3.

Allen, J., Edmonds, A., Patterson, S. and Smith, D. (2006) *Policing and the Criminal Justice System – Public Confidence and Perceptions: Findings from the 2004/05 British Crime Survey*, London: Home Office.

Allen, R. (2004) 'What Works in Changing Public Attitudes: Lessons from Rethinking Crime and Punishment', *Journal for Crime, Conflict and the Media* 1(3): 55–67.

——(2006) *From Punishment to Problem Solving: A New Approach to Children in Trouble*, London: Centre for Crime and Justice Studies.

——(2007) 'From Punishment to Problem-solving: A New Approach to Children in Trouble', in Z. Davies and W. McMahon (eds) *Debating Youth Justice: From Punishment to Problem-Solving?* London: King's College, 7–53.

——(2011) *Last Resort? Exploring the Reduction in Child Imprisonment 2008–11*, London: Prison Reform Trust.

All-Party Parliamentary Group on Women in the Penal System (2012) *Inquiry on Girls: From Courts to Custody*, London: Howard League.

Althusser, L. (1977) *Lenin and Philosophy and Other Essays*, London: NLB.

Anderson, B., Beinart, S., Farrington, D., Longman, J., Sturgis, P. and Utting, D. (2001) *Risk and Protective Factors Associated with Youth Crime and Effective Interventions to Prevent it*, London: Youth Justice Board.

Anderson, F., Worsley, R., Ninney, F., Maybanks, N. and Dawes, W. (2010) *Youth Survey 2009*, London: Youth Justice Board.

Annison, J. (2005) 'Risk and Protection', in T. Bateman and J. Pitts (eds) *The RHP Companion to Youth Justice*, Lyme Regis: Russell House, 119–24.

Ariès, P. (1962) *Centuries of Childhood*, Vintage: New York.

Armstrong, D., Hine, J., Hacking, S., Armaos, R., Jones, R., Klessinger, N. and France, A. (2005) *Children, Risk and Crime: The on Track Youth Lifestyles Surveys*, London: Home Office.

Armstrong, H. (2007) 'Ministerial Foreword', in Social Exclusion Task Force, *Reaching Out: Think Family*, London: The Stationery Office.

Arnull, E. and Eagle, S. (2009) *Girls and Offending – Patterns, Perceptions and Interventions*, London: Youth Justice Board.

Ashcroft, L. (2011) *Crime, Punishment & the People*, www.lordashcroft.com/pdf/03042011_crime_punishment_and_the_people.pdf, accessed 8 May 2013.

Ashford, B. (2007) *Towards a Youth Crime Prevention Strategy*, London: Youth Justice Board.

Ashton, J. and Grindrod, M. (1999) 'Institutional Troubleshooting: Lessons for Policy and Practice', in B. Goldson (ed.) *Youth Justice: Contemporary Policy and Practice*, Aldershot: Ashgate, 170–90.

Audit Commission (1996) *Misspent Youth*, London: Audit Commission.

——(2002) *Community Safety Partnerships: Learning from Audit, Inspection and Research*, London: The Stationery Office.

——(2004) *Youth Justice 2004*, London: The Stationery Office.

Austin, J. and Krisberg, B. (2002) 'Wider, Stronger and Different Nets: The Dialectics of Criminal Justice Reform', in J. Muncie, G. Hughes and E. McLaughlin (eds) *Youth Justice: Critical Readings*, London: Sage, 258–74.

Bailey, R. and Williams, B. (2000) *Inter-Agency Partnerships in Youth Justice: Implementing the Crime and Disorder Act 1998*, Sheffield: Joint Unit for Social Services Research, University of Sheffield.

Baker, K. (2005) 'Assessment in Youth Justice: Professional Discretion and the Use of Asset', *Youth Justice* 5(2): 106–22.

——(2008) 'Risk, Uncertainty and Public Protection: Assessment of Young People Who Offend', *British Journal of Social Work* 38(8): 1463–80.

——(2012) *Asset Plus Rationale*, London: Youth Justice Board.

Baker, K., Jones, S., Appleton, C. and Roberts, C. (n.d.) *Assessment, Planning Interventions and Supervision*, London: Youth Justice Board.

Baker, K., Jones, S., Roberts, C. and Merrington, S. (2002) *Validity and Reliability of Asset*, London: Youth Justice Board.

——(2003) *ASSET: The Evaluation of the Validity and Reliability of the Youth Justice Board's Assessment for Young Offenders*, London: Youth Justice Board.

Baker, K., Jones, S., Merrington, S. and Roberts, C. (2005) *Further Development of ASSET*, London: Youth Justice Board.

Bandura, A. (1976) *Social Learning Theory*, New York: Prentice Hall.

Barclay, G. and Mhlanga, B. (2000) *Ethnic Differences in Decisions on Young Defendants Dealt with by the Crown Prosecution Service*, London: Home Office.

Barclay, G., Munley, A. and Muntom, T. (2005) *Race and the Criminal Justice System: An Overview to the Complete Statistics 2003–2004*, London: Home Office.

Bateman, T. (2006) 'Youth Crime and Justice: Statistical "Evidence", Recent Trends and Responses', in B. Goldson and J. Muncie (eds) *Youth Crime and Justice*, London: Sage, 65–77.

——(2008) '"Target Practice": Sanction Detection and the Criminalisation of Children', *Criminal Justice Matters* 73(1): 2–4.

——(2011a) '"We Now Breach More Kids in a Week than We Used to in a Whole Year": The Punitive Turn, Enforcement and Custody', *Youth Justice* 11(2): 115–33.

——(2011b) 'Child Imprisonment: Exploring "Injustice by Geography"', *Prison Service Journal* 197: 10–14.

——(2011c) 'Punishing Poverty: The "Scaled Approach" and Youth Justice Practice', *Howard Journal of Criminal Justice* 50(2): 171–83.

——(2012a) 'Children in Conflict with the Law: An Overview of Trends and Developments – 2010/2011', National Association for Youth Justice, thenayj.org.uk/wp-content/files_mf/children_in_conflict_with_the_law_final_22.03.12.pdf, accessed 30 April 2013.

——(2012b) 'Who Pulled the Plug? Towards an Explanation of the Fall in Child Imprisonment in England and Wales', *Youth Justice* 12(1): 36–52.

——(2013) 'Childern in Conflict with the Law: An Overview of Trends and Developments – 2012', National Association for Youth Justice, thenayj.org.uk/wp-content/files_mf/nayj briefingchilderninconflict_withthelaw.pdf, accessed 28 August 2013.

Bateman, T. and Pitts, J. (2005) 'Conclusion: What the Evidence Tells Us', in T. Bateman and J. Pitts (eds) *The RHP Companion to Youth Justice*, Lyme Regis: Russell House, 248–58.

Beaumont, C. (2005) 'Work with Young People Whose Offending is Persistent: Intensive Supervision and Surveillance Programmes', in T. Bateman and J. Pitts (eds) *The RHP Companion to Youth Justice*, Lyme Regis: Russell House.

Beck, U. (1992) *Risk Society*, London: Sage.

Becker, H. (1963) *The Outsiders*, New York: Free Press.

Beckett, H., Campbell, C., O'Mahony, D., Jackson, J. and Doak, J. (2005) *Evaluation of the Youth Conference Pilot Scheme*, Belfast: Northern Ireland Office .

Beijerse, J.u. and Swaaningen, R.v. (2006) 'The Netherlands: Penal Welfarism and Risk Management', in J. Muncie and B. Goldson (eds) *Comparative Youth Justice*, London; Sage, 65–78.

Bell, A., Hodgson, M. and Pragnell, S. (1999) 'Diverting Children and Young People from Crime and the Criminal Justice System', in B. Goldson (ed) *Youth Justice: Contemporary Police and Practice*, London: Ashgate.

Benedict, R. (1961) *Patterns of Culture*, London: Routledge.

Berman, G. (2009) 'Anti-social Behaviour Order Statistics', Standard Note: SN/SG/3112, London: House of Commons Library.

——(2012) *Prison Population Statistics*, House of Commons London: Library.

Berridge, D., Brodie, I., Pitts, J., Porteous, D. and Tarling, R. (2001) *The Independent Effects of Permanent Exclusion from School on the Offending Careers of Young People*, London; Home Office.

BIBIC (British Institute for Brain Injured Children) (2005) *Ain't Misbehavin'*, London: BIBIC.

Birmingham Youth Offending Service (2004) *Birmingham Youth Justice Plan 2004–05*, Birmingham: Birmingham City Council.

Blagg, H. (1985) 'Reparation and Justice for Juveniles', *British Journal of Criminology* 25: 267–79.

Blagg, H., Derricourt, N., Finch, J. and Thorpe, D. (1986) *The Final Report on the Juvenile Liaison Bureau Corby*, Lancaster: University of Lancaster.

Blair, T. (1993) 'Why Crime is a Socialist Issue', *New Statesman*, 29 January, 27–28.

——(1997) Speech, Stockwell Park School, Lambeth, 8 December.

——(2002) 'Rebalancing of Criminal Justice System', speech, 18 June.

Blunkett, D. (2002) Statement on Street Crime, 20 March.

——(2003) 'Foreword', in Home Office, *A Guide to Anti-social Behaviour Orders and Acceptable Behaviour Contracts*, London: Home Office, 2.

Botley, M., Jinks, B. and Metson, C. (2010) *Young People's Views and Experiences of the Youth Justice System*, Leeds: Children's Workforce Development Council .

Bottoms, A. (1977) 'Reflections on the Renaissance of Dangerousness', *Howard Journal* 16: 70–96.

——(1995) *Intensive Community Supervision of Young Offenders: Outcomes, Process and Cost*, Cambridge: University of Cambridge Institute of Criminology.

——(2005) 'Methodology Matters', *Safer Society*, Summer: 10–12.

Bottoms, A., Brown, P., McWilliams, B., McWilliams, W. and Nellis, M. (1990) *Intermediate Treatment and Juvenile Justice*, London: HMSO.

Bourdieu, P. (1990) *The Logic of Practice*, Cambridge: Polity Press.

Bowling, B. and Phillips, C. (2002) *Racism, Crime and Justice*, Harlow: Longman.

Bradley, K. (2009) *The Bradley Report*, London: Royal College of Psychiatrists.

Bradley, T., Tauri, J. and Walters, R. (2006) 'Demythologising Youth Justice in Aotearoa/New Zealand', in J. Muncie and B. Goldson (eds) *Comparative Youth Justice*, London: Sage, 79–95.

Breese, C. (2013) 'New Study on how the Police use Stop and Search Powers in Notts', *Nottingham Post*, 27 February.

Bridges, A. (2004) *Joint Inspection of Youth Offending Teams: The First Phase Annual Report 2004*, London: HM Inspectorate of Probation.

Bright, M. (2002) 'Suicide Fear for Teen Victims of Blunkett's Get-tough Rules', *The Observer*, 7 July, 12.

Britton, N. (2000) *Black Justice? Race, Criminal Justice and Identity*, Stoke on Trent: Trentham Books.

Brogan, D. (2005) *An Assessment of Current Management Information Systems and the Scale of Anti-Social Behaviour Order Breaches Resulting in Custody*, London: Youth Justice Board.

Brown, S. (2005) *Understanding Youth and Crime (2nd Edition)*, Buckingham: Open University Press.

Buckland, G. and Stevens, A. (2001) *Review of Effective Practice with Young Offenders in Mainland Europe*, Canterbury: European Institute of Social Services.

Budd, T. and Sharp, C. (2005) 'Offending in England and Wales: First Results from the 2003 Crime and Justice Survey', *Findings*, 244, London: Home Office.

Budd, T., Sharp, C., Weir, G., Wilson, D. and Owen, N. (2005) *Young People and Crime: Findings from the 2004 Offending, Crime and Justice Survey*, London: Home Office.

Budd, T. and Sims, L. (2001) *Antisocial Behaviour and Disorder: Findings from the 2000 British Crime Survey*, London: Home Office.

Burfeind, J. and Bartusch, D. (2005) *Juvenile Delinquency: An Integrated Approach*, Sudbury, MA: Jones and Bartlett.

Burnett, R. and Appleton, C. (2004) 'Joined-Up Services to Tackle Youth Crime', *British Journal of Criminology* 44: 34–54.

Burnett, R. and Roberts, C. (2004) *What Works in Probation and Youth Justice*, Cullompton: Willan.

Burney, E. (2002) 'Talking Tough, Acting Coy: What Happened to the Anti-Social Behaviour Order?' *Howard Journal* 41(5): 469–84.

——(2005) *Making People Behave*, Cullompton: Willan.

——(2008) 'The ASBO and the Shift to Punishment', in P. Squires (ed.) *ASBO Nation: The Criminalisation of Nuisance*, Bristol: Policy Press, 135–48.

Campbell, S. (2002) *A Review of Anti-social Behaviour Orders*, London: Home Office.

Carlile, L. (2006) *An Independent Inquiry into the Use of Physical Restraint, Solitary Confinement and Forcible Strip Searching of Children in Prisons, Secure Training Centres and Local Authority Secure Children's Homes*, London: Howard League.

Case, S., Ellis, T., Haines, K., Hayden, C., Shalev, K. and Shawyer, A. (2011) 'A Tale of Two Cities: Young People, Anti-social Behaviour and Localised Public Opinion', *Crime Prevention and Community Safety* 13(3): 153–70.

Centre for Social Justice (2012) *Rules of Engagement: Changing the Heart of Youth Justice*, London: Centre for Social Justice.

Chambers, M., Ullmann, B., Waller, I. (2009) *Less Crime, Lower Costs: Implementing Effective Early Crime Reduction Programmes in England and Wales*, London: Policy Exchange.

Chapman, B., Mirrlees-Black, C. and Brawn, C. (2002) *Improving Public Attitudes to the Criminal Justice System: The Impact of Information*, London: Home Office.

Charman, S. and Savage, S.P. (1999) 'The New Politics of Law and Order: Labour, Crime and Justice', in M. Powell (ed.) *New Labour – New Welfare State?* London: Polity Press.

Cheetham, J. (1985) 'Juvenile Offenders and Alternatives to Custody in Northamptonshire: The Views of Magistrates and Social Workers', unpublished.

Children and Young People's Unit (2001) *Building a Strategy for Children and Young People*, London: Children and Young People's Unit.

——(2002) *Children's Fund Guidance*, London: DfES.

The Children's Society (1988) *The Line of Least Resistance*, London: The Children's Society.

——(1992) *Education for Citizenship: A Schools' Pack*, London: The Children's Society.

——(1993) *A False Sense of Security*, London: The Children's Society.

Choudhury, T. and Fenwick, H. (2011) 'The Impact of Counter-terrorism Measures on Muslim Communities', *International Review of Law, Computers & Technology* 25(3): 151–81.

Christie, N. (2000) *Crime Control as Industry*, London: Routledge.

Cicourel, A. (1968) *The Social Organisation of Juvenile Justice*, London: Heinemann.

Clancy, A., Hough, M., Aust, R. and Kershaw, C. (2001) *Ethnic Minorities' Experience of Crime and Policing: Findings from the 2000 British Crime Survey*, London: Home Office.

Clark, T. (2002) 'New Labour's Big Idea: Joined-up Government', *Social Policy & Society* 12: 107–17.

Clarke, J. (2002) 'Whose Justice? The Politics of Juvenile Control', in J. Muncie, G. Hughes and E. McLaughlin (eds) *Youth Justice: Critical Readings*, London: Sage, 284–95.

Clarke, J., Gewirtz, S. and McLaughlin, E. (eds) (2000) *New Managerialism New Welfare?* London: Sage.

Clarke, K. (2010) 'Foreword', in Ministry of Justice, *Breaking the Cycle*, London: The Stationery Office, 1–2.

Cohen, S. (1972) *Folk Devils and Moral Panics*, London: Paladin.

——(1985) *Visions of Social Control*, Cambridge: Polity Press.

Conservative Party (1979) *General Election Manifesto*, London: Conservative Party.

——(2010) *A Contract for Young People*, London: Conservative Party.

Corrigan, P. (1979) *Schooling the Smash Street Kids*, London: Macmillan.

Corrigan, P. and Leonard, P. (1978) *Social Work Practice Under Capitalism: A Marxist Approach*, London: Macmillan.

Craine, S. (1997) 'The "Black Magic" Roundabout: Cyclical Transitions, Social Exclusion and Alternative Careers', in R. MacDonald (ed.) *Youth, the 'Underclass' and Social Exclusion*, Basingstoke: Palgrave Macmillan, 130–52.

Crawford, A. and Burden, T. (2005) 'Involving Victims in Referral Orders and Youth Offender Panels: An Evaluation of Leeds Youth Service', in Centre for Criminal

Justice Studies, *Criminal Justice Review 2004–2005*, Leeds: Centre for Criminal Justice Studies.

Crawford, A. and Newburn, T. (2003) *Youth Offending and Restorative Justice*, Cullompton: Willan.

Crime Concern (2001) *Reducing Neighbourhood Crime*, Swindon: Crime Concern.

Crook, F. (2013) 'Tagging of Children', *Frances Crook's Blog*, 13 February, www.howardleague.org/francescrooksblog/tagging-of-children, accessed 9 May 2013.

Cross, N., Evans, J. and Minkes, J. (2003) 'Still Children First? Developments in Youth Justice in Wales', *Youth Justice* 2(3): 151–62.

Crowley, A. (1998) *A Criminal Waste*, London: The Children's Society.

Crown Prosecution Service (2006) *Narrowing the Justice Gap*.

Davies, B. (1986) *Threatening Youth*, Milton Keynes: Open University Press.

Davis, G., Boucherat, J. and Watson, D. (1988) 'Reparation in the Service of Diversion: The Subordination of a Good Idea', *British Journal of Criminology* 27: 127–34.

——(1989) 'Pre-court Decision-making in Juvenile Justice', *British Journal of Criminology* 29: 219–35.

Day, C., Ellis, M. and Harris, L. (2012) *High Need Families Project: Development and Piloting a New Parenting Intervention (The Helping Families Programme) for Children with Severe and Persistent Conduct Problems: Final Report*, London: Department for Education.

DCSF (Department for Children, Schools and Families) (2010) *Youth Crime Action Plan: Update*, London: DCSF.

Department for Constitutional Affairs (2006) *Delivering Simple, Speedy, Summary Justice*, London: DCA.

Department of Health (2000) *Framework for the Assessment of Children in Need and their Families*, London: The Stationery Office.

DfES (Department for Education and Skills) (2003) *Every Child Matters*, London: DfES.

——(2006) *The Common Assessment Framework for Children and Young People: Practitioners' Guide*, London: DfES.

DHSS (Department of Health and Social Security) (1983) 'Further Development of Intermediate Treatment', *Local Authority Circular* 83, 3, London: DHSS.

Dignan, J. (1992) 'Repairing the Damage: Can Reparation Work in the Service of Diversion?' *British Journal of Criminology* 32: 453–72.

——(2000) *Interim Report on Reparative Work and Youth Offending Teams*, London: Home Office.

——(2005) *Understanding Victims and Restorative Justice*, Maidenhead: Open University Press.

Dixon, J., Schneider, V., Lloyd, C., Reeves, A., White, C., Tomaszewski, W., Green, R. and Ireland, E. (2010) *Monitoring and Evaluation of Family Interventions (Information on Families Supported to March 2010)*, London: Department for Education.

Dominelli, L. (1998) 'Anti-oppressive Practice in Context', in R. Adams, L. Dominelli and M. Payne (eds) *Social Work: Themes, Issues and Critical Debates*, Basingstoke: Macmillan, 3–22.

Donzelot, J. (1979) *The Policing of Families*, Baltimore: Johns Hopkins University Press.

Drew, J. (2012) Presentation, *National Youth Justice Advisory Group Annual Practitioners Conference*, 13 June.

Duff, M. and Done, F. (2009) 'Re: Use of Custody Data', *Letter to Youth Court Panel Chairmen*, 28 September.

Eadie, T. and Canton, R. (2002) 'Practising in a Context of Ambivalence: The Challenge for Youth Justice Workers', *Youth Justice* 2(1): 14–26.

Earle, R. and Newburn, T. (2002) 'Creative Tensions? Young Offenders, Restorative Justice and the Introduction of Referral Orders', *Youth Justice* 1(3): 3–13.

East, K. and Campbell, S. (2000) *Aspects of Crime: Young Offenders 1999*, London: Home Office.

Eccles, P. (2001) 'Youth Inclusion – The Programme Most Likely?' discussion paper, Huddersfield: University of Huddersfield.

Ellis, T. and Boden, I. (2007) 'Is There a Unifying Professional Culture in Youth Offending Teams? A Research Note', *British Society of Criminology Conference papers*, 7, 6, britsoccrim.org/volume7/006.pdf.

Ellis, T., Pamment, N. and Lewis, C. (2009) 'Public Protection in Youth Justice? The Intensive Supervision and Surveillance Programme from the Inside', *International Journal of Police Science & Management* 11(4): 393–413.

Erikson, E. (1995) *Childhood and Society*, London: Vintage.

Eriksson, A. (2006) 'The Politicisation of Community Restorative Justice in Northern Ireland', www.restorativejustice.org/editions/2006/april06/erikssonarticle.

Ernst & Young (1999) *Reducing Delay in the Criminal Justice System: Evaluation of the Pilot Schemes*, London: Home Office.

Eshelby, G. (2011) 'County Durham Youth Offending Service Pre Reprimand Disposal', *Report to Durham County Council Overview and Scrutiny Committee*, 31 May.

Esping-Andersen, G. (1990) *The Three Worlds of Welfare Capitalism*, Oxford: Polity Press.

Evans, R. and Ellis, R. (1997) *Police Cautioning in the 1990s*, London: Home Office.

Farrington, D. (1996) *Understanding and Preventing Youth Crime*, York: Joseph Rowntree Foundation.

——(2002) 'Developmental Criminology and Risk-Focused Prevention', in M. Maguire, R. Morgan and R. Reiner (eds) *The Oxford Handbook of Criminology (Third Edition)*, Oxford: Oxford University Press, 657–701.

Feilzer, M. (2004) *The National Evaluation of the Youth Justice Board's Cognitive Behaviour Projects*, London: Youth Justice Board.

Feilzer, M., Appleton, C., Roberts, C. and Hoyle, C. (2004) *Cognitive Behaviour Projects: The National Evaluation of the Youth Justice Board's Cognitive Behaviour Projects*, London: Youth Justice Board.

Feilzer, M. and Hood, R. (2004) *Differences or Discrimination?* London: Youth Justice Board.

Fergusson, R. (2007) 'Making Sense of the Melting Pot: Multiple Discourses in Youth Justice Policy', *Youth Justice* 7(3): 179–94.

Field, S. (2007) 'Practice Cultures and the "New" Youth Justice in (England and) Wales', *British Journal of Criminology* 47(2): 311–30.

Fielder, C., Hart, D. and Shaw, C. (2008) *The Developing Relationship between Youth Offending Teams and Children's Trusts*, London: Youth Justice Board.

Fionda, J. (2005) *Devils and Angels: Youth Policy and Crime*, London: Hart.

Flanagan, R. (2007) *The Review of Policing: Interim Report*, Surbiton: The Police Federation.

——(2008) *The Review of Policing: Final Report*, Surbiton: The Police Federation.

Fletcher, H. (2005) *ASBOs: An Analysis of the First 6 Years*, London: ASBOConcern/Napo.

Foucault, M. (1979) *Discipline and Punish*, Harmondsworth: Peregrine.

——(1981) *The History of Sexuality, Vol. 1: The Will to Knowledge*, London: Pelican.

France, A. and Crow, I. (2002) *CTC – The Story So Far*, York: Joseph Rowntree Foundation.

Garland, D. (1990) *Punishment and Modern Society*, Oxford: Clarendon Press.

——(2001) *The Culture of Control*, Oxford: Oxford University Press.

Gelsthorpe, L. and Morris, A. (2002) 'Restorative Youth Justice: The Last Vestiges of Welfare?' in J. Muncie, G. Hughes and E. McLaughlin (eds) *Youth Justice: Critical Readings*, London: Sage, 238–53.

Gelsthorpe, L. and Sharpe, G. (2006) 'Gender, Youth Crime and Justice', in B. Goldson and J. Muncie (eds) *Youth Crime and Justice*, London: Sage, 47–61.

Gendrot, S. (2006) 'France: The Politicization of Youth Justice', in J. Muncie and B. Goldson (eds) *Comparative Youth Justice*, London: Sage, 48–64.

George, V. and Wilding, P. (1999) *British Society and Social Welfare: Towards a Sustainable Society*, Basingstoke: Macmillan.

Gervais, M.-C. (2008) *The Drivers of Black and Asian People's Perceptions of Racial Discrimination by Public Services: A Qualitative Study*, London: Department for Communities and Local Government.

Gibbs, P. and Hickson, F. (2009) *Children: Innocent Until Proven Guilty*, London: Prison Reform Trust.

Giddens, A. (1991) *Modernity and Self-Identity*, Cambridge: Polity.

Gilroy, P. (2002) 'Lesser Breeds without the Law', in J. Muncie, G. Hughes and E. McLaughlin (eds) *Youth Justice: Critical Readings*, London: Sage, 50–67.

Goldblatt, P. and Lewis, C. (eds) (1999) *Reducing Offending: An Assessment of Research Evidence on Ways of Dealing with Offending Behaviour*, London: Home Office.

Goldson, B. (1997) 'Children, Crime, Policy and Practice: Neither Welfare nor Justice', *Children & Society* 11: 77–88.

——(1999) 'Youth (In)justice: Contemporary Developments in Policy and Practice', in B. Goldson (ed.) *Youth Justice: Contemporary Policy and Practice*, Aldershot: Ashgate, 1–27.

——(ed.) (2000) *The New Youth Justice*, Lyme Regis: Russell House.

——(2002) *Vulnerable Inside*, London: The Children's Society.

——(2006) 'Penal Custody: Intolerance, Irrationality and Indifference', in B. Goldson and J. Muncie (eds) *Youth Crime and Justice*, London: Sage, 139–56.

——(2009) 'What "Justice" for Children in Conflict with the Law? Some Reflections and Thoughts', *Criminal Justice Matters* 76(1): 19–21.

——(2010) 'The Sleep of (Criminological) Reason: Knowledge—Policy Rupture and New Labour's Youth Justice Legacy', *Criminology and Criminal Justice* 10(2): 155–78.

Goldson, B. and Chigwada-Bailey, R. (1999) '(What) Justice for Black Children and Young People?' in B. Goldson (ed.) *Youth Justice: Contemporary Policy and Practice*, Aldershot: Ashgate, 51–74.

Goldson, B. and Coles, D. (2005) *In the Care of the State?* London: Inquest.

Goldson, B. and Muncie, J. (2006a) 'Critical Anatomy: Towards a Principled Youth Justice', in B. Goldson and J. Muncie (eds) *Youth Crime and Justice*, London: Sage, 203–31.

——(2006b) 'Rethinking Youth Justice: Comparative Analysis, International Human Rights and Research Evidence', *Youth Justice* 6(2): 91–106.

Goldson, B. and Peters, E. (2000) *Tough Justice: Responding to Children in Trouble*, London: The Children's Society.

Graham, J. (2010) 'Responding to Youth Crime', in D.J. Smith (ed.) *A New Response to Youth Crime*, Cullompton: Willan, 104–42.

Graham, J. and Bowling, B. (1995) *Young People and Crime*, London: Home Office.

Gramsci, A. (1971) *Selections from Prison Notebooks*, London: Lawrence and Wishart.

Gray, E., Taylor, E., Roberts, C., Merrington, S., Fernandez, R. and Moore, R. (2005) *Intensive Supervision and Surveillance Programme: The Final Report*, London: Youth Justice Board.

Greater Manchester Police Authority (2002) *Consultation for Best Value: Young People*, www.gmpa.gov.uk/consultation/young_people.htm.

Green, D. (2004) 'The Intensive Supervision and Surveillance Programme', www.civitas.org.uk/pdf/issp.pdf.

——(2006) 'Public Opinion Versus Public Judgment About Crime', *British Journal of Criminology* 46(1): 131–54.

Haines, K. (2000) 'Referral Orders and Youth Offender Panels: Restorative Approaches and the New Youth Justice', in B. Goldson (ed.) *The New Youth Justice*, Lyme Regis: Russell House, 58–80.

Haines, K. and Case, S. (2007) 'Individual Differences in Public Opinion about Youth Crime and Justice in Swansea', *The Howard Journal of Criminal Justice* 46(4): 338–55.

——(2012) 'Is the Scaled Approach a Failed Approach?' *Youth Justice* 12(2): 212–28.

Haines, K. and Charles, A. (2010) *The Swansea Bureau: Children First, Offenders Second*, Swansea: Swansea YOS/South Wales Police.

Haines, K. and Drakeford, M. (1998) *Young People and Youth Justice*, London: Macmillan.

Haines, K. and O'Mahony, D. (2006) 'Restorative Approaches, Young People and Youth Justice', in B. Goldson and J. Muncie (eds) *Youth Crime and Justice*, London: Sage, 110–24.

Hall, S., Critcher, C., Jefferson, T., Clarke, J. and Roberts, B. (1978) *Policing the Crisis: Mugging, the State and Law and Order*, Basingstoke: Macmillan.

——(2013) *Policing the Crisis: Mugging, the State and Law and Order (35th Anniversary Edition)*, Basingstoke: Palgrave Macmillan and Slough: National Foundation for Educational Research.

Halsey, K. and White, R. (2008) *Young People, Crime and Public Perceptions: A Review of the Literature* (LGA Research Report F/SR264), Slough: NFER.

Hancock, L. (1999) 'Community and State Responses to Crime and Disorder: Conflict, Compromise and Contradiction', *The British Criminology Conferences: Selected Proceedings*, Volume 2. London: Palgrave Macmillan.

——(2001) *Community, Crime and Disorder: Safety and Regeneration in Urban Neighbourhoods*, Basingstoke: Palgrave.

——(2006) 'Urban Regeneration, Young People, Crime and Criminalisation', in B. Goldson and J. Muncie (eds) *Youth Crime and Justice*, London: Sage, 172–86.

Harris, R. and Webb, S. (1987) *Welfare, Power & Juvenile Justice*, London: Tavistock.

Hart, D. (2012) 'Legal Aid Sentencing and Punishment of Offenders Act 2012: Implications for Children', www.thenayj.org.uk/wp-content/files_mf/briefinglaspo.pdf?, accessed 7 May 2013.

Hart, D. and Thompson, C. (2009) *Young People's Participation in the Youth Justice System*, London: National Children's Bureau.

Hazel, N. (2008) *Cross-national Comparison of Youth Justice*, London: Youth Justice Board.

——(forthcoming) *A History of Youth Justice*, London: Routledge.

Hazel, N., Hagell, A. and Brazier, L. (2002) *Young Offenders' Perceptions of their Experiences in the Criminal Justice System*, London: Policy Research Bureau.

Hearne, B. (2003) 'Speech to NACRO Annual Conference', Loughborough University, 10 April.

Hendrick, H. (2006) 'Histories of Crime and Youth Justice', in B. Goldson and J. Muncie (eds) *Youth Crime and Justice*, London: Sage, 3–16.

Herbert, N. (2011) Speech to Association of Chief Police Officers/Restorative Justice Council Conference, 22 February.

Hine, J. (2004) *Children and Citizenship*, London: Home Office.

Hine, J. and Celnick, A. (2001) *A One Year Reconviction Study of Final Warnings*, Sheffield: University of Sheffield.

HM Chief Inspector of Prisons (2001) *Annual Report 1999–2000*, London: The Stationery Office.

——(2002) 'Preface', in HM Inspectorate of Prisons, *Report on an Unannounced Follow-Up Inspection of HM Prison Eastwood Park*, London: HM Inspectorate of Prisons, 2–5.

HM Government (2006) *Reaching Out: An Action Plan on Social Exclusion*, London: Cabinet Office.

——(2007a) *PSA Delivery Agreement 24: Deliver a More Effective, Transparent and Responsive Criminal Justice System for Victims and the Public*, London: The Stationery Office.

——(2007b) *PSA Delivery Agreement 14: Increase the Number of Children and Young People on the Path to Success*, London: The Stationery Office.

——(2007c) *Children's Plan*, London: The Stationery Office.

——(2008) *Youth Crime Action Plan*, London: The Stationery Office.

Hodgson, P. and Webb, D. (2005) 'Young People, Crime and School Exclusion: A Case of Some Surprises', *The Howard Journal* 44(1): 12–28.

Holdaway, S., Davidson, N., Dignan, J., Hammersley, R., Hine, J. and Marsh, P. (2001) *New Strategies to Address Youth Offending: The National Evaluation of the Pilot Youth Offending Teams*, London: Home Office.

Holdaway, S. and Desborough, S. (2004) *The National Evaluation of the Youth Justice Board's Final Warning Projects*, London: Youth Justice Board.

Hollingsworth, K. (2012) 'Youth Justice Reform in the Big Society', *Journal of Social Welfare and Family Law* 34(2): 245–59.

Home Affairs Committee (1993) *Juvenile Offenders*, London: HMSO.

——(2007) *Young Black People and the Criminal Justice System*, London: The Stationery Office.

Home Office (1968) *Children in Trouble*, London: HMSO.

——(1980) *Young Offenders*, London: HMSO.

——(1985) 'The Cautioning of Offenders', *Home Office Circular 14/1985*, London: Home Office.

——(1988) *Punishment, Custody and the Community*, London: HMSO.

——(1990) 'The Cautioning of Offenders', *Home Officer Circular, 59/1990*, London: Home Office.

——(1992) *National Standards for the Supervision of Offenders in the Community*, London: Home Office.

——(1995) *Strengthening Punishment in the Community*, London: HMSO.

——(1996) *Criminal Statistics 1995 England and Wales*, London: Home Office.

——(1997a) *Consultation Paper: Tackling Youth Crime*, London: Home Office.

——(1997b) *No More Excuses*, Cm 3809, London: Home Office.

——(1998) *Youth Justice: The Statutory Principal Aim of Preventing Offending by Children and Young People*, London: Home Office.

——(2000) *Crime and Disorder Act 1998 – Community-Based Orders*, London: Home Office.

——(2001a) *Criminal Justice: The Way Ahead*, Cm 5074, London: Home Office.

——(2001b) *Criminal Statistics England and Wales 2000*, London: The Stationery Office.

——(2001c) *Establishing Referral Order Schemes: A Guidance Note for Youth Offending Teams*, London: Home Office.

——(2001d) *Statistics on Race and the Criminal Justice System 2000*, London: Home Office.

——(2002a) *Criminal Justice and Police Act 2001: Electronic Monitoring of 12–16 Year Olds on Bail and on Remand to Local Authority Accommodation*, London: Home Office.

——(2002b) *Criminal Justice and Police Act 2001 Section 130 Guidance – Secure Remands*, London: Home Office.

——(2002c) *Justice for All*, London: Home Office.

——(2003a) *Respect and Responsibility*, London: Home Office.

——(2003b) *Youth Justice – The Next Steps*, London: Home Office.

——(2003c) *Restorative Justice: The Government's Strategy*, London: Home Office.

——(2004a) *Defining and Measuring Anti-social Behaviour*, London: Home Office.

——(2004b) *Confident Communities in a Secure Britain*, London: Home Office.

——(2004c) *Every Child Matters: Next Steps*, Annex B, www.homeoffice.gov.uk/justice/ sentencing/youthjustice/index.html.

——(2005a) *Criminal Statistics*, London: The Stationery Office.

——(2005b) *Sentencing Statistics*, Londonl: The Stationery Office.

——(2006) *Statistics on Race and the Criminal Justice System – 2005*, London: The Stationery Office.

Home Office, Department of Health, Department for Education and Employment and Welsh Office (1998) *Establishing Youth Offending Teams*, London: Home Office.

Home Office, Lord Chancellor's Department, Attorney General's Office (2002) *Justice for All*, Cm5563, London: The Stationery Office.

Hope, T. (1998) 'Community Crime Prevention', in P. Goldblatt and C. Lewis (eds) *Reducing Offending: An Assessment of Research Evidence on Ways of Dealing with Offending Behaviour*, London: Home Office, 51–62.

Hough, M. and Mayhew, P. (1985) *Taking Account of Crime: Key Findings from the 1984 British Crime Survey*, London: Home Office.

Hough, M. and Roberts, J. (1998) *Attitudes to Punishment: Findings from the British Crime Survey*, London: Home Office.

——(2004) *Youth Crime and Youth Justice*, Bristol: Policy Press.

Howard, M. (1995) Speech to Conservative Party Conference.

Howard League (2010) *Life Inside 2010*, London: Howard League.

Hoyle, C. (2002) 'Securing Restorative Justice for "Non-Participating" Victims', in C. Hoyle and R. Young (eds) *New Visions of Crime Victims*, Oxford: Hart, 97–128.

Hudson, B. (1987) *Justice Through Punishment*, Basingstoke: Macmillan.

——(1996) *Understanding Justice*, Buckingham: Open University Press.

Hughes, G. and Follett, M. (2006) 'Community Safety, Youth and the "Anti-Social"', in B. Goldson and J. Muncie (eds) *Youth Crime and Justice*, London: Sage, 157–71.

Hughes, G., Leisten, R. and Pilkington, A. (1996) *An Independent Review of the Northamptonshire Diversion Unit*, Northampton: Nene College.

IARS and Gavrielides, T. (2011) *Consultation Response 1: Restorative Justice*, London; IARS.

Ignatieff, M. (1985) 'State, Civil Society and Total Institutions: A Critique of Recent Social Histories of Punishment', in S. Cohen and A. Scull (eds) *Social Control and the State*, Oxford: Blackwell.

Institute for Criminal Policy Research (2012) *Assessing Young People in Police Custody: An Examination of the Operation of Triage Schemes*, London: Home Office.

Ipsos-MORI (2005) *BME Communities' Expectations of Fair Treatment by the Criminal Justice System*, London: Home Office.

Jackson, S. (1999) 'Family Group Conferences and Youth Justice: The New Panacea?' in B. Goldson (ed.) *Youth Justice: Contemporary Policy and Practice*, Aldershot: Ashgate, 127–47.

Jacobson, J. and Kirby, A. (2012) *Public Attitudes to Youth Crime: Report on Focus Group Research*, London: Home Office.

Jamieson, C. (2002) 'Youth Justice in Scotland', Edinburgh: Scottish Executive.

Jamieson, J. (2006) 'New Labour, Youth Justice and the Question of "Respect"', *Youth Justice* 5(3): 180–93.

Jeffs, T. (1997) 'Changing their Ways: Youth Work and Underclass Theory', in R. MacDonald (ed.) *Youth, the 'Underclass' and Social Exclusion*, London: Routledge, 153–66.

Jenks, C. (1996) *Childhood*, London: Routledge.

Jennings, D. (2002) *One Year Juvenile Reconviction Rates: July 2000 Cohort*, London: Home Office.

Johnson, K. *et al.* (2001) *Cautions, Court Proceedings and Sentencing*, London: Home Office.

Johnstone, G. (2002) *Restorative Justice: Ideas, Values, Debates*, Cullompton: Willan.

Joint Chief Inspectors (2002) *Safeguarding Children: A Joint Chief Inspector's Report on Arrangements to Safeguard Children*, London: Department of Health.

Jones, T. and Newburn, T. (2002) 'Policy Convergence and Crime Control in the USA and the UK: Streams of Influence and Levels of Impact', *Criminology and Criminal Justice* 2(2): 173–203.

Justice Committee (2011) *The Proposed Abolition of the Youth Justice Board*, London: The Stationery Office.

Kautt, P. (2008) 'Ethnic Variation in Criminological Experiences: A Single and Multilevel Statistical Analysis of British Crime Survey Data', 2001–6: Full Research Report, *ESRC End of Award Report*, RES-163-25-0051, Swindon: ESRC.

Keightley-Smith, L. (2009) *The Dynamics of Multi-Agency Working in the Final Warning Scheme in the North East of England*, PhD thesis, University of Northumbria.

Keightley-Smith, L. and Francis, P. (2007) 'Final Warning, Youth Justice and Early Intervention: Reflections on the Findings of a Research Study Carried Out in Northern England', *Webb Journal of Current Legal Issues* 2, webjcli.ncl.ac.uk/2007/issue2/keightleysmith2.html.

Keith, B. (2006) *Report of the Zahid Mubarek Inquiry (Vol. 1)*, London: The Stationery Office.

Kelling, G. (1998) 'The Evolution of "Broken Windows"', in M. Weatheritt (ed.) *Zero Tolerance: What Does it Mean and is it Right for Policing in Britain*, London: The Police Foundation, 3–12.

Kemp, V., Sorsby, A., Liddle, M. and Merrington, S. (2002) *Assessing Responses to Youth Offending in Northamptonshire*, London: NACRO.

Kempf-Leonard, K. and Peterson, E. (2002) 'Expanding the Realms of the New Penology: The Advent of Actuarial Justice for Juveniles', in J. Muncie, G. Hughes and E. McLaughlin (eds) *Youth Justice: Critical Readings*, London; Sage, 431–50.

Kemshall, H. (2008) 'Risks, Rights and Justice: Understanding and Responding to Youth Risk', *Youth Justice* 8(1): 21–37.

Kershaw, C., Chivite-Matthews, N., Thomas, C. and Aust, R. (2001) *The 2001 British Crime Survey: First Results, England and Wales*, London; Home Office.

Kinsey, R., Lea, J. and Young, J. (1986) *Losing the Fight Against Crime*, Oxford: Blackwell.

Kuhn, T. (1970) *The Structure of Scientific Revolutions*, Chicago: University of Chicago Press.

Landau, S. and Nathan, G. (1983) 'Selecting Delinquents for Cautioning in the London Metropolitan Area', *British Journal of Criminology* 23: 128–49.

Lappi-Seppala, T. (2006) 'Finland: A Model of Tolerance?' in J. Muncie and B. Goldson (eds) *Comparative Youth Justice*, London: Sage, 177–95.

Lawrence Steering Group (2004) *5th Annual Report 2003–2004*, London: Home Office.

Lea, J. (2002) *Crime and Modernity*, London: Sage.

Lea, J. and Young, J. (1984) *What is to be Done About Law and Order?* Harmondsworth: Penguin.

Leicester YOT (Youth Offending Team) (2001) *Leicester Youth Justice Plan 2001–02*, Leicester: Leicester City Council.

Leonard, P. (1984) *Personality and Ideology*, London: Macmillan.

Lipscombe, S. (2012) 'The Age of Criminal Responsibility in England and Wales', Standard Note: SN/HA/3001, House of Commons Library.

Lipsky, M. (1980) *Street-Level Bureaucracy*, New York: Russell Sage Foundation.

Loeber, R., Wim Slot, N., van der Laan, P. and Hoeve, M. (2008) *Tomorrow's Criminals*, Aldershot: Ashgate.

Loxley, C., Curtin, L. and Brown, R. (2002) *Summer Splash Schemes 2000: Findings from Six Case Studies*, London: Home Office.

Lyon, J., Denison, C. and Wilson, A. (2000) *'Tell Them So They Listen': Messages from Young People in Custody*, London: Home Office.

MacDonald, R. (1997) 'Youth, Social Exclusion and the Millennium', in R. MacDonald (ed.) *Youth, the 'Underclass' and Social Exclusion*, Basingstoke: Palgrave Macmillan, 167–97.

MacDonald, R. and Marsh, J. (2005) *Disconnected Youth?* Basingstoke: Palgrave Macmillan.

Mackenzie, S., Bannister, J., Flint, J., Parr, S., Millie, A. and Fleetwood, J. (2010) *The Drivers of Perceptions of Anti-social Behaviour*, London: Home Office.

Macmillan, J. (1998) 'In Whose Interests? Politics and Policy', in S. Brown, *Understanding Youth and Crime*, Buckingham: Open University Press, 53–78.

Macpherson, W. (1999) *The Stephen Lawrence Inquiry*, Cm 4262–1, London: The Stationery Office.

Masters, G. (2005) 'Restorative Justice and Youth Justice', in T. Bateman and J. Pitts (eds) *The RHP Companion to Youth Justice*, Lyme Regis: Russell House, 179–85.

Mathiesen, T. (1974) *The Politics of Abolition*, Oxford: Martin Robertson.

Matrix Evidence (2012) *Risk-Based Interventions Pilot: Follow-Up*, London: Youth Justice Board.

Matthews, R. (2005) 'The Myth of Punitiveness', *Theoretical Criminology* 9(2): 175–201.

Mattinson, J. and Mirrlees-Black, C. (2000) *Attitudes to Crime and Criminal Justice: Findings from the 1998 British Crime Survey*, London: Home Office.

Matza, D. (1964) *Delinquency and Drift*, New York: Wiley.

May, T., Gyateng, T. and Hough, M. (2009) 'Ethnic Minority Young People: Differential Treatment in the Youth Justice System', *ESRC Research Report* RES-178-25-0008, London: King's College.

——(2010) *Differential Treatment in the Youth Justice System*, London: Equality and Human Rights Commission.

Mays, J. (1965) 'The Liverpool Police Liaison Officer Scheme', *The Sociological Review* 9: 185–200.

McAra, L. (2010) 'Models of Youth Justice', in D.J. Smith (ed.) *A New Response to Youth Crime*, Cullompton: Willan.

McAra, L. and McVie, S. (2005) 'The Usual Suspects? Street-life, Young People and the Police', *Criminal Justice* 5(1): 5–36.

——(2010) 'Youth Crime and Justice: Key Messages from the Edinburgh Study of Youth Transitions and Crime', *Criminology and Criminal Justice* 10(2): 179–209.

McCarthy, P., Laing, K. and Walker, J. (2004) *Offenders of the Future? Assessing the Risk of Children and Young People Becoming Involved in Criminal or Antisocial Behaviour*, London: DfES.

McLaughlin, E. and Muncie, J. (2000) 'The Criminal Justice System: New Labour's New Partnerships', in J. Clarke, S. Gewirtz and E. McLaughlin (eds) *New Managerialism New Welfare?* London: Sage, 169–85.

McLaughlin, E., Muncie, J. and Hughes, G. (2001) 'The Permanent Revolution: New Labour, New Public Management and the Modernization of Criminal Justice', *Criminal Justice* 1(3): 301–18.

McRobbie, A. and Thornton, S. (2002) 'Rethinking Moral Panic for Multi-mediated Social Worlds', in J. Muncie, G. Hughes and E. McLaughlin (eds) *Youth Justice: Critical Readings*, London: Sage, 68–79.

Merton, R. (1957) *Social Theory and Social Structure*, Glencoe: Free Press.

Miller, S. (2008) *Keeping on Track: Reducing Youth Offending: Prevention, Intervention, Diversion and Detention*, London: Liberal Democrat Party.

Milne, S. (2004) *The Enemy Within*, London: Verso.

Ministry of Justice (2010) *Breaking the Cycle*, London: The Stationery Office.

——(2011a) 'Reducing Reoffending', www.justice.gov.uk/youth-justice/reducing-re-offending, accessed 29 April 2013.

——(2011b) *Statistical Notice: Anti-Social Behaviour Orders (ASBO) Statistics England and Wales 2010*, London: Ministry of Justice.

——(2011c) *Breaking the Cycle: Government Response*, London: The Stationery Office.

——(2011d) *Statistics on Race and the Criminal Justice System 2010*, London: Ministry of Justice, The Stationery Office.

——(2012a) *Criminal Justice Statistics, England and Wales 2010*, London: The Stationery Office.

——(2012b) *Government Response to the Justice Committee's Report: The Proposed Abolition of the Youth Justice Board*, London: Ministry of Justice.

——(2012c) *Swift and Sure Justice: The Government's Plans for Reform of the Criminal Justice System*, London: Ministry of Justice.

——(2012d) *Referral Order Guidance*, London: Ministry of Justice.

——(2012e) *Reducing Reoffending*, www.jusice.gov.uk/youth-justice/reducing-re-offending (accessed 16 July 2013).

——(2012f) *Race and the Criminal Justice System 2010*, London: Ministry of Justice.

——(2013) *Youth Justice Statistics 2011/12 England and Wales*, London: Ministry of Justice.

Mirrlees-Black, C. (2000) *Confidence in the Criminal Justice System: Findings from the 2000 British Crime Survey*, London: Home Office.

Mirrlees-Black, C. and Allen, J. (1998) *Concern about Crime: Findings from the 1998 British Crime Survey*, London: Home Office.

Mirrlees-Black, C., Budd, T., Partridge, S. and Mayhew, P. (1998) *The 1998 British Crime Survey: England and Wales*, London: Home Office.

Moore, R. (2004) 'Intensive Supervision and Surveillance Programmes for Young Offenders: The Evidence Base so Far', in R. Burnett and C. Roberts (eds) *What Works in Probation and Youth Justice*, Cullompton: Willan, 159–79.

Moore, S. and Peters, E. (2003) *A Beacon of Hope: Children and Young People on Remand*, London: The Children's Society.

Moore, S. and Smith, R. (2001) *The Pre-Trial Guide*, London: The Children's Society.

Morgan, R. (2007a) 'A New Direction', *Safer Society* 32: 5–8.

——(2007b) 'The Government's Addiction to Stop-go Penal Politics is Destructive and Possibly Disastrous', *New Law Journal*, 2 March.

——(2012) 'Crime and justice in the "Big Society"', *Criminology and Criminal Justice* 12(5): 463–81.

Morgan Harris Burrows (2001) *Youth Inclusion Programme: Evaluation Overview*, unpublished.

——(2003) *Evaluation of the Youth Inclusion Programme*, Youth Justice Board, London.

MORI (2001) *Rethinking Crime and Punishment Survey*, London: MORI.

——(2002) *Youth Survey 2002*, London: Youth Justice Board.

——(2004) *MORI Youth Survey 2004*, London: Youth Justice Board.

Morris, A. and Giller, H. (1987) *Understanding Juvenile Justice*, London: Croom Helm.

Morris, A., Giller, H., Geach, H. and Szwed, E. (1980) *Justice for Children*, London: Macmillan.

Muncie, J. (1999a) 'Institutionalized Intolerance: Youth Justice and the 1998 Crime and Disorder Act', *Critical Social Policy* 19(2): 147–75.

——(1999b) *Youth and Crime: A Critical Introduction*, London: Sage.

——(2000) 'Pragmatic Realism? Searching for Criminology in the New Youth Justice', in B. Goldson (ed.) *The New Youth Justice*, Lyme Regis: Russell House, 14–34.

——(2001) 'Policy Transfers and "What Works": Some Reflections on Comparative Youth Justice', *Youth Justice* 1(3): 27–35.

——(2002) 'A New Deal for Youth? Early Intervention and Correctionalism', in G. Hughes, E. McLaughlin and J. Muncie (eds) *Crime Prevention and Community Safety: New Directions*, London: Sage, 142–62.

——(2004) *Youth and Crime*, 2nd edition, London: Sage.

——(2006) 'Governing Young People: Coherence and Contradiction in Contemporary Youth Justice', *Critical Social Policy* 26(4): 770–93.

——(2008) 'The "Punitive Turn" in Juvenile Justice: Cultures of Control and Rights Compliance in Western Europe and the USA', *Youth Justice* 8(2): 107–21.

——(2009) *Youth and Crime*, 3rd edition, London: Sage.

——(2011) 'Illusions of Difference: Comparative Youth Justice in the Devolved United Kingdom', *British Journal of Criminology* 51(1): 40–57.

Muncie, J. and Goldson, B. (2006) 'States of Transition: Convergence and Diversity in International Youth Justice', in J. Muncie and B. Goldson (eds) *Comparative Youth Justice*, London: Sage, 196–218.

——(2012) 'Towards a Global "Child Friendly" Juvenile Justice?', *International Journal of Law, Crime and Justice* 40(1): 47–64.

Muncie, J. and Hughes, G. (2002) 'Modes of Youth Governance: Political Rationalities, Criminalisation and Resistance', in J. Muncie, G. Hughes and E. McLaughlin (eds) *Youth Justice: Critical Readings*, London: Sage, 1–18.

Muncie, J., Hughes, G. and McLaughlin, E. (eds) (2002) *Youth Justice: Critical Readings*, London: Sage.

Murray, C. (1996) 'The Emerging British Underclass', in R. Lister (ed.) *Charles Murray and the Underclass: The Developing Debate*, London: IEA Health and Welfare Unit, 23–54.

Myhill, A. and Beak, K. (2008) *Public Confidence in the Police*, London: National Policing Improvement Agency.

NACRO (National Association for the Care and Resettlement of Offenders) (1987) *Time for Change: A New Framework for Dealing with Juvenile Crime and Offenders*, London: NACRO.

——(2001) *Lessons from Pilots: A Summary of the National Evaluation of the Pilot Youth Offending Teams*, London: NACRO.

——(2005) *A Better Alternative: Reducing Child Imprisonment*, London: NACRO.

——(2011) *Reducing the Number of Children and Young People in Custody*, NACRO Briefing Paper, London: NACRO, July.

National Assembly for Wales (2000) *Extending Entitlement*, Cardiff: National Assembly for Wales.

National Audit Office (2004) *Youth Offending: The Delivery of Community and Custodial Sentences*, London: The Stationery Office.

NAYJ (National Association for Youth Justice) (2002) *Working with Children in Trouble: The Philosophical Base*, www.nayj.org.uk/website/index.php?module=ContentExpree& func=display&ceid=1.

——(2006) *Manifesto for Youth Justice*, www.nayj.org.uk/website/index.php?module= ContentExpree&func=display&ceid=2.

——(2011) *For a Child Friendly Youth Justice System*, www.nayj.org.uk/wp-content/ files_mf/1332858575_magicfields_document_the_document_7_1.pdf, accessed 1 May 2013.

Nelken, D. (2006) 'Italy: A Lesson in Tolerance?' in J. Muncie and B. Goldson (eds) *Comparative Youth Justice*, London: Sage, 159–76.

Newburn, T. (1998) 'Tackling Youth Crime and Reforming Youth Justice: The Origins and Nature of "New Labour" Policy', *Policy Studies* 19(3/4): 199–211.

Newburn, T. and Jones, T. (2001) '"Policy Transfer" and Crime Control: Some Reflections on "Zero Tolerance"', Paper to the Annual Meeting of the American Political Science Association, San Francisco, CA, September.

Newburn, T., Masters, G., Earle, R., Goldie, S., Crawford, A., Sharpe, K., Netten, A., Hale, C., Uglow, S. and Saunders, R. (2001a) *The Introduction of Referral Orders into the Youth Justice System: First Interim Report*, London; Home Office.

Newburn, T., Earle, R., Goldie, S., Campbell, A., Masters, G., Crawford, A., Sharpe, K., Hale, C., Saunders, R., Uglow, S. and Netten, A. (2001b) *The Introduction of Referral Orders into the Youth Justice System: Second Interim Report*, London: Home Office.

Newburn, T., Crawford, A., Earle, R., Goldie, S., Hale, C., Hallam, A., Masters, G., Netten, A., Saunders, R., Sharpe, K. and Uglow, S. (2002) *The Introduction of Referral Orders into the Youth Justice System: Final Report*, London: Home Office.

Newbury, A. (2011) '"I Would Have Been Able to Hear What They Think": Tensions in Achieving Restorative Outcomes in the English Youth Justice System', *Youth Justice* 11(3): 250–65.

Northamptonshire YOT (Youth Offending Team) (2001) *Northamptonshire Youth Justice Plan 2001–01*, Northampton: Northamptonshire County Council.

Office for National Statistics (2012) *Focus on Public Perceptions of Policing, Findings from the 2011/12 Crime Survey for England and Wales*, London: The Stationery Office.

Owen, R. and Sweeting, A. (2007) *Hoodie or Goodie?* London: Victim Support.

PA Consulting (2002) *Reducing Delays*, www.reducing-delays.org.

Palmer, S. and Pitts, J. (2006) '"Othering" the Brothers: Black Youth, Racial Solidarity and Gun Crime', *Youth and Policy* 91: 5–22.

Parker, H. (1974) *A View from the Boys*, Newton Abbott: David & Charles.

Pearson, G. (1983) *Hooligan: A History of Respectable Fears*, Basingstoke: Macmillan.

Percy, A. (1998) *Ethnicity and Victimisation: Findings from the 1996 British Crime Survey*, London: Home Office.

Percy-Smith, J. (2000) 'Introduction: The Contours of Social Exclusion', in J. Percy-Smith (ed.) *Policy Responses to Social Exclusion*, Buckingham: Open University Press, 1–21.

Phillips, L. (2006) 'Foreword', in *Sentencing Guidelines Council and Sentencing Advisory Panel Annual Report 2005–06*, London: Sentencing Guidelines Secretariat, 2.

Phillips, L., Smith, R., Martin, M. and Mehta, P. (2012) *Evaluation of the YJB Pilot Resettlement Support Panel Scheme*, Cardiff: Welsh Government.

Pickford, J. (2000) 'Introduction: A New Youth Justice for a New Century', in J. Pickford (ed.) *Youth Justice: Theory and Practice*, London: Cavendish Publishing, xxi–lx.

Pitts, J. (1988) *The Politics of Juvenile Crime*, London: Sage.

——(1999) *Working with Young Offenders*, 2nd edition, Basingstoke: Macmillan.

——(2000) 'The New Youth Justice and the Politics of Electoral Anxiety', in B. Goldson (ed.) *The New Youth Justice*, Lyme Regis: Russell House, 1–13.

——(2001a) 'Korrectional Karaoke: New Labour and the Zombification of Youth Justice', *Youth Justice* 1(2): 3–16.

——(2001b) *The New Politics of Youth Crime*, Basingstoke: Palgrave.

——(2002) 'Amnesia and Discontinuity', Speech to National Association of Youth Justice Conference, Milton Keynes, 14 June.

——(2003) 'Youth Justice in England and Wales', in R. Matthews and J. Young (eds) *The New Politics of Crime and Punishment*, Cullompton: Willan, 71–99.

——(2008) *Reluctant Gangsters*, Cullompton: Willan.

——(2011) 'Riotous Assemblies', *Youth & Policy* 107.

Pollock, L.A. (1983) *Forgotten Children*, Cambridge: Cambridge University Press.

Poulantzas, N. (1978) *Political Power and Social Classes*, London: Verso.

Power, A. and Tunstall, R. (1997) *Dangerous Disorder: Riots and Violent Disorders in 12 Areas of Britain 1991–92*, York: YPS.

Pragnell, S. (2001) 'Report to Northamptonshire Youth Offending Team Steering Group', unpublished.

——(2005) 'Reprimands and Final Warnings', in T. Bateman and J. Pitts (eds) *The RHP Companion to Youth Justice*, Lyme Regis: Russell House, 77–82.

Pratt, J. (1989) 'Corporatism: The Third Model of Juvenile Justice', *British Journal of Criminology* 29: 236–54.

——(2000) 'The Return of the Wheelbarrow Men; or, the Arrival of Postmodern Penality?' *British Journal of Criminology* 40: 127–45.

——(2002) 'Corporatism: The Third Model of Juvenile Justice', in J. Muncie, G. Hughes and E. McLaughlin (eds) *Youth Justice: Critical Readings*, London: Sage, 404–12.

Public Accounts Committee (2011) *The Youth Justice System in England and Wales: Reducing Offending by Young People*, London: The Stationery Office.

Respect Task Force (2006) *Respect Action Plan*, London: The Stationery Office.

Reynolds, F. (1985) 'Juvenile Offending in Northamptonshire 1982–83', unpublished.

Riots Communities and Victims Panel (2012) *After the Riots: The Final Report of the Riots Communities and Victims Panel*, London: Riots Communities and Victims Panel.

Roberts, C., Baker, K., Merrington, S. and Jones, S. (2001) *Validity and Reliability of ASSET: Interim Report to the Youth Justice Board*, Oxford: Centre for Criminological Research.

Roberts, J. and Hough, M. (2013) 'Sentencing Riot-Related Offending: Where Do the Public Stand?' *British Journal of Criminology*, online, 24 January, doi: 10.1093/bjc/azs069.

Rock, P. (2002) 'On Becoming a Victim', in C. Hoyle and R. Young (eds) *New Visions of Crime Victims*, Oxford: Hart, 1–21.

Rodger, J. (2012) 'Rehabilitation Revolution in a Big Society?' in A. Silvestri (ed) *Critical Reflections: Social and Criminal Justice in the First Year of Coalition Government*, London: Centre for Crime and Justice Studies, 18–19.

Rutherford, A. (1992) *Growing Out of Crime: The New Era*, Winchester: Waterside Press.

——(1996) *Transforming Criminal Policy*, Winchester: Waterside Press.

Rutter, M., Giller, H. and Hagell, A. (1998) *Anti-Social Behaviour by Young People*, Manchester: Fields Press.

Saini, A. (1997) *'So What's the Point of Telling Anyone?'* Leicester: De Montfort University.

Salisbury, H. and Upson, A. (2004) 'Ethnicity, Victimisation and Worry about Crime: Findings from the 2001/02 and 2002/03 British Crime Surveys', *Findings 237*, London: Home Office.

Scarman, L. (1982) *The Scarman Report*, Harmondsworth: Penguin.

Schrag, L. (2003) 'Restorative Justice in Northern Ireland: An Outsider's Perspective', Paper to Best Practices in Restorative Justice Conference, Simon Fraser University, 1–4 June.

Schur, E. (1973) *Radical Non-Intervention*, New Jersey: Prentice-Hall.

Schweinhart, L. (2003) 'Validity of the High/Scope Preschool Education Model', www.highscope.org/Research/preschoolvalidity.pdf, accessed 11 April 2006.

Scottish Executive (2002) *National Standards for Scotland's Youth Justice Services*, Edinburgh: Scottish Executive.

——(2004) *Getting it Right for Every Child*, Edinburgh: Scottish Executive.

Scraton, P. and Haydon, D. (2002) 'Challenging the Criminalisation of Children and Young People: Securing a Rights-based Agenda', in J. Muncie, G. Hughes and E. McLaughlin (eds) *Youth Justice: Critical Readings*, London: Sage, 311–28.

Sentencing Guidelines Council (2009) *Overarching Principles – Sentencing Youths*, London: Sentencing Guidelines Council.

Seymour, M. (2004) 'Juvenile Justice in the Republic of Ireland', www.esc-eurocrim.org/files/juvenile_justice_in_the_republic_of_ireland.doc.

Shapland, J., Johnstone, J., Sorsby, A., Stubbing, T., Jackson, J., Hibbert, J. and Howes, M. (2001) *Evaluation of Statutory Time Limit Pilot Schemes in the Youth Court*, Sheffield: University of Sheffield.

Sharp, D. (2006) 'Serve and Protect? Black Young People's Experiences of Policing in the Community', in D. Wilson and G. Rees (eds) *Just Justice*, London: The Children's Society, 5–13.

Sharpe, G. and Gelsthorpe, L. (2009) 'Engendering the Agenda: Girls, Young Women and Youth Justice', *Youth Justice* 9(3): 195–208.

Sherman, L. and Strang, H. (2008) *Restorative Justice*, London: Youth Justice Board.

Simes, J. and Chads, K. (2002) *Prison Population Brief England and Wales: May 2002*, London: Home Office.

Smith, D. (1999) 'Social Work with Young People in Trouble: Memory and Prospect', in B. Goldson (ed.) *Youth Justice: Contemporary Policy and Practice*, Aldershot: Ashgate, 148–69.

——(2000a) 'Corporatism and the New Youth Justice', in B. Goldson (ed.) *The New Youth Justice*, Lyme Regis: Russell House, 129–43.

Smith, D.J. (2004) *The Links Between Victimization and Offending*, Centre for Law and Society, Edinburgh: University of Edinburgh.

Smith, D.J., McVie, S., Woodward, R., Shute, J., Flint, J. and McAra, L. (2001) *The Edinburgh Study of Youth Transitions and Crime: Key Findings at Ages 12 and 13*, Edinburgh: University of Edinburgh.

Smith, J., Balls, E. and Straw, J. (2008) 'Foreword', in HM Government, *Youth Crime Action Plan*, London: The Stationery Office, 1–2.

Smith, R. (1985) 'The Catch-all Term of Reparation', *Community Care*, 25 July, 8.

——(1989) *Diversion in Practice*, MPhil thesis, University of Leicester: Leicester.

——(1987) 'The Practice of Diversion', *Youth and Policy* 19: 10–14.

——(1989) *Diversion in Practice*, MPhil thesis, University of Leicester: Leicester.

——(1995) 'Margaret Thatcher: Soft on Crime', unpublished.

——(2000b) 'Order and Disorder: The Contradictions of Childhood', *Children & Society* 14: 3–10.

——(2001) 'Foucault's Law: The Crime and Disorder Act 1998', *Youth Justice* 1(2): 17–29.

——(2002a) 'Evaluation of Northampton Youth Offending Team', unpublished.

——(2002b) 'The Wrong End of the Telescope: Child Protection or Child Safety?' *Journal of Social Welfare and Family Law* 24(3): 247–61.

——(2003) *Youth Justice: Ideas, Policy, Practice*, 1st edition, Cullompton: Willan.

——(2006) 'Actuarialism and Early Intervention in Contemporary Youth Justice', in B. Goldson and J. Muncie (eds) *Youth Crime and Justice*, London: Sage, 92–109.

——(2010) 'Children's Rights and Youth Justice: 20 Years of No Progress', *Child Care in Practice* 16(1): 3–18.

——(2011a) 'Developing Restorative Practice: Contemporary Lessons from an English Juvenile Diversion Project of the 1980s', *Contemporary Justice Review* 14(4): 425–38.

——(2011b) *Doing Justice to Young People*, Cullompton: Willan.

Smith, R. and Fleming, J. (2011) *Welfare + Rights: UR Boss Legal Service*, London: Howard League.

Smithson, H. (2004) *Effectiveness of a Dispersal Order to Reduce ASB Amongst Young People: A Case Study Approach in East Manchester*, Sheffield: Sheffield Hallam University.

Social Exclusion Unit (1998) *Bringing Britain Together: A National Strategy for Neighbourhood Renewal*, London: The Stationery Office.

——(1999a) *Bridging the Gap*, London: The Stationery Office.

——(1999b) *Teenage Pregnancy*, London: The Stationery Office.

——(2000) *The Social Exclusion Unit Leaflet*, London: Cabinet Office.

——(2001a) *Preventing Social Exclusion*, London: The Stationery Office.

——(2001b) *National Strategy for Neighbourhood Renewal*, London: The Stationery Office.

——(2002) *Reducing Re-offending by Ex-Prisoners*, London: The Stationery Office.

——(2003) *A Better Education for Children in Care*, London: Office of the Deputy Prime Minister.

Solomon, E. (2009) 'New Labour and Crime Prevention in England and Wales: What Worked?' *IPC Review* 3: 41–65.

Solomon, E. and Garside, R. (2008) *Ten Years of Labour's Youth Justice Reforms: An Independent Audit*, London: Centre for Crime and Justice Studies.

Soothill, K., Francis, B. and Fligelstone, R. (2002) *Patterns of Offending Behaviour: A New Approach*, London: Home Office.

Souhami, A. (2007) *Transforming Youth Justice*, Cullompton: Willan.

Squires, P. (ed.) (2008) *ASBO Nation*, Bristol: Policy Press.

Squires, P. and Stephen, D. (2005) *Rougher Justice*, Cullompton: Willan.

Standing Conference for Youth Justice (2010) *Custody for Children: The Impact*, www.scyj.org.uk/.../the_impact_of_custody–position_paper_FINAL.pdf, accessed 1 May 2013.

Stevens, M. and Crook, J. (1986) 'What the Devil is Intermediate Treatment?' *Social Work Today* 18(2): 10–11.

Strang, H. and Braithwaite, J. (eds) (2001) *Restorative Justice and Civil Society*, Cambridge: Cambridge University Press.

Straw, J. and Michael, A. (1996) *Tackling the Causes of Crime: Labour's Proposals to Prevent Crime and Criminality*, London: Labour Party.

Summerfield, A. (2011) *Children and Young People in Custody 2010–11*, London: The Stationery Office.

Sure Start (2000) *What is Sure Start?* London: Sure Start.

Sutherland, A. (2009) 'The "Scaled Approach" in Youth Justice: Fools Rush In …', *Youth Justice* 9(1): 44–60.

Tarling, R., Burrows, J. and Clarke, A. (2001) *Dalston Youth Project Part II (11–14): An Evaluation*, London: Home Office.

Taylor, I. (1981) *Law and Order: Arguments for Socialism*, London: Macmillan.

Taylor, L., Lacey, R. and Bracken, D. (1979) *In Whose Best Interests?* London: The Cobden Trust/MIND.

Telford, M. and Santatzoglou, S. (2011) '"It was about Trust" – Practitioners as Policy Makers and the Improvement of Inter-professional Communication within the 1980s Youth Justice Process', *Legal Studies* 32(1): 58–77.

Thompson, R., Holland, J., Henderson, S., McGrellis, S. and Sharpe, S. (1999) *Youth Values: A Study of Identity, Diversity and Social Change*, London: South Bank University.

Thornton, D., Curran, C., Grayson, D. and Holloway, V. (1984) *Tougher Regimes in Detention Centres*, London: HMSO.

Thorpe, D. (1984) 'Does the Northamptonshire Model Work? – Some Preliminary Results', in H. Fox and R. Williams (eds) *Diversion – Corporate Action with Juveniles*, Northampton: Northamptonshire County Council, 40–42.

Thorpe, D., Smith, D., Green, C. and Paley, J. (1980) *Out of Care*, London: George Allen and Unwin.

Travis, A. (2002) 'Youth Jail Taken Off the Critical List', *The Guardian*, 15 October.

United Nations (1985) *The United Nations Standard Minimum Rules for the Administration of Juvenile Justice (Beijing Rules)*, Geneva: United Nations.

——(1989) *Convention on the Rights of the Child*, Geneva: United Nations.

UN Committee on the Rights of the Child (2002) *Concluding Observations of the Committee on the Rights of the Child: United Kingdom of Great Britain and Northern Ireland*, Geneva.

——(2008) *Concluding Observations of the Committee on the Rights of the Child: United Kingdom of Great Britain and Northern Ireland*, Geneva.

Upson, A. (2005) 'Patterns of Crime', in S. Nicholas, D. Povey, A. Walker and C. Kershaw (eds) *Crime in England and Wales 2004/2005*, London: Home Office.

Vickerstaff, S. (2003) 'Apprenticeship in the Golden Age: Were Youth Transitions Really Smooth and Unproblematic Back Then?' *Work, Employment and Society* 17(2): 269–87.

Victim Support (2013) 'Restorative Justice', www.victimsupport.org.uk/About-us/Policy-and-research/Position-statements/Restorative-justice, accessed 7 May 2013.

Walker, S. (2012) *National Standards Trial: April 2012–April 2013*, London: Youth Justice Board.

Walker, S. and Harvey-Messina, L. (2012) 'Implementation of the LASPO Act 2012 Key Stakeholder Information', www.justice.gov.uk/downloads/youth-justice/courts-and-orders/laspo/implementation-laspo-act.ppt, accessed 7 May 2013.

Walklate (2004) *Gender, Crime and Criminal Justice*, 2nd edition, Cullompton: Willan.

Walther, A. (2006) 'Regimes of Youth Transitions', *Young* 14(2): 119–39.

Warner, N. (2001) 'Foreword', in Youth Justice Board, *The Preliminary Report on the Operation of the New Youth Justice System*, London: Youth Justice Board.

Weber, M. (1957) *The Theory of Social and Economic Organisation*, Glencoe: The Free Press.

Webster, C. (2006) '"Race", Youth Crime and Justice', in B. Goldson and J. Muncie (eds) *Youth Crime and Justice*, London: Sage, 30–46.

Webster, C., Simpson, D., MacDonald, R., Abbas, A., Cieslik, M., Shildrick, T. and Simpson, M. (2004) *Poor Transitions: Social Exclusion and Young Adults*, Bristol: Policy Press.

White, M. (2002) 'Anti-crime Plan for Urban Youth Under Threat', *The Guardian*, 16 August.

Whitehead, P. and Arthur, R. (2011) '"Let No One Despise your Youth": A Sociological Approach to Youth Justice under New Labour 1997–2010', *International Journal of Sociology and Social Policy* 31(7/8): 469–85.

Whiting, E. and Cuppleditch, L. (2006) *Re-offending of Juveniles: Results from the 2004 Cohort*, London: Home Office.

Wilcox, A. (2003) 'Evidence-Based Youth Justice? Some Valuable Lessons from and Evaluation for the Youth Justice Board', *Youth Justice* 3(1): 21–35.

——(2004) *The National Evaluation of the Youth Justice Board's Restorative Justice Projects*, London: Youth Justice Board.

Williams, B. (1997) *Working with Victims of Crime: Policies, Politics and Practice*, London: Jessica Kingsley.

——(2000) 'Victims of Crime and the New Youth Justice', in B. Goldson (ed.) *The New Youth Justice*, Lyme Regis: Russell House, 176–92.

——(2005) 'Working with Victims in Youth Justice', in T. Bateman and J. Pitts (eds) *The Russell House Companion to Youth Justice*, Lyme Regis: Russell House, 210–15.

Willis, P. (1977) *Learning to Labour*, Farnborough: Saxon House.

Willow, C. (1999) *It's Not Fair*, London: The Children's Society.

Wilson, D. (2006) '"Playing the Game": The Experiences of Young Black Men in Custody', in D. Wilson and G. Rees (eds) *Just Justice*, London: The Children's Society, 14–21.

Wilson, D. and Rees, G. (eds) (2006) *Just Justice*, London: The Children's Society.

Wilson, E. and Hinks, S. (2011) *Assessing the Predictive Ability of the Asset Youth Risk Assessment Tool Using the Juvenile Cohort Study (JCS)*, London: Ministry of Justice.

Wood, M. (2004) 'Perceptions and Experiences of Antisocial Behaviour', *Findings 252*, London: Home Office.

——(2005) *Perceptions and Experience of Antisocial Behaviour: Findings from the 2003/2004 British Crime Survey*, London: Home Office.

Woolf, L. (2002) 'Court of Appeal Sentencing Guidelines', 19 December.

Worrall, A. (1999) 'Troubled or Troublesome? Justice for Girls and Young Women', in B. Goldson (ed.) *Youth Justice: Contemporary Policy and Practice*, Aldershot: Ashgate, 28–50.

Yarrow, S. (2005) *The Experiences of Young Black Men as Victims of Crime*, London: Criminal Justice System Race Unit.

Young, R. (2002) 'Testing the Limits of Restorative Justice: The Case of Corporate Victims', in C. Hoyle and R. Young (eds) *New Visions of Crime Victims*, Oxford: Hart, 133–71.

Youth Justice Board (1999) *Speeding Up Youth Justice*, Youth Justice Board, London.

——(2000) *National Standards for Youth Justice*, London: Youth Justice Board.

——(2001) *Youth Justice Board for England and Wales Corporate Plan 2001–02 to 2003–04 and Business Plan 2001–02*, London: Youth Justice Board.

——(2002) *Youth Justice Board Review 2001/02: Building on Success*, London: Youth Justice Board.

——(2004a) *National Standards for Youth Justice*, 2nd edition, London: Youth Justice Board.

——(2004b) 'Written Evidence to the House of Commons Home Affairs Select Committee', www.publications.parliament.uk/pa/cm200405/cmselect/cmhaff/80ii/80we 51.htm.

——(2004c) *Sustaining the Success*, London: Youth Justice Board.

——(2004c) *Race Audit and Action-planning Toolkit for Youth Offending Teams*, London: Youth Justice Board.

——(2005a) 'Supplementary Written Evidence to the House of Commons Home Affairs Select Committee', www.publications.parliament.uk/pa/cm200405/cmselect/cmhaff/80/80we28.htm.

——(2005b) *Strategy for the Secure Estate for Children and Young People*, London: Youth Justice Board.

——(2005c) *Annual Report and Accounts 2004/05*, London: Youth Justice Board.

——(2005d) *Corporate and Business Plan 2005/06 to 2007/08*, London: Youth Justice Board.

——(2005e) *Bail Supervision and Support*, London: Youth Justice Board.

——(2006a) *Youth Justice Annual Statistics 2004/05*, London: Youth Justice Board.

——(2006b) *Common Assessment Framework: Draft Guidance for Youth Offending Teams*, London: Youth Justice Board.

——(2008) *Assessment, Planning Interventions and Supervision*, London: Youth Justice Board.

——(2009) *The Scaled Approach and the Youth Rehabilitation Order*, London: Youth Justice Board.

——(2010a) *National Standards for Youth Justice Services*, London: Youth Justice Board.

——(2010b) *Youth Justice: The Scaled Approach*, London: Youth Justice Board.

——(2011) 'Written Evidence from the Youth Justice Board for England and Wales', Justice Committee, 22 November.

——(2012) *YJB Corporate Plan 2012–15 and Business Plan 2012/13*, London: Youth Justice Board.

——(2013) *National Standards for Youth Justice Services*, London: Youth Justice Board.

Youth Justice Board and Ministry of Justice (2012) *Youth Justice Statistics 2010/11*, London: Ministry of Justice.

Youth Justice Board and Welsh Assembly Government (2004) *All Wales Youth Offending Strategy*, London: Youth Justice Board.

Index